Jung's Nietzsche

Gaia Domenici

Jung's Nietzsche

Zarathustra, The Red Book, and "Visionary" Works

palgrave
macmillan

Gaia Domenici
University College London
London, UK

ISBN 978-3-030-17669-3 ISBN 978-3-030-17670-9 (eBook)
https://doi.org/10.1007/978-3-030-17670-9

This Palgrave Macmillan imprint is published by the registered company Springer Nature Switzerland AG
The registered company address is: Gewerbestrasse 11, 6330 Cham, Switzerland

For Massi.
In memory of my grandfather, Aldo Viviani (1925–2019), the first person to have ever spoken to me about Nietzsche, Zarathustra, *and the German language.*

Foreword: Between Deserts by Sonu Shamdasani

Writing in 1973, Walter Kaufmann called for scholarly and perceptive studies of aspects of Nietzsche's thought and influence that had been inadequately explored, such as his influence on the work of Freud, Adler, and Jung.[1] Nevertheless, the take-up of this call in Jung studies was slow. A potential watershed moment was the publication in 1989, long awaited in some quarters, of Jung's five-year *Mahabharata*-length seminar on Nietzsche's *Thus Spoke Zarathustra*,[2] run partially concurrent with Martin Heidegger's Nietzsche lectures. What new insights might this provide regarding Jung's engagement with Nietzsche's life and work, and the formative role of his reading of *Zarathustra* in the elaboration of his own work? What new hermeneutic approaches might Jung's complex psychology open to the imagery of Nietzsche's text? For a number of readers, the opportunity to engage finally with Jung's seminars on *Zarathustra* was cause for consternation. From the perspective of the current state of the historical understanding of *Zarathustra*, how could someone versed in Nietzsche's work for decades, familiar with his cultural milieu, acquainted with some people who knew him, engaged with the same philosophical forebears, notably Schopenhauer, and grappling with similar theological issues apparently misread the text so profoundly, and at such length?[3]

The consternation was not helped by a minimal scholarly apparatus that did not draw on the significant body of Nietzsche scholarship, nor attempt to contextualise Jung's engagement with Nietzsche and Zarathustra in particular. Thankfully, the dearth of serious scholarship in this area began to be rectified in the 1990s, notably in studies by Paul Bishop and Martin

Liebscher.[4] However, the riddle posed by Jung's *Zarathustra Seminars* in part still remained.

The publication in 2009 of Jung's *The Red Book: Liber Novus* opened a new entrance into this labyrinth, from which Gaia Domenici's *Jung's Nietzsche: Zarathustra, The Red Book, and 'Visionary' Works* has now emerged.[5] *Liber Novus* had arisen from a period in Jung's life which he dubbed, in retrospect, his confrontation with the unconscious and with his soul. It revealed that a significant part of this undertaking involved his confrontation with Nietzsche. In his *Zarathustra Seminar*, Jung noted 'I read *Zarathustra* for the first time with consciousness in the first year of the war, in November 1914, 20 years ago; then suddenly the spirit seized me and carried me to a desert country in which I read *Zarathustra*'.[6]

Jung's Nietzsche guides the reader to this desert, and through it, to intermodulating deserts of *Liber Novus* and *Zarathustra*. As we can now grasp, Jung's reading took place at a pivotal moment, after his initial active imaginations between the autumn of 1913 and the summer of 1914, and while he was conceiving of and commencing turning this into the base of a self-styled prophetic work for publication (for which *Thus Spoke Philemon* could have been a mimetically conceivable title) through editing his material and adding a second layer of commentary and lyrical elaboration. In *Liber Novus*, Jung was also, as he put it, led into 'the desert of my own self'.[7] In such deserts, Jung noted, 'the ancients found "the abundance of visions, the fruits of the desert, the wondrous flowers of the soul."'[8]

Jung's Nietzsche reconstructs Jung's formation of a tradition of 'visionary works' (in effect, desert works) which he claimed were marked by their figuration of the contents of the collective unconscious—of which *Zarathustra* was a paradigmatic example, and to which arguably his own *Liber Novus* belonged. It demonstrates the manner in which Jung understood Nietzsche's *Zarathustra* by analogy to his own experiences, as portrayed in *Liber Novus*, and that this provides the missing hermeneutic key to understanding his reading of *Zarathustra* in his seminar. Impacted and in part shaped by Jung's first 'conscious' reading of *Zarathustra*, it in turn at the same time reframed his understanding of the latter, refigured as Nietzsche's *Liber Novus*. The questions opened up here refigure not only Jung's reading of *Zarathustra* in his seminar, but his understanding of Nietzsche as a whole, including how he later came to frame this in his biographical memoir included in *Memories, Dreams, Reflections*. Developing from this, *Jung's Nietzsche* shows how Jung's 'overcoming' of the alternatives to Christianity presented by Nietzsche led to his formulation of a psychology which could recover the original significance of Christianity in a form which was nevertheless suited for modernity. Drawing upon and resituating recent work in Jung and Nietzsche scholarship, it simultaneously forms a major contribution to the study of the reception of Nietzsche's work and to Jung studies.

University College London
London, UK

Sonu Shamdasani

Notes

1. Walter Kaufmann, *Nietzsche. Philosopher, Psychologist, Antichrist* (Princeton, Princeton University Press, 1974), p. 94.
2. C. G. Jung, *Nietzsche's Zarathustra: Notes of the Seminar Given in 1934–9*, ed. James Jarrett (Bollingen Series, Princeton, Princeton University Press, 1988).
3. See Graham Parkes, "Nietzsche and Jung: Ambivalent Appreciations," in Jacob Golomb, Weaver Santaniello, and Ronald Lehrer, eds., *Nietzsche and Depth Psychology* (Albany, SUNY Press, 1999), pp. 205–227.
4. Paul Bishop, *The Dionysian Self: C. G. Jung's Reception of Nietzsche* (Berlin, Walter de Gruyter, 1995), Martin Liebscher, *Libido und Wille zur Macht. C.G. Jungs Auseinandersetzung mit Nietzsche* (Basel, Schwabe, 2011).
5. C. G. Jung, *The Red Book: Liber Novus*, ed. Sonu Shamdasani, trs. Mark Kyburz, John Peck and Sonu Shamdasani (Philemon Series, New York, W. W. Norton, 2009; *A Reader's Edition*, 2011).
6. C. G. Jung, *Nietzsche's Zarathustra*, p. 381.
7. C. G. Jung, *The Red Book: Liber Novus* (*A Reader's Edition*, p. 141).
8. Ibid., p. 143.

Acknowledgements

I wish to thank all the many people who have made this dream of mine come true. First of all, I must express gratitude to my husband, Massi, my parents, Franco and Emma, and my brother, Niki, for their constant love and support. I then have to thank my cousin Laura, my uncles and aunties, my grandmother, my father-, mother- and brother-in-law, and my best friends, Sonia and Michela, for their supportive presence in my life.

I am then grateful for all the beautiful minds and souls that have helped me through my research: Sonu Shamdasani, Martin Liebscher, and Giuliano Campioni—my research would not even exist without their teachings and support, and there are no words to express my gratitude for having them in my both academic and personal life. There are also so many lovely friends and colleagues I am lucky enough to have crossed my path with: starting from the *Seminario Permanente Nietzscheano* (in particular Stefano Busellato, Luca Lupo, Selena Pastorino, Carlotta Santini, Irene Treccani), I would then love to thank Helmut Heit, Hannah Große Wiesmann, and the group of the *Nietzsche-Lektüretage* (in particular Tobias Brücker), and, last but not least, my 'Jungian' soul mates from *Phanês: Journal and Network for Jung History* (Alessio De Fiori, Ernst Falzeder, Matei Iagher, Ollie Knox, Christine Maillard, Dee McQuillan, Armelle Line Peltier, Tommaso Priviero, Quentin Schaller, Florent Serina, Josh Torabi, Christopher Wagner, Alex Woodcock, Dangwei Zhou).

Moreover, I would like to thank Thomas Fischer, Bettina Kaufmann, Andreas Jung, and the *Stiftung der Werke von C.G. Jung*, for granting me permission to consult Jung's Library in Küsnacht twice, for providing me with precious information, and for allowing me to use archival material in this book. I would also like to thank the *Staatsarchiv Basel—Stadt*, for allowing me to consult Jung's school curricula, and refer to the results of such consultation in this book.

Lastly, I must thank Paul Bishop, not only for his outstanding research and publications, but also for the valuable tips and information he has given me, which have been extremely helpful for my research.

Contents

Abbreviations

Nietzsche[1]

AC	*The Anti-Christ* (1888)
BVN	*Briefe von Nietzsche*
DD	*Dithyrambs of Dionysus* (1888–1889)
EH	*Ecce Homo* (1888)
eKGWB	*Digital Critical Edition* (edited by P. D'Iorio, 2009–)
FW	*The Gay Science* (1882/1887)
GD	*Twilight of the Idols* (1888)
GM	*Genealogy of Morals* (1887)
GT	Birth of Tragedy (1872)
JBG	*Beyond Good and Evil* (1886)
KGW	*Kritische Gesamtausgabe der Werke Nietzsches* (edited by Giorgio Colli and Mazzino Montinari. Berlin/New York: De Gruyter, 1967–)
KSA	*Kritische Studienausgabe* (edited by Giorgio Colli and Mazzino Montinari. Berlin/New York: De Gruyter, 1980–)
M	*Daybreak* (1881)
MA I	*Human, All Too Human I* (1878)
MA II	*Human, All Too Human II* (1879)
NcW	*Nietzsche contra Wagner* (1888–1889)
NF	*Nachgelassene Fragmente*
UBDS	*David Strauß: the Confessor and the Writer* (1873)
UBHL	*On the Use and Abuse of History for Life* (1874)

UBSE	*Schopenhauer as Educator* (1874)
UBWA	*Richard Wagner in Bayreuth* (1876)
WA	*The case of Wagner* (1888)
WL	*On Truth and Lie in an Extra-Moral Sense* (1873)
WM	*Miscellaneous Maxims and Opinions* (MA II, 1979)
WS	*The Wanderer and His Shadow* (MA II, 1879)
Za	*Thus Spoke Zarathustra* (1883–1885)

Jung[2]

CW	*The Collected Works of C. G. Jung*, translated by Gerhard Adler and R.F.C. Hull. London: Routledge, 1953–
MDR	*Memories, Dreams, Reflexions* (1962), recorded and edited by Aniela Jaffé, translated by Richard and Clara Winston. New York: Vintage Books, 1989
RB	*The Red Book: Liber Novus* (1913–1959). Edited and Introduced by Sonu Shamdasani, Translated by Mark Kyburz, John Peck, and Sonu Shamdasani. New York/London: W. W. Norton & Company, 2009
SNZ	*Nietzsche's Zarathustra: Notes of the Seminar Given in 1934–1939*. Edited by James L. Jarret in two parts. London: Routledge, 1989 (2nd edition, 1994)
WSL	*Wandlungen und Symbole der Libido. Beiträge zur Entwicklung des Denkens* (1912). Leipzig and Vienna: Franz Deuticke, 1925 (2nd edition)

Freud

CPW	*The Complete Psychological Works of Sigmund Freud*, eds. James Strachey and Anna Freud. London: The Hogarth Press 1906–1974.
GW	*Gesammelte Werke in achtzehn Bänden mit einem Nachtragsband*, ed. Anna Freud et al. London/Frankfurt am Main: S. Fischer 1940–1961

Notes

1. References to works and *Nachlaß* will be given according to the KSA numbers of volume and page. When not directly translated by the author of this book, the translation used will be given among the references at the end of each chapter.

   References to Nietzsche's letters will be given according to the eKGWB enumeration criteria.
2. Archetypes are always capitalised, except when referred to in citations (in which case, their original spelling is kept).

CHAPTER 1

Introduction

> *In spite of these trepidations I was curious, and finally resolved to read him.* Thoughts Out of Season *was the first volume that fell into my hands. I was carried away by enthusiasm, and soon afterward read* Thus Spake Zarathustra. *This, like Goethe's* Faust, *was a tremendous experience for me.* Zarathustra *was Nietzsche's* Faust, *his No. 2, and my No. 2 now corresponded to Zarathustra though this was rather like comparing a mole hill with Mount Blanc. And* Zarathustra*—there could be no doubt about that—was morbid. Was my No. 2 also morbid? This possibility filled me with a terror which for a long time I refused to admit, but the idea cropped up again and again at inopportune moments, throwing me into a cold sweat, so that* in the end I was forced to reflect on myself. (MDR: 102)[1]

1.1 A Life-Long Confrontation

1.1.1 Jung's Educational Background

On 14 November 1913, Jung heard the voice of his 'soul' for the third time. He felt confused, having no idea whose voice that could be, and still trying to figure out the meaning of the catastrophic visions he had been seized with a few weeks earlier. He asked the voice if it was 'God' speaking; if 'God' was 'a child, a maiden'; to which the voice replied: 'You are lying to yourself! You spoke so as to deceive others and make them believe in you. You want to be a prophet and chase after your ambition' (RB I, 2,

G. Domenici, *Jung's Nietzsche*,
https://doi.org/10.1007/978-3-030-17670-9_1

'Soul and God': 233). The question of being a 'prophet', as well as the meaning of the 'prophets' for our time will be a major issue of Jung's thinking. Such a question and what Aniela Jaffé has defined as 'question of *meaning*' (Jaffé 1967: 12. See also Bishop 2014: 75–78) come together in Jung's approach to his own existence and writing. But what does it mean to be a 'prophet', according to Jung? And who are the 'prophets' of our time?

Carl Gustav Jung was born on 26 July 1875 in Kesswil on Lake Constance. After only six months, his family moved to Laufen (near the Falls of the Rhine), where they lived until he was four years old. In 1879, Jung's family moved again, this time to a village near Basel (Klein-Hüningen), where they settled and he received his education (MDR: 6–15). Although his family was not a rich or an influential one, he had the chance to attend excellent schools, namely *Unteres* and *Oberes Gymnasium* in Basel (formerly known as *Pädagogium*). According to Jung's high school curricula—which are all still available for consultation, alongside teachers' assessments and grades, at *Staatsarchiv Basel-Stadt*—he never attended philosophy classes during his studies at *Oberes Gymnasium.* Yet his philosophical education took place at that time, thanks to private readings in his father's library, which kept the 17-year-old Jung strongly involved, while he was mainly concerned about the theological issue on God and the question of evil. According to his memoires, it was not easy to find texts from philosophers in the library of Johan Paul Achilles Jung who, being a parson, regarded them as 'suspect because they thought'. Nevertheless, the young boy managed to first come across the second edition of the *General Dictionary of the Philosophical Sciences* [*Allgemeines Handwörterbuch der philosophischen Wissenschaften, nebst ihrer Literatur und Geschichte*] (Leipzig, 1832) by Wilhelm Traugott Krug, and then *Christian Dogmatics* [*Christliche Dogmatik*] (Zurich, 1869) by Alois Emanuel Biedermann. At the same time, he read several pieces of English literature and engaged with more specific philosophical matters by dealing with Pythagoras, Heraclitus, Empedocles, Plato, and Meister Eckhardt, all authors that he particularly enjoyed. Jung then faced other philosophers, whose ideas he did not find equally stimulating, that is Schoolmen and St Thomas—whose Aristotelian intellectualism appeared to him 'more lifeless than a desert', as well as Hegel, whose language sounded 'as arrogant as it was laborious'. The 'great find resulting from [his] researches was Schopenhauer', however, who 'was the first to speak of the suffering of the world, which visibly and glaringly surrounds us, and of confusion, passion, evil—all those things which the others hardly seemed to notice and always tried to resolve into all-embracing harmony and comprehensibility'. Because he was engaging with Schopenhauer's philosophy so much, and was struggling to find a negotiation between a 'blind' Will and the intellect, Jung eventually sympathised with Kant, who allowed him to solve his problem: Schopenhauer 'had committed the deadly sin of hypostatizing a metaphysical assertion, and of endowing a mere noumenon, a *Ding an sich*, with special qualities' (MDR: 60–72). Jung read Eduard von Hartmann, too (ibid.: 101). Plato also appears in Jung's Greek programme during his third and fourth year at *Oberes Gymnasium*. As reported by his teacher, Theodor Plüss, the class had to read: *Euthyphron* (chapters 1–8), *Apology* (first speech), *Phaedo* (chapters 1–13, 63–67, with particular stress on Socrates's personality).[2]

The reason why Jung was so concerned with the issue of evil, was because he was going through a crucial religious crisis, having experienced that 'god' could not be reduced to the concept of 'goodness', but had to include evil in his attributes. Therefore, at the age of 16, Jung was looking for earlier thinkers who could back him up on his hypothesis. Facing the issue from a theological perspective did not seem to work for him, nor were his father's 'expatiations' fruitful; he found them 'sentimental-sounding and usually incomprehensible as well as uninteresting'. The problems with his father culminated when they had to deal with the concept of the Trinity, which the parson preferred to skip, claiming that he understood 'nothing of it' himself. At this point, the young Jung was more and more concerned, and still seeking answers. Probably sensing this anxiety, Emilie Preiswerk-Jung, Jung's mother, suggested that he read Goethe's *Faust*. The book 'poured into [his] soul like a miraculous balm', for the protagonist appeared to him as 'someone who takes the devil seriously and even concludes a blood pact with him—with the adversary who has the power to frustrate God's plan to make a perfect world'. Nonetheless Jung never sympathised with the character of Faust, whose behaviour he judged to be far too naïve; rather, he likened himself more to the figure of Mephistopheles, who seemed to him 'cheated in quite a different sense: he had not received his promised rights because Faust, that somewhat characterless fellow, had carried his swindle through right into the Hereafter'. Mephistopheles made 'the deepest impression' on Jung, who immediately put him in connection with the 'mystery of the mothers' in terms of 'initiation'. Due to the fact that he had highlighted the role of evil in a wider world perspective, Goethe appeared to Jung as a 'prophet', but 'having dismissed Mephistopheles by a mere trick' was something Jung could not forgive the German writer for (MDR: 36–60).

According to Jung's German and Greek teacher, in his first year at *Oberes Gymnasium*, Emanuel Probst, some pieces by Goethe had already been part of the German programme. Still among Jung's school curricula, it is possible to verify what a key role the classics have played in his educational background more broadly. The main authors treated were: Ovid, Caesar, Livius, Cicero, Catullus, Tibullus, Tacitus, Xenophon, Homer, Lysin, Sophocles Aeschylus, Schiller, Chamisso, Uhland, Shakespeare, Molière, Bernardin de Saint-Pierre, Delille, Claris de Florian, Madame de Staël, Guisot, Lamartine, Casimir Delavigne, Thiers, A. Dumas père, V. Hugo, E. About, Lafontaine, Töpffer, and others. In fact, keen interest and familiarity for both ancient and modern classics shine through all of Jung's work, as well as his lexical choices. Furthermore, during his university years (still in Basel), Jung was a fellow of the prestigious fraternity 'Zofingia'—of which several well-known personalities, such as Jacob Burckhardt, had previously been members—where various topics were discussed on a regular basis, ranging from philosophy to science, and of course literature. Bearing this in mind, and considering the famous legend which believes Jung to be an illegitimate great-grandson of Goethe's (MDR: 35), the weight of Jung's humanistic education might have gone further than a mere scholastic reading of texts. In this sense, it is thus arguable that he regarded himself as belonging to a humanistic tradition, by the side of the scientific legacy traditionally connected to his profession as a psychiatrist. Over the past decade, the significance of the humanities for a complete understanding of Jung's depth psychology has been exhaustively explored by Paul Bishop, with particular regard to Goethe, Weimar Classicism, and German Idealism (Bishop 2008, 2012, 2014, 2017). The amount of classics kept in Jung's library is indeed astonishing (see Shamdasani 2012). However, to this day, the effective weight of Jung's school education had yet to be explored. Looking at Jung's school programmes, the impact of not only German Classicism but also the Antiquities on Jung's upbringing can be considered high enough to regard Jung belonging to a humanistic tradition as a matter of fact.

1.1.2 Nietzsche's Presence in the Evolving of Jung's Thinking

Jung's humanistic background emerges especially through the references to several authors who assiduously occur in his published works. Among these, a crucial role is played by Nietzsche, particularly as the author of *Thus Spoke Zarathustra* [Also *Sprach Zarathustra*] (1883–1885), a work which definitely impressed Jung throughout his lifetime. Besides Jung's 1934–1939 seminar, expressly dedicated to a psychological interpretation of *Zarathustra*, this work appears to be mentioned, among his published texts, 'at least 87 times', as reported by Paul Bishop (1995b). Sometimes the purpose of such mentions is to show Nietzsche as a clinical case; at other times, the philosopher appears to Jung as anticipating some of the key concepts of analytical psychology and revealing deep and aware experiences with what he calls the 'unconscious'.[3]

As mentioned above, Jung grew up and studied in Basel. In particular, he attended *Oberes Gymnasium*, which was quite a prestigious school. Among its teachers, it could be proud of some of the most influential thinkers of the nineteenth century, such as Jacob Burckhardt and Friedrich Wilhelm Nietzsche. During Jung's years as a student, Professor Nietzsche had already retired and was spending his last days in a state of insanity in Germany (in his mother's house in Naumburg until 1897, then with his sister in Weimar, where he died on 25 August 1900). In Basel, his name was still associated with madness, and a certain dread of going through a similar destiny arose in Jung, according to his memoires, who hesitated for a long time before approaching Nietzsche's texts, despite his intellectual curiosity. Rumours concerning Nietzsche and his eccentricity might have affected Jung's reception of him. During his university years, after having postponed his planned reading, Jung eventually decided to start from Nietzsche's *Untimely Mediations* [*Unzeitgemässe Betrachtungen*] (1873–1876), then he moved on to *Zarathustra*. Although Bishop has observed that Jung's own *Untimely Meditations* volume does not present reading marks at all (Bishop 1995b: 273), some excerpts have been copied by Jung at the time of his first reading of the text, possibly in preparation for his lecture at the *Zofingiaverein*, a student fraternity of which he was a member.[4]

As reported by Jung in *Memories, Dreams, Reflexions*, since his first reading of the book, *Zarathustra* appeared to him as a 'morbid' text, where a confrontation with what he will later call the 'unconscious' seemed to play the main role. Despite a possible reinterpretation of his first experience with Nietzsche's text, due to his old age at the time of recalling his memories, linking *Zarathustra* with Nietzsche's innermost reality remains a steady element in Jung's understanding of the text. Indeed, such a psychological reading of the work, in spite of a mild evolution during the development of Jung's theories, can be considered as consistent in his thinking. Jung's first extended discussion on *Zarathustra* was in his medical dissertation, where, in the chapter 'Of Great Events', he recognised an example of *cryptomnesia*—a case of unconscious plagiarism—from *Blätter aus Prevorst* by Justinus Kerner (1831–1835) (CW 1: §§ 140–142 and 180–184). In order to prove his hypothesis, Jung had a short correspondence with Elisabeth Förster-Nietzsche, the philosopher's sister, who confirmed that both herself and her brother had engaged with readings from Kerner's works during their childhood (Bishop 1993, 1995b: 280).

The mild evolution of Jung's interpretation of *Zarathustra*, instead, goes parallel with his view on poetry, whose categories—he never stopped believing—*Zarathustra* could fit into. In 1912, Nietzsche, alongside other authors, was often quoted by Jung to contrast Freud's idea of poetic creation with his own theory. In 1907, Freud's understanding of creation was that of a poet's *personal* experience, brought about by his or her *past*, and with no other aim than to solve the tension caused by a repressed memory in order to move on in life (*Der Dichter und das Phantasieren*). In 1912, Jung proposed to regard poetry as the product of a *collective* experience, or better, of the encounter with the collectivity present in oneself. His idea is namely that poetry can result from *introversion*, that is, from the 'regression' of the libido through introspection. In this process, mythological representations can spontaneously occur, demonstrating the continuity of representative ability in humans. The meaning of such representations, therefore, is now to be read in connection with the *future*, since the core of their creative power lies in their universal *symbolic* nature. To endorse his theory, Jung quotes from *Der Dichter und das Phantasieren*, where Freud defines myths as 'distorted vestiges of the wishful phantasies of whole nations, the [age-long] dreams of youthful humanity', and compares it with aphorism 13 from Nietzsche's *Human, All Too Human* [*Menschliches, Allzumenschliches*] (1878), which reads, indeed: 'in sleep and in dreams we pass through the whole thought of earlier humanity'. In this sense, Jung makes use of Nietzsche to reverse Freud's view advocating that 'infantile thinking and dream-thinking are simply a recapitulation of earlier evolutionary stages'. In fact, Jung's purpose is to extend Freud's conceptualisation by stressing the 'archaic' contents of the unconscious over their closeness to the dreamer's personal past: 'All this shows how much the products of the unconscious have in common with mythology. We should therefore have to conclude that any introversion occurring in later life regresses back to infantile reminiscences which, though derived from the individual past, generally have a slight archaic tinge' (CW 5: §§ 21–40; WSL: 25). Later on, Freud made use of the same quotation from Nietzsche's *Human, All Too Human* in the fifth edition of his *Interpretation of Dreams* (1919):

> We can guess how much to the point is Nietzsche's assertion that in dreams 'some primaeval relic of humanity is at work which can now scarcely reach any longer by a direct path'; and we may expect that the analysis of dreams will lead us to a knowledge of man's archaic heritage, of what is physically innate in him. Dreams and neuroses have seemed to have preserved more mental antiquities than we could have imagined possible; so that psycho-analysis may claim a high place among the sciences which are concerned with the reconstruction of the earliest and most obscure periods of the beginning of the human race. (CPW, vol. 5: VII [B])

Other than as a forerunner of his theory of dreams, Nietzsche is mentioned by Jung in *Wandlungen und Symbole der Libido* quite frequently, to support his own new view on mythology. In this sense, Jung takes as examples some of Nietzsche's aphorisms, as well as *Dithyrambs of Dionysus* [*Dionysos-Dithyramben*] (1888–1889), among pieces by Goethe and Hölderlin, which seem to anticipate the importance of introversion, as well as to reveal a certain experience with the collective unconscious.

Moreover, according to Freud, the only ability of an artist was to convert his suffering to creative energy, so the only task of a psychoanalyst should be to help him solve his personal conflicts. Therefore, speculation on art was to be excluded from the framework of psychological investigation (*Drei Abhandlungen zur Sexualtheorie* [1900–1905]; *Eine Kindheitserinnerung des Leonardo da Vinci* [1910]; *Der Wahn und die Traüme in W. Jensens 'Gradiva'* [1906/1912]; *Das Interesse an der Psychoanalyse* [1913]). In contrast, since the poet appears as a real *medium* between the external world and the collective unconscious, analysing artistic creation is not only justified by Jung and depth psychology, but also exalted. A few years later, in regard to the relation between poetry and psychology, Jung will write: 'Although the two things [psychology and art in general] cannot be compared, the close connections which undoubtedly exist between them call for investigation. These connections arise from the fact that the practice of art is a psychological activity and, as such, can be approached from a psychological angle' (CW 15: § 97). A few paragraphs below, in order to contrast Freud's 'reductive method', which approaches the artist in terms of pathological subject only, he will once more take Nietzsche as an example:

> The results are no doubt very interesting and may perhaps have the same kind of scientific value as, for instance, a post-mortem examination of the brain of Nietzsche, which might conceivably show us the particular atypical form of paralysis from which he died. But what would this have to do with *Zarathustra*? Whatever its subterranean background may have been, is it not a whole world in itself, beyond the human, all-too-human imperfections, beyond the world of migraine and cerebral atrophy? (ibid.: § 103)

Although this way of regarding art as a link to collectivity remains the same, in the 1920s Jung's focus is mainly directed towards the relation between the artist's *personality* and his or her unconscious, as well as on work creation *typology*. It is safe to say that his opinion on *Zarathustra* follows such a development. In *Psychological Types* [*Psychologische Typen*] (1921), Nietzsche is frequently taken as an example for an introverted type, and his *Birth of Tragedy* [*Die Geburt der Tragödie*] (1872) aids Jung to define the categories of introverted intuition and extraverted sensation from the relation between Apollinian and Dionysian (CW 6: §§ 223–242). Furthermore, Jung mentions *Zarathustra* in order to show the antithesis between a poet's typological attitude, namely introversion, and the contents of the collective unconscious. He explains:

> But what creative minds bring up out of the collective unconscious also actually exists, and sooner or later must make its appearance in collective psychology. Anarchism, regicide, the constant increase and splitting off of a nihilistic element on the extreme Left, with a programme absolutely hostile to culture—these are phenomena of mass psychology, which were long ago adumbrated by poets and creative thinkers. (ibid.: § 322)

Zarathustra is then considered as separated from 'the collection of philosophical aphorisms, which are accessible to philosophical criticism because of their predominantly intellectual method', in order to oppose Bergson's 'intuitive method', which appears to Jung as rather an 'intellectual' one. Jung argues that 'Nietzsche made far greater use of the *intui-*

tive source and in so doing freed himself from the bonds of the intellect in shaping his philosophical ideas'; this is why his 'intuition' brought about a 'work of art' rather than a philosophical work, 'largely inaccessible to philosophical criticism' (ibid.: § 540; italic added). In *Introduction à la Métaphysique* (1903), Henri Bergson stated: 'By intuition is meant the kind of *intellectual sympathy* by which one places oneself within an object in order to coincide with what is unique in it and consequently inexpressible'. The opposite approach to reality, according to Bergson, is 'analysis', which 'on the contrary [...] reduces the object to elements already known, that is, to elements common both to it and other objects' (Bergson 1903: 7).[5] Jung criticises the intellectual element in Bergson's position, highly influenced by Neoplatonism. In fact, by Jung's definition, intuition corresponds to an irrational function.

Such a stress on the artist's relation to collectivity culminates in Jung's reading of *Zarathustra* in terms of *inflation* from the 1930s on. During Jung's development on his archetypes theory (as will be explored in details in the next section), Nietzsche appears to Jung as identified with the archetype of the 'Wise Old Man', thus becoming a direct spokesman for the unconscious. In *'Ulysses': A Monologue* (1932b), Jung compares Joyce's character of Ulysses, namely 'a true demiurge who has freed himself from entanglement in the physical and mental world and contemplates them with detached consciousness', to Nietzsche's Zarathustra and Goethe's Faust: 'the higher self who returns to his divine home after blind entanglement in *samsara*' (CW 15: § 192). *Zarathustra's* pathological side, that is the prophetical representation of psychic disorders of its author, is associated by Jung with Picasso's figure of Harlequin (1932a):

> Harlequin is a tragically ambiguous figure [...]. He is indeed the hero who must pass through the perils of Hades, but will not succeed? That is the question I cannot answer. Harlequin gives me the creeps—he is too reminiscent of that "motley fellow, like a buffoon" in *Zarathustra*, who jumped over the unsuspecting rope-dancer (another Pagliacci) and thereby brought about his death. Zarathustra then spoke the words that were to prove so horrifyingly true of Nietzsche himself: "Your soul will be dead even sooner than your body: fear nothing more!" Who the buffoon is, is made plain as he cries out to the rope-dancer, his weaker *alter ego*: "To one better than yourself you bar the way!" He is the greater personality who bursts the shell, and this shell is sometimes—the brain. (CW 15: § 214)

Still in similar terms, *Zarathustra* is linked with Goethe's *Faust* in the Foreword to Suzuki's *Introduction to Zen Buddhism* (1939), where Jung describes both works as 'wholeness' experiences, where the predominance of the unconscious makes them much closer to Eastern creations than to the European literary tradition. This also explains why their comprehension appears so difficult for a European mind (CW 11: §§ 905–906). Ultimately, with the arrival of the totalitarian regimes, *Zarathustra's* prophetical capacity increases its meaning and comes to represent a mirror for the infamous European happenings of the twentieth century. In this sense, in *Wotan* (1936), behind *Zarathustra's* Dionysian leitmotif, Jung senses a hidden reference to the destructive archetype of Wotan, that is, to the collective psychology of the Germans in the 1930s (CW 10: § 373. See Liebscher 2001a). Similarly, after the war, in *After the Catastrophe* (1945), in order to explain Hitler's rise in Europe, Jung utilises a few metaphors from *Zarathustra*: just like Nietzsche's incapability to accept his Shadow has prevented him from recognising the divine as an independent entity, and has led him to project such perfection onto the *Übermensch*, so the Germans have not been able to recognise their Shadow in Hitler and have idealised him. Now their feeling of guilt is the same as Nietzsche's 'pale criminal' (Za I, 6, KSA 4: 45–47) (CW 10: §§ 400–443).[6]

As already argued, the original opinion on *Zarathustra* as a product of Nietzsche's encounter with his innermost nature does not seem to change throughout Jung's life; at the same time, a certain fear of going through a similar destiny seems to increase during Jung's reading of *Zarathustra*. In this sense, Jung's experience with Nietzsche does not stop on the intellectual level and can be defined in terms of a real *confrontation*. It is not to forget that Nietzsche also appears to be determinant in Jung's characterisation of the archetype of the *Self*. According to what he reports in his seminar on *Zarathustra*, Jung decided to read *Zarathustra* for the second time in 1914, when he was indeed concerned with the problematic nature of the Self. Nietzsche's understanding of the Self—or the way Jung perceived it—framed Jung's conceptualisation. The passages where Nietzsche dwelled upon this idea seemed 'very important' to him, 'yet'—he concludes—'I could not make use of it because one misses in *Zarathustra* the concept of the unconscious' (SNZ I: 391).

1.2 Jung's Psychological Understanding of Nietzsche

1.2.1 Jung's Seminar on Zarathustra*: A Problematic Reading*

During the years 1934–1939, in Zurich, Jung gave a seminar entirely dedicated to a psychological reading of *Zarathustra*. Apparently, the proposal came from some enthusiastic participants in his previous seminar on Christiana Morgan's visions, wishing to take on a similar analysis on Nietzsche's work. Jung accepted the challenge of a new seminar and dedicated nearly five years to a meticulous analysis of Nietzsche's text. The official language of the seminar was English, and the used translation was by Thomas Common (New York: The modern Library, the year of publication missing in Jung's volume), with the only exception of the chapter 'The Night Song', which Jung decided to read in German from his *Kleinoktav-Gesamtausgabe* (Leipzig: Naumann and Kröner, 1899–1911), 'because it is of such a musical quality that it expressed something of the nature of the unconscious which is untranslatable' (SNZ II: 1142).

Jung's interpretation is grounded on two presuppositions, namely *Zarathustra* as the representation of Nietzsche's meeting with the unconscious, and the character of Zarathustra as the 'Wise Old Man', that is to say, one of the possible manifestations of the *Spirit* archetype (SNZ I: 3–37). In support of the former hypothesis, Jung refers to a specific testimony of Nietzsche's, that is, his description of *Zarathustra's* composition as an experience of independence from his own will. In *Ecce Homo*, the philosopher describes the origin of his work in terms of 'inspiration', particularly stressing the speed of his writing (EH III, 25, KSA 6: 339–340). Autonomy and impulsivity led Jung to link Nietzsche's writing to an unconscious process. In order to endorse the possibility of Zarathustra being an archetype, Jung quotes from the poem *Sils Maria*, where one is told that 'the one became two', and Zarathustra would 'pass by' Nietzsche (FW *Anhang*, 13, KSA 3: 649). According to Jung, such a dualistic perception reflects Nietzsche's experience of Zarathustra as separate from himself, yet belonging to his mind, thus manifesting the very essence of an archetypal encounter. Furthermore, Jung highlights Nietzsche's highly poetic tone as an example of *inflation*, namely of his identification with the archetype of the 'Wise Old Man'. In fact, Jung's analysis might be summarised in terms of a fight, within Nietzsche's mind, between 'I' and the unconscious, where the latter tries consistently to be recognised by the former, but, not being able to succeed, is each time either rejected or projected. Behind Nietzsche's experience, the *Self* tends indeed to become manifest and to lead him to the completion of his *individuation process.* By virtue of 'darwinistic' and 'materialistic' prejudices, however, the philosopher appears to Jung as incapable of dealing with the idea of an incorporeal entity independent from his conscience, and fails to recognise any of its manifestations. At the same time, Nietzsche is also *seized* by the archetype of the *Wise Old Man*, namely the only unconscious manifestation that he is able to accept. As a philosopher on the one hand, and as an introverted, intuitive type on the other, he is more likely to admit the spirit as an autonomous phenomenon, rather than a possible sensual appearance of the *Anima* or any other archetype. Precisely for this reason, however, the encounter with the unconscious does not present any of those protections which a good relation with one's own Anima or Animus could guarantee, and may therefore lead to the catastrophic identification with the autonomous power experienced.

According to Jung, therefore, Nietzsche is 'inflated' with the character of Zarathustra and cannot accept his *Shadow*, which is consequently projected onto figures such as 'the last man' or 'the ugliest man', as well as onto all the characters and situations that appear inferior, dark, feminine, corporeal or chthonic, irrational. In fact, the spirit represents height, sunlight, masculinity, and logic or rational thinking. In the same way, all of the feminine aspects of the Anima are either incorporated by Zarathustra himself (the clearest example is giving by his love for dance), or projected onto a form of immature eroticism emerging through images such as the dancing girls or the doves. *Zarathustra* appears to Jung as depicting the evolving of Nietzsche's contradictory attitude towards the experience he is living: on the one hand, through the death of God, he tries to deny what cannot be grasped within the framework of the conscience; on the other hand, through his strong and blind exaltation of dance and corporeality, he seems to project this denied divine attitude onto a materialistic view of the world. But the unconscious cannot be denied or rejected, and through an *enantiodromia*—Jung utilises this phrase, which he attributes to Heraclitus, in order to represent the transformation of a term to its opposite—it ends up turning one's conscious attitude to its opposite. Therefore, Nietzsche's projected Shadow takes its revenge on the 'I' by turning Nietzsche's introverted intuition into its opposite, that is, the extraverted sensation of the 'Dionysian orgy' which the book seems to culminate with (SNZ I: 143).

From the point of view of Nietzsche's philosophy, such an understanding of his text might appear as a *misreading*, and a few scholars have already brought out the most relevant aspects of this interpretation, as well as investigated possible mediators for Jung's reception of Nietzsche. Three relevant articles to be pointed out are, alphabetically: Martin Liebscher, 'Zarathustra – Der Archetypus des "Alten Weisen"' (2002); Peggy Nill, 'Die Versuchung der Psyche: Selbstwerdung als schöpferisches Prinzip bei Nietzsche und C. G. Jung' (1988), and Graham Parkes, 'Nietzsche and Jung: Ambivalent Appreciations' (1999). The most significant points of such a misreading concern Jung's apparent lack of awareness towards *Zarathustra's* parodistic purposes (notably highlighted by Hans Gadamer in 1986; see Nill 1988), as well as the questionability of its fundamental assumptions. Moreover, to consider Zarathustra as a manifestation of the Old Wise Man archetype is not obvious at all (Liebscher 2002: 245). In addition to this, a few further details may be added. First of all, despite the description proposed in *Ecce Homo*, Nietzsche's *Nachlaß* presents a significant number of pages that show how slow-paced and accurate Nietzsche's writing was. Of course, Jung is aware of how important it was for Nietzsche to re-elaborate and develop his images, but he takes such an accuracy for an example of the rejection of the unconscious, instead of acknowledging the philosopher's 'philological' background and his consistent search for stylistic perfection. On more than one occasion, Jung emphasises Nietzsche's need for rational explanations, as well as complex constructions, of unexplainable manifestations and worrying signals; such explanations and constructions, however, would be better understood when contextualised within Nietzsche's philological quest and his striving for what he will later call 'the economy of the great style', namely a style capable of 'holding together its strength', as opposed to the weakness of the style of the *décandence* (AC *Vorwort*, KSA 6, 167). Then it is questionable whether or not Zarathustra was actually experienced as an independent reality. To rely on Nietzsche's poem is not sufficient evidence for any archetypal experience in his 'meeting' with Zarathustra. Again, Nietzsche's *Nachlaß* presents different re-elaborations of *Sils Maria*, which lets one guess a poetic intent, rather than a hasty collection of unusual encounters. Moreover, even if the assumption of Zarathustra's representing the Wise Old Man archetype was admitted, it would not still be easy to include Nietzsche within the category of inflation: several times he recognises to be part of his contemporary scene, thus showing no refusal of the Shadow, but rather a full awareness of his own inferiority. In

Ecce Homo, he declares: 'Granting that I am a decadent, I am the opposite as well' (EH I, 2, KSA 6: 266). Finally, a position of total rejection of the unconscious in Nietzsche is not to be taken for granted, since he frequently questions the nature of concepts such as 'soul' or 'ego'—especially in relation to their possible materialistic meaning—and depicts them as delusions (JGB 12–23, KSA 5: 26–39). It is also equally difficult to consider Nietzsche's view as influenced by Darwinism, if one thinks of his strong criticism of Darwin: according to Nietzsche, if one wanted to postulate finality, this should not be found in the struggle for life, as Darwin puts it, but rather in the power's self-overcoming (GD IX, 14, KSA 6: 120. On a detailed analysis of Nietzsche's criticisms of Darwin, see Johnson 2010).

Even regarding the philosophical content of Jung's understanding of *Zarathustra*, a few details must be pointed out. As I have dealt with this issue in details elsewhere (see Domenici 2014b), I will just briefly sketch the main points of criticism. First of all, throughout his seminar, Jung believed in Nietzsche's *Übermensch*, a symbol for the wholeness represented by the Self. However, if one wanted to find such a wholeness in Nietzsche's philosophy, then it would be his conception of an exalted Dionysian, rather than this hypothetical man. The *Übermensch* is more likely to be somehow understood as Nietzsche's perception of what Jung would call 'individuated man'. He represents indeed the one who has experienced the uncontrollable totality of a Dionysian becoming and has learnt how to cope with it, by loving his necessary condition and turning the violence of imposition into creative power. Precisely in similar terms, Jung's individuation process leads to first discover the Self as the sense of totality, and then to accept it and to let it act on one's own personality, thus allowing it to 'realise'; or, in Nietzsche's vocabulary, to become 'who one is'. Another problematic point of Jung's philosophical understanding of *Zarathustra*, lastly, concerns the absence of consciousness in Nietzsche's representation of feminine elements, which would remain on an unconscious level, being therefore either integrated in Zarathustra's personality (like the aforementioned dance) or projected onto erotic scenes. However, studies have been conducted, where Nietzsche's attention to the feminine was brought out. In particular, one of the most important figures of Nietzsche's philosophy is Ariadne (see Deleuze 1965; Krell 1986: 14–31): not only is she the protagonist of the dithyramb 'Klage der Ariadne' (DD 7, KSA 6: 398–402), but her characterisation occurs in several unpublished fragments dating from the time of *Zarathustra*. Above all, while commenting on 'The Night Song' in *Ecce Homo*, Nietzsche writes:

> Nothing like this has ever been composed, ever been felt, ever been *suffered* before: this is how a god suffers, a Dionysus. The answer to this sort of dithyramb of solar solitude in the light would be Ariadne… Who besides me knows what Ariadne is! … Nobody until now has been able to solve riddles like this, I doubt anyone has ever seen riddles here.—Zarathustra rigorously determines his task—it is mine as well—, and there can be no mistake about what he *means*: he is *affirmative* to the point of justification, to the point of salvation, even for everything past. (EH III, Za 8, KSA 6: 348)

Finally, one should not forget that Nietzsche calls Cosima Wagner 'Ariadne' in some of his very last letters (3 January 1889, eKGWB 1241, 1242, 1242a).

Since the 1990s, several studies have been conducted about Jung's relationship to Nietzsche. Some of these are more content-oriented, such as Gerhardt Schmitt's *Zyklus und Kompensation: Zur Denkfigur bei Nietzsche und Jung* (1998), Patricia Dixon's *Nietzsche and Jung: Sailing a Deeper Night* (1999), and Lucy Huskinson's *Nietzsche and Jung. The Whole Self in the Union of Opposites* (2004); others focus more on Jung's reception of Nietzsche, such as Paul Bishop's *The Dionysian Self: C. G. Jung's Reception of Friedrich Nietzsche* (1995a) and Martin Liebscher's *Libido und Wille zur Macht. C.G. Jungs Auseinandersetzung mit Nietzsche* (2012). These last two texts, along with the many articles that both Bishop (e.g. 1993, 1994, 1995b, 1999) and Liebscher (2001a, 2001b, 2002, 2003, 2006) have written on the subject, are milestones of the scholarly research on Nietzsche and Jung, given their historical approach to both Nietzsche and Jung, and their critical analysis of Jung's relationship to Nietzsche. However, albeit thoroughly deconstructed and analysed, Jung's apparent misreading of *Zarathustra* has, to this day, been left unsolved. Something that, starting from Romano Màdera's essay, 'Nietzsche e Jung: Mitografie del senso perduto' (1989) has been sufficiently stressed in the existing literature (especially by Huskinson) is Jung's projection of his own fear of madness onto Nietzsche; such fear of madness, however, does not exhaust the complexity of Jung's understanding of *Zarathustra*. In addition to this, there is a vast array of analytical-psychological studies on Nietzsche and Jung, mostly focused on *Zarathustra*, published in Germany and Italy (e.g. Gay and Schiffmüller 2013; Innamorati 1991; Lindner 2010;

Pezzella 1995; Rocci 1999). Also in these cases, Jung's *Seminar on Nietzsche's Zarathustra* is deconstructed and analysed, but Jung's fear of becoming mad is not sufficiently considered in relation to his own understanding of *Zarathustra* as an *experience*. Even more importantly, none of the above studies have been able, as yet, to explain why Jung's opinion of Nietzsche changes dramatically after 1914 and, from a forerunner of his theories, Nietzsche becomes Jung's favourite case study to represent the consequences of a *failed individuation*. As will be shown in the next sections, the answer to both Jung's peculiar reading of *Zarathustra* and the shift in his relationship with Nietzsche lies in Jung's very own *experience* of *Liber Novus*.

1.2.2 The 'Red Book': Liber Novus

About 20 years before Jung's *Zarathustra* seminar, in 1912, Jung went through a complicated period, in both a personal and a professional sense. It is now common knowledge that his estrangement from Freud's psychoanalysis took place at that time, as well as the publication of *Wandlungen und Symbole der Libido*, which indicated the beginning of a new theory.[7] In 1913, Jung was literally assailed by visions, which he transcribed at first in his *Black Books*. At that time, he realised a certain need for solitude and introspection, and decided to take up on the challenge that such fantasies were presented to him with such violent assault, by letting them flow into his life. A little later, these were even collected and re-elaborated by him in a new work (although he did not stop with the *Black Books* transcription), which he decided to call *Liber Novus*. Later on, he started to illustrate such fantasies in the 'calligraphic volume' of *Liber Novus*. Jung worked consistently on this work until the end of the 1920s, and continued to reflect on such an experience until the last days of his life. In fact, in 1916, Jung had other fantasies which gave birth to the 'Septem Sermones ad Mortuos', while *Liber Novus*' 'Epilogue' was written in 1959. Jung's unusual piece of work remained unpublished until 2009, when Sonu Shamdasani, after several years of research, persuaded the Jungs to release it for publication. Shamdasani gave it the name 'The Red Book', because that ('das rote Buch', in German) was the phrase used by Jung and his closest acquaintances to refer to the monumental book, because of its huge red leather cover (Shamdasani 2009, RB: 193–226). *Liber Novus* is written in folio, with gothic characters and miniatures, and is divided into three parts: *Liber Primus*, *Liber Secundus*, *Scrutinies* (which includes 'Epilogue' and

'Appendices'). Regarding its general contents, it should be noted that it is composed of visions and commentaries. Furthermore, Jung frequently quotes from the Bible; in a few visions the style reaches poetical tones; symbols and metaphors are recurrent throughout. The protagonist is Jung's 'I' and the main story is told in first person. If one wanted to bring out 'philosophical' contents more broadly, it could be stated that *Liber Novus* can be represented as teaching and symbolising the experience of a *transformation*. Indeed, the process can be summarised as a continuative development from the perspective of the *sense* [Sinn] to the *nonsense* [Unsinn]—which can be placed as its own Shadow—towards the realisation of a *supreme meaning* [Übersinn]. If accepted, the nonsense can be integrated by the sense and become one with it, creating a new and superior perspective; if not accepted, the only consequence is that it turns into *absurdity* [Widersinn], leading any developmental attempt to failure (see Nante 2010). The most significant symbol of the supreme meaning is the 'Birth of a New God', which, in terms of Jung's later psychology, represents the discovery of the Self [Selbst].

1.2.3 Jung's Zarathustra *or Nietzsche's* Liber Novus?

It can be stated that, similarly to Jung's *Liber Novus*, *Zarathustra* was written in quite a dark period of its author's life. After Nietzsche's disappointment with Wagner's ideology—with his consequent estrangement from the Bayreuth environment—and the worsening of his health conditions—which led him to retire from his professorship position in Basel in 1879—in 1882, he went through one of the deepest and saddest failures of his life, namely the end of his friendship with Paul Ree and Lou von Salomé, along with a severe refusal from her to his insistent marriage proposals. Right after that, he travelled intensively around Engadin (Switzerland), Italy, and Provence, published the first four parts of the *Gay Science* [*Die fröhliche Wissenschaft*] (1882/1887), and came across a few meaningful intuitions, highly significant for his philosophy henceforth. Such intuitions were collected and published in four separate parts around the period 1883–1885, titled *Also sprach Zarathustra*.

The first part of *Zarathustra* consists of a *Prologue* and 22 'Speeches'; all of the other 'books' are characterised by speeches and narrations, with the addition of a few dreams and visions of Zarathustra. The main stylistic features are utilisation of the dithyramb; several mythological or literary references; an abundance of symbols and metaphors, often making a parody of Luther's Bible. Zarathustra is the actual protagonist, but apart from his speeches, the text is written in third person. If one wanted to sum up the main philosophical concept of the book, the 'death of God' should certainly be highlighted. Such a phrase alludes to the most extreme nihilistic perspective, consequently bringing about two different reactions: a negative and a positive one. The negative reaction can in turn be categorised into two: on the one hand, it corresponds to the attitude of the 'last man', that is, to the attitude of someone who does not care about the 'death of God', despite acknowledging that he is responsible for it. On the other hand, a negative, 'passive' nihilistic attitude is also represented by the 'higher man', who not only is more than aware about his own responsibility but also *suffers* because of such situation, yet is not strong enough to overcome it. The only way to overcome nihilism—meaning the only possibility of achieving the necessary strength to overcome the 'death of God'—lies in the thought of the 'eternal return' and its actual acceptance; the full realisation of such a possibility is symbolised by the figure of the *Übermensch*, that is, of the one who has said 'yes' to life in all of its positive and negative sides, namely in all of its lack of meaning. This figure represents the only possible positive response to the 'death of God'.

In Jung's own *Zarathustra* volume, among several underlinings and annotations, it is possible to find many references to *Liber Novus*. One could then argue that Jung's unusual reading of *Zarathustra* was originated by a sort of confusion in his mind between Nietzsche's text and his own *Liber Novus*, that is to say, Jung read *Zarathustra* as if it was Nietzsche's *Liber Novus*. Both texts are indeed similar to each other not only because of their style and, in a sense, of their contents but also because Nietzsche and *Zarathustra* appear in Jung's work. Most of the times, this appearance is implicit and occurs just through hidden quotations or references to Nietzsche's main concepts. Besides, it is also possible to find a few explicit quotations, and, even more importantly, Nietzsche appears in a vision as a proper character. Thanks to *Liber Novus*, furthermore, it is now possible to better understand all those passages in Jung's seminar on *Zarathustra* which seem to be completely obscure and far away from Nietzsche's purpose. What characterises Jung's reading of *Zarathustra*, it can be stated, is precisely a hidden allusion to his *Liber Novus*, which might have led him to overlook some significant philosophical differences and analyse the text from a mere psychological standpoint. It is known that Jung had already read *Zarathustra* before his first visions, but this does not invalidate this hypothesis: firstly—as anticipated—Jung's impression of

Zarathustra as a 'prophetical' representation of Nietzsche's encounter with his innermost and dangerous personality originates from his very first reading and remains the same throughout his life; secondly, the urge he felt in 1914 to reread the text and have a further confrontation with its author is a matter which cannot be disregarded. Regarding the first reason, it is true that *Memories, Dreams, Reflexions* represents Jung's retrospective reconsideration of his life and cannot be considered as a reliable testimony; however, Jung arguably linked *Zarathustra* with Nietzsche's madness already at the time of his first reading, due to Nietzsche's reputation in Basel, as has been discussed above. As to the second point, it can be even argued that, as pointed out above, 1914 marks the division between two different levels in Jung's reading: before that time, it was the encounter with a 'prophet' and the eternal aspects of his innermost nature to be stressed; after that, when Jung had to mention Nietzsche in his published texts, his focus was exclusively directed onto the psychic danger of experiencing the 'collective unconscious'. From 1914 onwards, Nietzsche increasingly becomes a model to show the meaning and the consequences of a failed individuation.

Both texts can surely be considered as personal *experiences*, and in several letters Nietzsche refers to his *Zarathustra* in terms of 'solitude' and 'incomprehension' (emblematic is Nietzsche's letter to Overbeck dating 12 February 1887; BVN 1887, eKGWB, 798). Moreover, both the fourth part of *Zarathustra* and the entire *Liber Novus* were originally meant for a closed group of readers, and not for an official publication. Emma Jung, Toni Wolff, Cary Baynes, Wolfgang Stockmayer were the only people certainly involved by Jung in his adventure, although it is still possible that someone else had knowledge of it. Jung discussed with them the possibility of a publication but then refused, feeling that the right time for letting his experience be known had yet to come. Similarly, Nietzsche withdrew the only few copies available of *Zarathustra*, IV, and regretted about having given them to someone not ready for his philosophy. Precisely such a proximity in the relation between author and text might have led Jung to 'confuse' Nietzsche's *Zarathustra* with his *Liber Novus*. Finally, as Luca Lupo has observed, it is also possible to link the personal component of both *Zarathustra* and *The Red Book* to the question of the truth and the insufficiency of science which, as will be fully explored in the following chapters of this book, is a crucial element to understand not only *Liber Novus* and *Zarathustra*, but also Jung's relationship with Nietzsche (Lupo 2012).

1.3 Misreading or 'Revaluation'?

1.3.1 The 'Unconscious' as a Perspective

Arguing that Jung read *Zarathustra* as if it was Nietzsche's *Liber Novus* is not meant as a negative criticism; in fact it opens up a new interpretative perspective. As I have shown elsewhere, there are sufficient arguments to consider *Zarathustra* as Nietzsche's attempt to reflect the paradoxical complexity of a Dionysian becoming, which creates and destroys its own values, and overcomes itself in its own self-affirmation process (Domenici 2014a). On this premise, then, a psychological reading mirrors one of the possible *will to power* perspectives and, therefore, sticks to the *Zarathustra* purpose. As Martin Liebscher has convincingly pointed out, Jung's interpretation can be read as a form of *transvaluation*, according to Nietzsche, whereas reading Nietzsche from a pure psychological position would mean a certain presumption, which, in Nietzsche's words, could be expressed as a form of 'will to truth'. This means precisely to impose only one perspective on the totality of the will to power possibilities (Liebscher 2012: 155–164. Jung's perspective has been also described in terms of 'will to truth' by Huskinson 2004: 151–157). In this sense, to read *Zarathustra* as the mere product of an ill mind would be nothing but reductionism, meaning it might *also* be that, but considering Nietzsche's psychological processes as the *only* way his text should be taken on would be nothing but a mistake. In fact, following a multi-perspective reading does not exclude the possibility of Jung's interpretations being true or at least plausible, it just does not admit this single view as 'the' *truth*. *Zarathustra's* subtitle is *A Book for All and None*, indeed, meaning that a multiple reading was originally thought of as its main feature. Giorgio Colli, to this extent, has stressed the *esoteric* shade of the text, besides its immediate *exoteric* meaning:

> *Thus Spoke Zarathustra* is "a Book for All" and with that Nietzsche has meant to start off a revolutionary reform within philosophical argumentation [...]. This work, therefore, may also be regarded as a large scale fight; but what remains remote, hidden, unaccessible, at the bottom of it, muddies the clarity of communication. The contemptuous, Heraclitean, coldness, from which such an expression pours, perpetuates towards a kind of ambiguity, that can be only externally connected to a symbolic relation, a gap between signifier and signified. Therefore, it is also a "Book for None". (Colli 1980: 113–114; translation is my own)

Nietzsche himself has publicly highlighted the unavoidability of interpretation in *Beyond Good and Evil* [*Jenseits von Gut und Böse*] (1886), which was published only one year after the publication of the last part of *Zarathustra*: 'Everything profound loves masks. The most profound things of all even have a hatred for images and allegories'. Indeed, in any kind of conversation—even, and above all, when it comes to dialoguing with a written text—every given information is mediated, thus filtered by the listener—or the reader—and the original meaning of a word, a phrase, a sentence tends to slightly vary. Consequently, the deeper the meaning, the more likely its original sense is misunderstood. So, Nietzsche concludes in his aphorism: 'Every profound spirit needs a mask; even more, around every profound spirit a mask is continuously growing, thanks to the constantly false, that is, *shallow* interpretation of every word, every step, every sign of life he gives' (JGB 40, KSA 5: 57–58). Already at the time of *Zarathustra* composition, while meditating on the perfect 'style' to express particularly profound concepts, Nietzsche had written down, in form of a personal note: 'The more abstract the truth to teach, the more we need to firstly seduce our senses, in order to grasp it' [Je abstrakter die Wahrheit ist, die man lehren will, um so mehr muß man erst die Sinne zu ihr verführen] (NF 1[45] July–August 1882, KSA 10: 23; translation is my own). Thinking of how significant it was for him to preserve a 'philological' approach to both writing and reading, one could argue that *Zarathustra* was also meant to be read 'slowly' (M *Vorrede* § 5, KSA 3: 17). A 'slow' reading may prevent one from misunderstanding the author's original intention. At the same time, however, since mediation seems to be unavoidable, the creation of a new meaning accompanies any reading. It might not be a case that Nietzsche's biggest stress on *revaluation* arises at first during his writing of *Zarathustra*, III, in parallel with his deepest reflections on the eternal return (Brobjer 2010). Furthermore, Jung is not the only one who has approached Nietzsche in a psychological way; as is well-known, Lou von Salomè's biography of Nietzsche is oriented to an analysis of his personality in the first place (Andreas von Salomè 1894); other popular or less popular biographies have been written since then, with a similar focus. Just to give a few examples, Karl Löwith suggested reading the most significant characters in *Zarathustra* as characters of Nietzsche's dialogue with himself (Löwith 1935–1956: 188–189); Werner Ross proposed to call Nietzsche's philosophy of years 1872–1873 'Tiefenphilosophie', an analogy of depth psychology [Tiefenpsychologie] indeed. He understands Nietzsche's philosophy 'as a philosophy indeed, that bores its courses under all previous systems and from there wants them to burst in the air' (Ross 1979: 370; translation is my own).

Moreover, it is highly remarkable that Jung worked on his *Liber Novus* while developing most of the key concepts of his depth psychology. Hence, if it is true that Jung experienced Nietzsche as part of a particular tradition to which he himself felt to belong, then investigating Nietzsche's presence in *Liber Novus* might make clearer his overall influence on Jung's theories.[8] As mentioned above, Jung's humanistic education is an essential element to understand and contextualise most of his thoughts, especially in the case of a work whose organisation mirrors a medieval manuscript, and which presents similarities with William Blake's work—given by the association of paintings and text—by the side of 'unreferenced citations and allusions to works of philosophy, religion, and literature' (Shamdasani 2009, RB: 202–203). On the other hand, *Liber Novus* itself contributes to shed new light on Jung's unusual interpretation of *Zarathustra* and by so doing gives even more value to Nietzsche's expectations regarding his text. An accurate analysis of such a reading is therefore worthy and interesting, even from a Nietzschean perspective. Ultimately, bringing out Nietzsche's presence within Jung's innermost experiences does not mean depriving *Liber Novus* of its value. On the contrary, it can help highlight some elements which Jung felt the need to confront with. Therefore, such an analysis does not seem to be disrespectful towards Jung's intent, either. As Paul Bishop has put it, throughout *Liber Novus* 'we find a number of concerns that are reminiscent of texts from the period of German Idealism, and provide the cultural historical context for approaching Jung's long-withheld masterpiece'. Becoming aware 'of this context does not detract from Jung's inventiveness or originality; on the contrary, it enables us to appreciate his achievement all the better'. Nor can it be stated 'that Jung marshalled a number of sources when he undertook to produce *The Red Book,* along the model that he took a previously existing pack of cards and simply reshuffled them'. In fact, Bishop concludes, 'Jung is working on the same intellectual and experiential terrain as the German Idealists (in the broadest sense of the term), including Goethe and Schiller. *Their* problems are *his* problems; equally, *his* problems are *ours*' (Bishop 2012: 337).

1.3.2 Structure of the Work

Since the publication of *Liber Novus*, only a few studies have dealt with its relation to Nietzsche (most remarkably Bishop 2017: 207–210; Lupo 2012; Schmitt 2011). Among these, only Schmitt has exclusively dealt with the symbology underpinning *Liber Novus* and *Zarathustra*. However, a systematic investigation on Nietzsche's actual presence in *Liber Novus* from a historical-philological perspective is still missing. This study is aimed to explore such a presence in details, considering *Liber Novus* as a pre-context for Jung's later understanding of *Zarathustra*. The approach adopted in this research is based, on the one hand, on Colli and Montinari's historical-critical method in relation to Nietzsche's philosophy, widely promoted by Giuliano Campioni and the Italian school and, on the other hand, on Sonu Shamdasani's historical approach to Jung. For this reason, this research is mostly focused on Jung's literary sources, to be found not only in Nietzsche but in the whole tradition of the so-called visionary artists. With such an approach, Jung's seemingly obscure later interpretation of Nietzsche becomes, if not clear, at least more accessible. This is the case, for instance, with Jung's understanding of the lions and the poisonous serpents in *Zarathustra*, which can be fully explained solely by reading Jung's comments on his own copy of *Zarathustra* and integrating such comments with similar motifs or comments from *Liber Novus* (see Domenici 2015, 2018).

What such an analysis primarily requires is to find a common ground that could have offered elements to both *Liber Novus* and *Zarathustra*. As anticipated, Jung describes his very first reading of Nietzsche's text as 'a tremendous experience', exactly as had happened with Goethe's *Faust*. In fact, 'Zarathustra was Nietzsche's Faust, his No. 2', that is to say, that part of its author's personality which did not depend on his historical belonging, on his 'here and now', but referred to an inner and uncontrollable other reality, timeless and incorporeal. The first time Jung went through the experience of a 'No. 2' was exactly within himself, and the reason why *Zarathustra* was terrifying him so much, was that his '"No. 2" now corresponded to Zarathustra'. This had a strong effect on him, who eventually claimed: 'in the end I was forced to reflect on myself'. However, it is not so obvious to admit that such a link between Nietzsche's 'No. 2' and his own 'No. 2' would have been possible, if Jung had not already read *Faust*. Surely, as he tells Aniela Jaffè, Nietzsche's mental conditions were well-known in Basel during Jung's school days, so that the association Nietzsche-folly—hence the association Zarathustra-Nietzsche's 'No. 2'—was taken for granted by everyone (MDR: 101–102). But the first time that an author's 'No. 2' was related to a work of his in Jung's mind, was with Goethe.

As will be exhaustively argued in the first chapter, Jung has also frequently regarded other works in similar terms: Dante Alighieri's *Commedia*, Richard Wagner's *Ring*, *Tristan* and *Parsifal*, Carl Spitteler's *Olympian Spring* (and not seldom *Prometheus and Epimetheus*), William Blake's poetry and paintings, and so on. In 1930, Jung specifically takes such works as examples for the 'mode of artistic creation' defined by him as *visionary*, namely where 'the experience that furnishes the material for artistic expression [...] is something strange that derives its existence from the hinterland of man's mind, as if it had emerged from the abyss of prehuman ages [...]' and 'to which' the artist 'may easily succumb' (CW 15: §§ 139–141). Besides the authors mentioned above, Jung frequently associates inner experiences also to Hölderlin's *Song of Destiny* [*Schicksalslied*] (*Hyperion*) (CW 5: §§ 619–620; CW 9, 1: § 576; CW 15: § 178) and Vischer's *Auch Einer* (CW 6: § 627). In particular, among all of these authors, those most frequently (and significantly) put by Jung in connection with *Zarathustra* are: Goethe, Hölderlin, Spitteler, and Vischer. For this reason, both the contents and style of such 'visionary' works will be measured with *Zarathustra* and *Liber Novus*. Furthermore, parallels, or even common historical contingencies in the lives of such authors will be also highlighted. To conclude this first part, a return to *Liber Novus* is necessary, in order to answer the question as to whether such a work could ever fit in the same category as well. The answer is given by Jung himself, who describes the feeling of intense anxiety during his first visions in the same way he had described his 'No. 2', *Faust* and *Zarathustra* experiences (RB I: 231; RB 'Scrutinies' § 2: 336). Apart from these descriptions, historical-environmental details also should be noted, if one intended to consider *Liber Novus* as a 'visionary' work: a few of mutual acquaintances with Nietzsche's, a brief argument with Spitteler, important mediators (such as Burckhardt and Bachofen) to the same tradition of 'visionary' authors, as well as Basel, where Jung lived and studied until the end of his university career, and whose buildings had been shared also by Nietzsche and Spitteler. As argued by Bishop, ultimately, a few significant elements recurring in *Liber Novus* have been apparently inspired by Goethe, Vischer, Hölderlin, and German Classicism (Bishop 2012). Occasionally, the text presents a few references to Spitteler as well.

In the second chapter, Nietzsche's presence in Jung's *Liber Novus* is thoroughly investigated. First, all of the implicit and often general allusions to Nietzsche are presented and contextualised through philological archive work, referring to Jung's personal underlinings and annotations in his complete Nietzsche's *Kleinoktav-Gesamtausgabe*. Jung read *Zarathustra* at least three times: during his university years in Basel, in 1914, and at the time of his Zurich seminar. According to him, all of the main annotations presented in his personal copy were written down in 1914, as he was majorly concerned with the problem of the Self, as already mentioned (SNZ I: 391). Nevertheless, it is arguable that several inscriptions belong to a later period, due to his intense referring to problematics which do not appear relevant at the time of *Liber Novus*, but will become central in the following years. Indeed, a few marginalia present phrases that remarkably recall Jung's seminar comments.[9] Somewhere else in his *Zarathustra* copy, Jung refers to the archetypes, making it easier to put such references in connection with his 1930s reading; since those concepts had still to be developed in 1914. In a few cases, however, it might be difficult to distinguish between annotations of 1914 and 1930, if not impossible. This all means that a philological research is not to be read as an incontrovertible piece of evidence to determine whether or not Jung was actually referring to *Zarathustra* while writing *Liber Novus* or to *Liber Novus* while commenting on *Zarathustra*. Nonetheless, having such a huge amount of annotations in almost all of Nietzsche's works makes such a hypothesis more than plausible. The focus of this chapter is mainly directed on images such as: desert, lion, serpent, dwarf, and sun path. Moreover, the explicit references to, as well as quotation from, Nietzsche—and particularly *Zarathustra*—are analysed from the philosophical point of view of what was called Jung's 'confrontation' with Nietzsche. Whereas the first part of this chapter concerns symbols and metaphors exclusively, the second part focuses on three essential aspects of Jung's understanding of Nietzsche: folly, the relation between teaching and imitating, the question of the 'death of God'.

In the third chapter, Jung's seminar on *Zarathustra* is confronted with *Liber Novus*. In particular, all those passages in which Jung's interpretation does not come across as extremely coherent with Nietzsche's philosophy are compared with those *Liber Novus* lines which Jung is most likely to refer to. This is firstly the case with Jung's stress on Nietzsche's failed individuation and the presuppositions of such a theory: Zarathustra as the 'Old Wise Man', Nietzsche's *Übermensch* as a symbol for the Self, Nietzsche's solitude and his negation of the unconscious. A second point of this study regards Jung's tendency to overanalyse some animal figures which do not play any essential role in the understanding of *Zarathustra*, but appear quite significantly in *Liber Novus*. The main elements of this last part are: the couple serpent-bird; the black scarab; frogs, toads and swamp; lion and doves.

As has been pointed out throughout this introduction, it is important to keep the field of interpretation as open as possible in the cases of both *Zarathustra* and *Liber Novus*. Furthermore, if one agrees with Sonu Shamdasani that 'the role of Philemon in Jung's work has analogies to that of Zarathustra in Nietzsche's work and Virgil in Dante's' (Shamdasani 2009, RB: 202), it really makes sense to let Zarathustra 'have a dialogue' with Philemon and confront the crucial aspects of their 'teachings'. In order to draw our conclusions, Nietzsche's understanding of the 'death of God' will be compared with Jung's need for the 'birth of a new God'; so their consequential interpretation of Christianity will become a major question. Finally, the meaning of 'self-overcoming' for both authors, and in both *Zarathustra* and *Liber Novus*, will be considered.

Notes

1. The text was first published by Aniela Jaffé, *Erinnerungen, Träume, Gedanken* in 1962, after Jung's death. Although it has been considered a valuable biography by several authors, its historical reliability is highly questionable, as significant changes and omissions have been made by its editors (Shamdasani 1995/2003). However, the text can be still regarded as a suggestive testimony of Jung's rethinking his childhood memories.
2. On a detailed reconstruction of Jung's reception of Schopenhauer, see Liebscher (2014). One of the first studies on Jung and Schopenhauer to be mentioned was written by James Jarrett (1981). Luca Lupo has also postulated the possibility of a Schopenhauerian inspiration for *The Significance of the Father in the Destiny of the Individual* (1909–1949, CW 4: §§ 693–744) and *Synchronicity: An Acausal Connecting Principle* (1952b, CW 8: §§ 816–997), to be found in Schopenhauer's writing *Transcendent Speculation on the Apparent Deliberateness in the Fate of the Individual* (Lupo 2013).
3. In this context, I am not going to take any philosophical position in regard to the existence of the unconscious. In fact, every time the word 'unconscious' appears in this text, it has to be understood in relation to Jung's own understanding of the word. To have a historical excursus on the development of the concept of the unconscious in philosophy, see (alphabetically): Buchholz and Gödde (eds., 2005); Gödde (1999); Nicholls and Liebscher (eds., 2010).
4. I have to sincerely thank Thomas Fischer for this information.

5. On Jung's reception of Bergson, see Shamdasani (2003: 227–230); Gunter (1982); and Pilard (2015).
6. Paul Bishop has drawn an interesting distinction between Jung's and Freud's understandings of Nietzsche's 'Of The Pale Criminal': whereas the latter dwells upon the idea of 'madness before the deed'—thus stressing the individuality of sense of guilt—, the latter seems to be more interested in analysing the meaning of a form of 'madness after the deed', namely its relation to a collective sense of guilt (Bishop 1999).
7. Jung's writing on libido, unconscious, and the archetypes are numerous. His theory has been developed slowly, and sometimes it does not provide precise definitions. Nonetheless it is possible to find a certain coherency within Jung's exposition. To have a detailed excursus on Jung and 'the science question', see Shamdasani (2003: 87–99).
8. The closeness of Weimar Classicism to Nietzsche's philosophy has been the main argument of a couple of texts edited by Paul Bishop (2004). A certain proximity between Nietzsche, Weimar environment, and its most influential characters, such as Goethe, Schiller, and Hölderlin, has been debated by Baioni (1981), Vivarelli (1989), and von Seggern (2005). Although it is undeniable to regard Goethe and Hölderlin as relevant figures both in Nietzsche's writings—which quite often offer several explicit as well as implicit allusions to them—and in his student years—when he used to refer to Hölderlin as his 'favourite poet'—, it is not easy to defend Jung's opinion. Surely Nietzsche considered Goethe as an extraordinary man (GD IX, 49, KSA 6: 151–152), and exalted his personality in several occasions. But his anti-German position, started off especially after his estrangement from Wagner and, above all, from the Wagnerians, is too strong to postulate a sense of belonging to German Idealism.
9. One of such cases is represented by a curious anecdote. During one of my researches at Jung's library in Küsnacht, I found a headed paper of Jung's with a couple of I-Ching hexagrams written down, in the middle of Förster-Nietzsche and Gast's postface at the end of *Zarathustra*. It is known that Jung came across Chinese philosophy and horoscope later than *Liber Novus*, it is therefore likely that the paper dates back to the 1930s. Furthermore, in the aforementioned Förster-Nietzsche and Gast's postface, all of the most significant lines referring to Nietzsche's fear of illness and contagion are underlined, and a few marginalia present phrases occur in Jung's seminar comments. This all endorses the hypothesis of those reading marks' belonging to the time of Jung's *Zarathustra* seminar.

References

Andreas von Salomè, Lou. 1894. *Friedrich Nietzsche in seinen Werken*. Vienna: Verlag von Carl Konegen.

Baioni, Giuliano. 1981. La filologia e il sublime dionisiaco. Nietzsche e le 'Considerazioni inattuali'. In *Considerazioni Inattuali (Italian translation of Unzeitgemäße Betrachtungen, 1873–1876)*, ed. F.W. Nietzsche, V–LXII. Turin: Einaudi.

Bergson, Henri. 1903. *An Introduction to Metaphysics*. Translated by T. E. Hulme. New York and London: G. P. Putnam's Sons, 1912.

Biedermann, Alois Emanuel. 1869. *Christliche Dogmatik*. Zurich: Orell, Füssli, & Co.

Bishop, Paul. 1993. The Jung/Förster-Nietzsche Correspondence. *German Life and Letters* 46: 319–330.

———. 1994. The Members of Jung's Seminar on Zarathustra. *Spring* 56: 92–122.

———. 1995a. *The Dionysian Self: C. G. Jung's Reception of Friedrich Nietzsche*. Berlin and New York: De Gruyter.

———. 1995b. Jung's Annotation of Nietzsche's Works: An Analysis. *Nietzsche-Studien* 24: 271–314.

———. 1999. Estrangement from the Deed and the Memory Thereof: Freud and Jung on the Pale Criminal in Nietzsche's *Zarathustra*. *Orbis Litterarum* 54: 424–438.

———, ed. 2004. *Nietzsche and Antiquity. His Reaction and Response to the Classical Tradition*. Rochester, NY: Camden House.

———. 2008. *Analtytical Psychology and German Classical Aesthetics: Goethe, Schiller, and Jung. Vol. 1, The Development of the Personality*. 2 vols. London and New York: Routledge.

———. 2012. Jung's *Red Book* and Its Relation to Aspects of German Idealism. *The Journal of Analytical Psychology* 57: 335–353.

———. 2014. *Carl Jung*. London: Reaktion Books.

———. 2017. *On the Blissful Island with Nietzsche and Jung: In the Shadow of the Superman*. Oxon and New York: Routledge.

Bishop, Paul, and R.H. Stephenson, eds. 2004. *Friedrich Nietzsche and Weimar Classicism*. Rochester, NY: Camden House.

Brobjer, Thomas H. 2010. The Origin and Early Context of the Revaluation Theme in Nietzsche's Thinking. *The Journal of Nietzsche's Studies* 19 (Spring): 12–29.

Buchholz, Michael B., and Günter Gödde, eds. 2005. *Macht und Dynamik des Unbewussten: Auseinandersetzungen in Philosophie, Medizin und Psychoanalyse*. Giessen: Psychosozial Verlag.

Colli, Giorgio. 1980. *Scritti su Nietzsche*. Milan: Adelphi, 1995.

Deleuze, Gilles. 1965. *Nietzsche, sa vie, son œuvre: avec un exposé de sa philosophie*. Paris: PUF, 2005.

Dixon, Patricia E. 1999. *Nietzsche and Jung: Sailing a Deeper Night*. New York: Peter Lang.

Domenici, Gaia. 2014a. Eine 'göttlich künstliche' Sprache. Zarathustra als Beispiel für Nietzsches Lebenskunst. *Nietzscheforschung* 21: 231–240.

———. 2014b. Overleaping oder Surpassing? Die problematische Lektüre der Geschichte des Seiltänzers bei C. G. Jung. In *Nietzsches Zarathustra Auslegen. Thesen, Positionen und Entfaltungen zu "Also sprach Zarathustra" von Friedrich Wilhelm Nietzsche*, ed. Murat Ates, 207–219. Marburg: Tectum Verlag.

———. 2015. Il 'ruggito del leone morale'. C. G. Jung si confronta con *Zarathustra*. In *Prospettive. Omaggio a Giuliano Campioni*, ed. Paolo D'Iorio, Maria Cristina Fornari, Luca Lupo, and Chiara Piazzesi, 197–202. Pisa: ETS.

———. 2018. 'Crush the Head of the Serpent and it will Bite you in the Heel'. A Reconstruction of Jung's Interpretation of the Poisonous Serpents in *Zarathustra* through *Liber Novus*. *Phanês: Journal for Jung History* 1: 1–27. https://doi.org/10.32724/phanes.2018.Domenici.

Freud, Sigmund. 1906–1974. *The Complete Psychological Works of Sigmund Freud*. Edited by J. Strachey and A. Freud. London: The Hogarth Press.

———. 1925–1928. *Gesammelte Schriften von Sigm. Freud*. Leipzig, Vienna, Zurich: Internatioaler Psychoanalitischer Verlag.

Freud, Sigmund, and C.G. Jung. 1974. *Briefwechsel*. Edited by William McGuire and Wolfgang Sauerländer. Frankfurt am Main: Fischer.

Gadamer, Hans. 1986. Das Drama Zarathustra. *Nietzsche-Studien* 15: 1–15.

Gay, Marco, and Isolde Schiffermüller, eds. 2013. *Lo Zarathustra di Nietzsche: C. G. Jung e lo scandalo dell'inconscio*. Bergamo: Moretti & Vitali.

Gödde, Günter. 1999. *Traditionslinien des Unbewußten: Schopenhauer, Nietzsche, Freud*. Tübingen: Edition Diskord.

Goethe, Johann Wolfgang. 1772–1832. *Faust*. Stuttgart and Tübingen, 1835.

Gunter, P.Y.A. 1982. Bergson and Jung. *Journal of the History of Ideas* 43: 635–652. Reprinted. In *Jung in Context. A Reader*, ed. Paul Bishop, 265–282. London and New York: Routledge.

Hölderlin, Friedrich. 1946–. *Sämtliche Werke*, 6 Bände. Stuttgart: W. Kohlhammer Verlag.

Huskinson, Lucy. 2004. *Nietzsche and Jung. The Whole Self in the Union of Opposites*. Hove and New York: Brunner-Routledge.

Innamorati, Marco. 1991. La presenza dello Zarathustra di Nietzsche nelle opere di Jung. *Giornale storico di psicologia dinamica* 29: 73–93.

Jaffé, Aniela. 1967. *Der Mythus vom Sinn im Werk von C. G. Jung*. Translated by R. F. C. Hull. New York: G. P. Putnam's Sons, 1971.

Jarrett, James. 1981. Schopenhauer and Jung. *Spring: An Annual of Archetypal Psychology and Jungian Thought* 81: 193–202.

Johnson, Dirk R. 2010. *Nietzsche's Anti-Darwinism*. New York: Cambridge University Press.
Jung, Carl Gustav. 1902. *On the Psychology and Pathology of So-called Occult Phenomena*. Collected Works of C. G. Jung. Vol. 1, §§ 1–150.
———. 1905. *Cryptomnesia*. Collected Works of C. G. Jung. Vol. 1, §§ 166–186.
———. 1909/1949. *The Significance of the Father in the Destiny of the Individual*. Collected Works of C. G. Jung. Vol. 4, §§ 693–744.
———. 1912. *Psychology of the Unconscious. A study of the Transformations and Symbolisms of the Libido. A contribution to the History of the Evolution of Thought*. New York: Moffat, Yard and Company, 1917.
———. 1917. *On the Psychology of the Unconscious*. Collected Works of C. G. Jung. Vol. 7, §§ 1–201.
———. 1921. *Psychological Types*. Collected Works of C. G. Jung. Vol. 6.
———. 1922/1931. *On the Relation of Analytical Psychology to Poetry*. Collective Works of C. G. Jung. Vol. 15, §§ 97–132.
———. 1930/1950. *Psychology and Literature*. Collected Works of C. G. Jung. Vol. 15, §§ 133–162.
———. 1932a. *Picasso*. Collective Works of C. G. Jung. Vol. 15, 204–214.
———. 1932b. *'Ulysses': A Monologue*. Collective Works of C. G. Jung. Vol. 15, §§ 163–203.
———. 1934. *Archetypes of the Collective Unconscious*. Collected Works of C. G. Jung. Vol. 9, 1, §§ 1–86.
———. 1936. *Wotan*. Collected Works of C. G. Jung. Vol. 10, §§ 371–399.
———. 1939. Foreword to Suzuki's *Introduction to Zen Buddhism*. Collective Works of C. G. Jung. Vol. 11, §§ 538–557.
———. 1945. *After the Catastrophe*. Collected Works of C. G. Jung. Vol. 10, §§ 400–443.
———. 1952a. *Symbols of Transformation*. Collected Works of C. G. Jung. Vol. 5.
———. 1952b. *Synchronicity: An Acausal Connecting Principle*. Collected Works of C. G. Jung. Vol. 8, §§ 816–997.
———. 1989. *Nietzsche's Zarathustra: Notes of the Seminar Given in 1934–9*. 2nd ed. Edited by James L. Jarrett in Two Parts. London: Routledge, 1994.
———. 1996. *The Psychology of Kundalini Yoga. Notes of the Seminar given in 1932*. Edited by Sonu Shamdasani. Princeton: Princeton University Press.
———. 2009. *The Red Book: Liber Novus*. Edited and Introduced by Sonu Shamdasani, Translated by Mark Kyburz, John Peck, and Sonu Shamdasani. New York and London: W. W. Norton & Company.
Jung, Carl Gustav, and Aniela Jaffé. 1962. *Memories, Dreams, Reflections by Carl Gustav Jung*. Recorded and Edited by Aniela Jaffé. New York: Vintage Books, 1989.

Kerner, Justinus Andreas Christian. 1831–1835. *Blätter aus Prevorst; Originalien und Lesefrüchte für Freunde des inneren Lebens, mithgeteilt von dem Herausgeber der Seherin von Prevorst*. Karlsruhe.

Krell, David Farrell. 1986. *Postponements, Woman, Sensuality, and Death in Nietzsche*. Bloomington: Indiana University Press.

Krug, Wilhelm Traugott. 1832. *Allgemeines Handwörterbuch der philosophischen Wissenschaften, nebst ihrer Literatur und Geschichte*. 2nd ed. Leipzig: Brodhaus.

Liebscher, Martin. 2001a. 'Wotan' und 'Puer Aeternus'. Die Zeithistorische Verstrickung von C. G. Jungs Zarathustrainterpretation. *Nietzsche Studien* 30: 329–350.

———. 2001b. Jungs Abkehr von Freud im Lichte seiner Nietzsche-Rezeption. In *Zeitenwende-Wertewende. Internationaler Kongreß der Nietzsche-Gesellschaft zum 100. Todestag Friedrich Nietzsches vom 24.-27. August 2000 in Naumburg*, 255–260. Protokollband des Naumburger Nietzsche-Kongresses. Berlin: Akademie Verlag.

———. 2002. Zarathustra – Der Archetypus des 'Alten Weisen'. *Nietzscheforschung* 9: 234–245.

———. 2003. Die 'unheimliche Ähnlichkeit'. Nietzsches Hermeneutik der Macht und analytische Interpretation bei Carl Gustav Jung. *Ecce Opus* 81: 37–50.

———. 2006. *Nietzsche und Jung*. Review of Lucy Huskinson, *The Whole Self in the Union of Opposites* (2004). *Nietzsche Studien* 35: 393–397.

———. 2012. *Libido und Wille zur Macht. C.G. Jungs Auseinandersetzung mit Nietzsche*. Basel: Schwabe.

———. 2014. Schopenhauer und Jung. In *Schopenhauer-Handbuch. Leben, Werk, Wirkung*, ed. Daniel Schubbe and Matthias Kossler, 312–316. Stuttgart: Metzler.

Lindner, Michael. 2010. 'Ein tiefstes Erlebnis'. C. G. Jungs Lektüre von Nietzsches 'Also sprach Zarathustra' anhand seiner Seminare 1934–39. In *Nietzsche und die Tiefenpsychologie*, ed. Roman Lesmeister and Elke Metzner, 107–120. Freiburg and Munich: Verlag Karl Alber.

Löwith, Karl. 1935–1956. *Nietzsches Philosphie der ewigen Wiederkehr des Gleichen (1935–1956)*. Hamburg: Meiner, 1978.

Lupo, Luca. 2012. 'Also spricht meine Seele'. Lo *Zarathustra* di Nietzsche nel *Libro rosso* di Jung: la verità come vita tra esperienza ed esperimento. In *Teorie e pratiche della verità in Nietzsche*, ed. Pietro Gori and Paolo Stellino. Pisa: ETS.

———. 2013. A 'mighty Hand': Father, God, and Chance: Jung Reads Schopenhauer's 'Transzendente Spekulation über die anscheinende Absichtlichkeit im Schicksale des Einzelnen'. *In Schopenhauer-Jahrbuch* 94: 203–216.

Màdera, Romano. 1989. Nietzsche e Jung: Mitografie del senso perduto. *Aut Aut* 229–230: 111–123.

Nante, Bernardo. 2010. *'El libro rojo' de C. G. Jung. Claves por la comprension de una obra inexplicable*. Madrid: Siruela.

Nicholls, Angus, and Martin Liebscher, eds. 2010. *Thinking the Unconscious. Nineteenth-Century German Thought*. Cambridge: Cambridge University Press.
Nietzsche, Friedrich Wilhelm. 1878. *Human, All Too Human I*. Translated by Alexander Harvey. Chicago: Charles H. Kerr & Company, 1908.
———. 1888–1889. *Dithyrambs of Dionysus*. www.thenietzschechannel.com.
———. 1899–1911. *Kleinoktav-Gesamtausgabe*. Leipzig: Naumann und Kröner.
———. 1930 [1883–1885]. *Thus Spake Zarathustra*. Translated by Thomas Common. New York: The Modern Library.
———. 1967–. *Kritische Gesamtausgabe der Werke Nietzsches*. Edited by Giorgio Colli and Mazzino Montinari. Berlin and New York: De Gruyter.
———. 1980–. *Kritische Studienausgabe*. Edited by Giorgio Colli and Mazzino Montinari. Berlin and New York: De Gruyter.
———. 2009–. *Digital Critical Edition*. Edited by P. D'Iorio.
Nill, Peggy. 1988. Die Versuchung der Psyche: Selbstwerdung als schöpferisches Prinzip bei Nietzsche und C. G. Jung. *Nietzsche-Studien* 17: 250–279.
Parkes, Graham. 1999. Nietzsche and Jung: Ambivalent Appreciations. In *Nietzsche and Depth Psychology*, ed. Jacob Golomb, Weaver Santaniello, and Ronal L. Lehrer, 205–227. Albany: SUNY Press.
Pezzella, Mario, ed. 1995. *Lo spirito e l'ombra. I seminari di Jung su Nietzsche*. Bergamo: Moretti & Vitali.
Pilard, Nathalie. 2015. *Jung and Intuition: On the Centrality and Variety of Forms of Intuition in Jung and Post-Jungians*. Oxon and New York: Routledge, 2018.
Rocci, Giovanni. 1999. *La maschera e l'abisso. Una lettura junghiana di Nietzsche*. Rome: Bulzoni Editore.
Ross, Werner. 1979. *Der ängstliche Adler. Friedrich Nietzsches Leben*. Munich: Kastell Verlag GmbH, 1997/98.
Schmitt, Gerhard. 1998. *Zyklus und Kompensation: Zur Denkfigur bei Nietzsche und Jung*. Frankfurt am Main: Peter Lang.
———. 2011. Vom Übermensch und Übersinn: Nietzsches Metaphorik im *Roten Buch*. *Recherches germaniques* 8 (special edition): 117–133.
Schopenhauer, Arthur. 1851. *Parerga and Paralipomena: Short Philosophical Essays*. 2 vols. Translated by E. F. J. Payne. Oxford: Caledonian Press, 1974.
von Seggern, Hans. 2005. *Nietzsche und die Weimarer Klassik*. Tübingen: Francke Verlag.
Shamdasani, Sonu. 1995. Memories, Dreams, Omissions. *Spring: A Journal of Archetype and Culture* 57, Reprinted. In *Jung in Context. A Reader*, ed. Paul Bishop, 33–50. London and New York: Routledge, 2003.
———. 1998. *Cult Fictions. C.G. Jung and the Founding of Analytical Psychology*. London: Routledge.
———. 2003. *Jung and the Making of Modern Psychology. The Dream of a Science*. Cambridge and New York: Cambridge University Press.
———. 2005. *Jung Stripped Bare: By His Biographers, Even*. London: Karnac.

———. 2009. 'Introduction' and 'Footnotes'. In *The Red Book: Liber Novus*, ed. C.G. Jung. Edited and Introduced by Sonu Shamdasani, Translated by Mark Kyburz, John Peck, and Sonu Shamdasani. New York and London: W. W. Norton & Company.

———. 2012. *A Biography in Books*. New York and London: Norton and Company.

Spitteler, Carl. 1881. *Prometheus und Epimetheus. Ein Gleichnis*. Jena: Eugen Diederichs, 1906.

———. 1900. *Olympischer Frühling*. Jena: Eugen Diederichs, 1910.

———. 1906. *Imago*. Jena: Eugen Diederichs, 1922.

Suzuki, Daisetz Deitaro. 1934. *Die grosse Befreiung: Einführung in den Zen Buddhismus*. Leipzig: C. Weller, 1939.

Vigna, Francesco. 2011. *La depressione creativa. Dal Libro rosso di Jung alla modernità*. Rome: Moretti&Vitali.

Vischer, Friedrich Theodor. *Auch Einer. 1878*. Leipzig: Heffe & Becker Verlag.

Vivarelli, Vivetta. 1989. Empedokles und Zarathustra. Verschwendeter Reichtum und Wollust am Untergang. *Nietzsche-Studien* 18: 509–536.

CHAPTER 2

'Visionary' Works and *Liber Novus*

He who sleeps in the grave of the millennia dreams a wonderful dream. He dreams a primordially ancient dream. He dreams of the rising sun.

If you sleep this sleep and dream this dream in this time of the world, you will know that the sun will also rise at this time. For the moment we are still in the dark, but the day is upon us.

He who comprehends the darkness in himself, to him the light is near. He who climbs down into his darkness reaches the staircase of the working light, fire-maned Helios. (RB II, 5, 'Dies II': 272)

2.1 'Visionary' Works

2.1.1 *Jung's Definition and Characterisation*

As anticipated, Jung makes a distinction between *psychological* and *visionary* works in *Psychology and Literature* (1930/1950):

For the sake of clarity I would like to call the one mode of artistic creation *psychological*, and the other *visionary*. The psychological mode works with materials drawn from man's conscious life—with crucial experiences, powerful emotions, suffering, passion, the stuff of human fate in general. All this is assimilated by the psyche of the poet, raised from the commonplace to the level of poetic experience, and expressed with a power of conviction that gives us a greater depth of human insight by making us vividly aware of those everyday happenings which we tend to evade or to overlook because we perceive them only dully or with a feeling of discomfort. The raw mate-

G. Domenici, *Jung's Nietzsche*,
https://doi.org/10.1007/978-3-030-17670-9_2

> rial of this kind of creation is derived from the contents of man's consciousness, from his eternally repeated joys and sorrows, but clarified and transfigured by the poet. There is no work left for the psychologist to do [...]. The gulf that separates the first from the second part of *Faust* marks the difference between the psychological and the visionary modes of artistic creation. Here everything is reversed. The experience that furnishes the material for artistic expression is no longer familiar. It is something strange that derives its existence from the hinterland of man's mind, as if it had emerged from the abyss of prehuman ages, or from a superhuman world of contrasting light and darkness. It is a primordial experience which surpasses man's understanding and to which in his weakness he may easily succumb. (CW 15: §§ 139–141)

Within such a 'visionary' mode of artistic creation, Goethe is not alone with his *Faust II*: Nietzsche's *Zarathustra* and *Dithyramb of Dionysus* belong to the same category, as well as Dante's *Commedia*; Wagner's *Ring*, *Tristan*, and *Parsifal*; Spitteler's *Olympian Spring* [*Olympischer Frühling*] (1900–1906); Blake's *Poetry and Paintings*; the *Shepherd* of Hermas; Francesco Colonna's *Hypnerotomachia*; 'Jacob Boehme's poetic-philosophic stammerings'; 'the magnificent but scurrilous imagery of E. T. A. Hoffman's tale *The Golden Bowl*'. Furthermore, in 'more restricted and succinct form', this primordial experience is said to constitute 'the essential content of Rider Haggard's *She* and *Ayesha*, of Benoît's *L'Atlantide*, of Alfred Kubin's *Die andere Seite*, of Meyrink's *Das grüne Gesicht*, of Goetz's *Das Reich ohne Raum*, and of Barlach's *Der tote Tag*', although 'the list might be greatly extended' (ibid.: § 142). Interestingly, a few years earlier, Jung had suggested that the participants in his seminar on analytical psychology should choose and read one of these following texts as examples of the Anima in literature: *She*, *L'Atlantide*, *Das grüne Gesicht* (Jung 1925: 127–128). Even more interesting, Hermas, Nietzsche, Wagner, Dante, and Goethe had been already gathered together by Jung in 1921, as representing the tradition of 'the relativity of the symbol' (CW 6: §§ 408–412).

Elsewhere in his writings, Jung expands the list of 'visionary' works just sketched on *Psychology and Literature*. The most remarkable 'visionary' additions are: Spitteler's *Prometheus and Epimetheus* [*Prometheus und Epimetheus*] (1881); Hölderlin's *Song of Fate* [Schicksalslied] (from *Hyperion*, 1797/1798, 1789); Vischer's novel *Auch Einer* (1879). In *Psychological Types*, Jung analyses Spitteler's metric novel as the representation of 'the introverted and extraverted lines of development in one and the same individual, though the poet has embodied it in two independent figures and their typical destinies' (CW 6: § 276). According to such an interpretation, Prometheus would represent introversion and Epimetheus extraversion. In the following few paragraphs, while commenting on Prometheus's soul appearing as a feminine entity, 'separate from his individual ego', he states:

> And, just as the unconscious world of mythological images speaks indirectly, through the experience of external things, to the man who surrenders wholly to the outside world, so the real world and its demands find their way indirectly to the man who has surrendered wholly to the soul; for no man can escape both realities. If he is intent only on the outer reality, he must live his myth; if he is turned only towards the inner reality, he must dream his outer, so-called real life. (ibid.: § 280)

Prometheus has to indeed experience the 'real world'; whereas his brother needs to 'live his myth'. Jung then compares Spitteler's representation of the myth with Goethe's *Prometheus Fragment* (1773), and argues that whereas Spitteler appears to embody an 'introverted type', Goethe 'belongs more to the extraverted [...] type'. Despite many similarities concerning the two Promethean figures and their peculiar relationships with their 'soul[s]', 'one essential difference remains. Goethe's Prometheus is a creator and artist, and Minerva [his soul] inspires his clay images with life. Spitteler's Prometheus is suffering, rather than creative; only his soul is creative, but her work is secret and mysterious'. Differently from Goethe's, Spitteler's Pandora represents the 'equivalent' of the amount of Prometheus's libido withdrawn from the outer world; she is a product of the unconscious to balance Prometheus's introversion. The jewel 'she wants to give to mankind to ease their sufferings' is 'an unconscious mirror-image that *symbolizes* the real work of the soul of Prometheus', 'it is a *God-redeemer*, a renewal of the sun'. Indeed, it 'symbolizes a renewal of God, a new God, but this takes place in the divine sphere, i.e., in the unconscious'. Since Epimetheus represents 'the relation to the world', the 'rational attitude and orientation to objects', Pandora's gift cannot find its place among humans, for these are 'incapable of appreciating the true value and significance of the jewel'. Promethean and Epimethean sides, therefore, appear 'dissociated', and the rebirth of the God can only take place at the end of the story, when the 'enantiodromia' leads Epimetheus to negotiate with Behemoth and allow him to take away the divine children: 'psychologically, this means that the collective, undifferentiated attitude to the world stifles a man's highest values and becomes a destructive force, whose influence increases until the Promethean side, the ideal and abstract attitude, places itself at the service of the soul's jewel and, like a true Prometheus, kindles for the world a new fire' (CW 6: §§ 288–311; see also §§ 434–435). Still in the same section, Jung compares Spitteler's work with *Parsifal*, *Zarathustra*, *Faust II*. In all of these works, 'the solution of the problem [...] is *religious*. It is therefore not surprising that Spitteler too is drawn towards a religion setting', even though here 'the specifically religious problem loses in depth, though gaining in mythological richness and archaism'. Differently from Nietzsche and Goethe, Spitteler does not seem to be conscious of 'the meaning of the symbol' in his work; *Zarathustra* and *Faust*, therefore, appear 'far more satisfying *aesthetically* than Spitteler's *Prometheus*, though the latter, as a more or less faithful reflection of actual processes of the collective unconscious, has a deeper *truth*'. A different and deeper level of awareness, according to Jung, will be achieved by Spitteler in his later *Olympian Spring* [*Olympischer Frühling*] (1906–1909), where 'the renewal of God' will play the main role (ibid.: §§ 324–326). Lastly, in order to show how important it is to accept the uniting symbol—represented in Spitteler's novel by the third son of God, Messias—Jung cites from Blake's poem *The Marriage of Heaven and Hell* (1790), which 'summarizes to simplify the fundamental ideas of Spitteler': 'These two classes of men are always upon earth ... the Prolific and the Devouring ... Religion is an endeavour to reconcile the two' (ibid.: § 460).

Another 'visionary' author is Hölderlin, who had already been quoted in *Wandlungen und Symbole der Libido*, in order to endorse Jung in his representation of libido regression. Among all his poems, 'Song of Fate' seemed to represent the most significant example of 'divine heavenly bliss' [göttlich-infantile Seligkeit]. At that time, however, what interested Jung were the psychic consequences of a too deep introversion of the libido, and the first stanza of Hölderlin's poem was quoted and interpreted as a symbol of such danger. It reads, indeed: 'You move up there in the light / On easeful ground, blessed Geniuses! / Bright divine airs / Touch you lightly [/ As the player's fingers Her holy strings]'. In his 1952 version, Jung develops the symbolic meaning of Hölderlin's poem in terms of 'renewal'. This time, he quotes from the second stanza: 'Fateless, like the sleeping / Infant, breathe the heavenly ones, / Chastely guarded / In modest bud; their spirits / Blossom eternally, / And the quiet eyes / Gaze out in placid / Eternal Serenity'. So, Jung concludes, 'it is enviable prerogative of the gods to enjoy everlasting infancy'. According to the poem, 'Hölderlin was never able to forget this first and greatest happiness whose haunting presence estranged him from real life' (CW 5: §§ 619–620; WSL: 377; Jung cites only the first four lines of the stanza). In 1950, in *A Study in the Process of Individuation* (1934/1950), Jung compares the drawing of a mandala with Hölderlin's poem and writes, right before reporting its verses:

> The numerous wavy lines or layers in the mandala could be interpreted as representing the formation of layers of skin giving protection against outside influences. [...] In our mandala the cortices are boundary lines marking off the inner unity and protecting it against the outer blackness with its disintegrating influences, personified by the serpent. The same motif is expressed by the petals of the lotus and by the skins of the onion: the outer layers are withered and desiccated, but they protect the softer, inner layers. The lotus seat of the Homs-child, of the Indian divinities, and of the Buddha must be understood in this sense. Hölderlin makes use of the same image. (CW 9, 1: § 576; translation modified)

In *Psychological Types*, Jung takes Hölderlin's *Patmos* as an example of 'redeeming symbol': 'Near is God / And hard to apprehend. / But where danger is, there / Arises salvation also'. As shown in the poem, even the divine might be dangerous, when in excess; the symbol therefore arises as 'the saving factor', the element 'which embraces both conscious and unconscious and unites them' (CW 6: § 446). Furthermore, in '*Ulysses*': *A Monologue* (1932), Hölderlin is associated with Nietzsche, Goethe, and Joyce, for his *prophetical* capacity towards modernism (CW 15: § 178).

The last author to be considered part of the same category of 'visionary' authors is Friedrich Theodor Vischer. Jung writes, in *Psychological Types*:

> His [the introverted type's] ideal is a lonely island where nothing moves except what he permits to move. Vischer 's novel, *Auch Einer*, affords deep insight into this side of the introverted psychology, and also into the underlying symbolism of the collective unconscious. (CW 6: § 627)

Among these 'visionary' works, a few of them deserve particular attention, since they are consistently compared with *Zarathustra* by Jung. These are: *Faust II*; *Song of Fate* (therefore *Hyperion*), *Olympian Spring*, and *Prometheus and Epimetheus*; *Auch Einer*. To give a few examples, the 'destructive element in the Epimethean attitude' is compared by Jung with Nietzsche's 'Ass Festival in *Zarathustra*' in *Psychological Types* (CW 6: § 312; see also § 322). However, it is in his seminar on *Zarathustra*, that Jung highlights such proximity quite significantly. So, referring to *Prometheus and Epimetheus*, he argues that 'there are quite certainly primordial experiences in *Faust*, but others are taken from his [Spitteler's] wide mystical reading' and 'only by analysing [*Olympian Spring*] as we are analysing *Zarathustra*, could we make out which is the genuine experience and which is elaboration' (SNZ I: 224; 7 November 1934). On 5 June 1935, the 'Bush soul'—of which Nietzsche's relation to Zarathustra is an example, according to Jung—is compared to *Auch Einer* motto *Die Tücke des Objekts* (ibid.: 528). A similar statement had already been made on 30 January 1935, in regard to *Zarathustra* chapter 'Of the Afterworldsmen' ('Backworldsmen', as translated by Thomas Common in Jung's edition), and to Nietzsche's criticism of such disregard of the body of 'afterworldmen'. So, Jung had expressed himself: '[y]ou will then observe that the German philosopher tells about the *die Tücke des Objekts*. And the more you curse them, the more you see speech figures which insinuate life into them' (ibid.: 352). In *Zarathustra*, it is stated indeed: 'Beyond the sphere of their body and this earth they now fancied themselves transported, these ungrateful ones. But to what did they owe the convulsion and rapture of their transport? To their body and this earth' (Za I, 3, KSA 4: 37, translation by Thomas Common). *Zarathustra* as an experience will be associated with Vischer's *Auch Einer* also in *Memories, Dreams Reflexions*, where Jung will express his retrospective fear of going through a destiny similar to Nietzsche's one, by stating: 'I feared I might be forced to recognize that I too was another such strange bird [daß ich wie Nietzsche "Auch Einer" war]' (MDR: 102). While analysing 'On the Blissful Islands', Jung compares Zarathustra's animals with Prometheus's, and establishes that as the tiger represents the latter's Anima, so the lioness embodies Zarathustra's. Moreover, he adds that 'In *Prometheus* the lion is the will to power, and the dog is the sentimentality, the weakness, the craving for love and tenderness' (SNZ II: 871; 26 February 1936). In the following session, Jung compares Nietzsche's representation of one of Zarathustra's 'Blissful Islands' to a mandala 'in which the god expresses himself', exactly as in Hölderlin's *Song of Fate*, that he quotes in this occasion as well, and explains: 'So the god of the underworld, or the water world, which is the collective unconscious, brings up that Happy Island upon which the god is seated; on that flower he can be nursed. You may remember, perhaps, that the German poet Hölderlin uses exactly the same image of the god' (ibid.: 887; 4 March 1936). Lastly, on 7 December 1938, Jung compares Joyce's and Spitteler's experiences to Nietzsche's, even though these authors appear to him as if trying to deny the power of the unconscious over their works (ibid.: 1445–1446).[1]

As already argued, what seems to keep *Zarathustra* and *Faust II* together is their capacity to reveal their authors as *prophets*. Leaving the unconscious component aside, it is truly remarkable that a few significant peculiarities occur in all these 'visionary' works. In the next sections of this chapter, the focus will be directed on such works, aiming to draw stylistic similarities, common ground, and mediations.

2.1.2 Return to Mythology

At a first glance, such 'visionary' works do not seem to share significant common features concerning their style. Indeed, *Faust* and *Olympian Spring* are metric poems; *Hyperion* and *Prometheus* are free verse poems—the former is even written in the form of an epistolary novel; *Auch Einer* belongs to the genre of novels more broadly; *Zarathustra* presents a mixed style, which cannot unequivocally fit into one precise category. However, since Jung could grasp a certain similarity in all of these works, it is arguable to wonder whether there is something to be noticed in them, apart from their presumable reflecting 'the hinterland of man's mind, as if it had emerged from the abyss of prehuman ages' (CW 15: § 141). In fact, a few recurrent motifs in their style deserve to be highlighted; above all, they all present highly *symbolic* patterns, particularly recalling the Bible and the *mythology* of ancient Greece. Mythology in general seems to be the most significant element in all of these 'visionary' works. Finally, it can be stated that a peculiarity also concerns the authors' relation with these texts: *Faust*, *Hyperion*, *Zarathustra IV* were never considered ready to be shared with readers.

Goethe, in particular, worked on *Faust* throughout the period 1772–1832, that is to say, from his first elaborations of *Urfaust* until his death. His first publication of *Faust, a Fragment* [*Faust, ein Fragment*] (1790) was followed by the first edition of *Faust I*, in 1808, to which a second edition followed in years 1828–1829. In *Faust II*, along with the protagonist's political rise, his cognitive development is also represented. This is moved by the feminine ideal, which is depicted by Goethe through the most traditional figures from Greek mythology, such as the mothers or Helena. Besides, significant biblical motifs are also recurrent: Mephistopheles embodies a hellish figure who played with Faust's thirst for knowledge by betting with God against Faust's salvation. The whole work evokes angels and devils recurrently, and the very last scene of the book describes a traditional fight between celestial and hellish potencies, contending for Faust's soul. As pointed out by Burton Feldman, the utilisation of mythology in Goethe's *Faust* differentiates from 'subsequent romantic use of the myth', for the fact that he neither dissolves nor subordinates the 'Nordic, Pagan and Christian myths' one to the other; rather, Goethe 'seeks a balance between these contrasting and often contradictory mythic elements that later writers either deliberately destroy or lose'. When it comes to advocating one of the other tendencies—namely retaining 'older myths', yet subordinating 'them decisively to Christian and modern purposes'—the author mentions Wagner, Novalis, and Hölderlin, indeed (Feldman 1972: 262). In this sense, it can be stated that *Hyperion* represents the modern quest for the lost Greek society—utterly unattainable for the moderns—and the conflict provoked by such quest in the German reality of the late eighteenth century. The plot describes a young Greek, educated to classics, who decides to fight against the Turkish army during the 'Orlov Revolt' (1770), one of the very first attempts to achieve independence. The aim of the protagonist is to restore Greece's cultural and religious atmosphere, motivated by his passion for history and legends from his country. The story is spaced out by a journey to Europe with a relatively short break in Germany, and the structure of the novel is composed of letters from Hyperion to Bellarmin, his closest friend, as well as of a few letters to Diotima, the woman Hyperion is in love with. The temporal structure is a circular one, and Greek and German experiences merge consistently throughout the novel. As argued by Feldman, 'Hölderlin [...] takes literally what romantic mythologists from Herder on taught but never practiced so intensely: that myth must be livingly experienced to be understood, and that regaining such mythic depth and life may help redeem modern man'. In the poem, such a motif comes together with one of Hölderlin's more mature topics, that is, 'waiting for divine appearance'. This latter topic appears to be still a romantic and Christian one, albeit re-elaborated in the direction of what could be called the 'leading' role of the poet: the Gods might indeed 'not have vanished, but may have only withdrawn because of man's own indifference, corruption, and "forgetfulness"'; the poet is the balancing element which enlightens human minds through his/her works (ibid.: 329–330).

The whole plot of *Auch Einer* boasts to be—in an openly anti-Hegelian and anti-idealistic polemic—a criticism against any aesthetic conception being grounded on 'ideal' and trying to freeze the 'real' through the illusion of pre-established harmony. Ironically, the novel plays on the impossibility to escape destiny, in which *objects* deceitfully seem to impose on the subject that is ignoring them ['die Tücke des Objekts'] (see Althaus 2011). A few references to ancient Greece—especially to Greek drama—are to be found in this novel as well. In particular, mythological references play one of the main roles in the novel, as the centre of the story concerns the fictitious *myth* about an ancient tribe living by the Lake Zurich, the so-called *Pfahldorfgeschichte*. In this story, life and tradition of such a tribe are made up in detail; above all, their religious system and rituals are described meticulously, through their profession of belief in a goddess called 'Selinur', 'the great mother of all things, who lives in the moon, who weaved on the sacred spindle earth and water and air and grass and trees and animals and men, and to these she often appeared as a white cow' (Vischer 1878, Part One: 139–140; translation of Vischer's writings is my own throughout). Among its goals, this work is indeed aimed to emphasise the necessity of abandoning realism and ideal-radicalisms, promoting, instead, what someone has defined as 'poetical real-idealism'. This represents an alternative approach to reality, which borrows much of its essence from Prutz's and Schlegel's views. In this sense, the entire world can be read as a poem in which each single human individual is a poet, even when not aware, and possesses all the necessary tools to interpret it from his or her own perspective. This is why symbology, cosmology, and mythology achieve such a decisive role in Vischer's works, and in *Auch Einer* in particular. As Paul Bishop remarks, 'In a letter to David Friedrich Strauß of 27 May 1838, Vischer once defined himself as "a cross between philosophy and poetry" (Zwitter *zwischen Philosophie und Poesie*), and as "an amphibian of idealism and realism" (Amphibium *zwischen Idealismus und Realismus*)' (Bishop 2012: 354).

It is safe to say Spitteler's *Olympian Spring*—for which he was awarded the Nobel Prize in 1919—presents mythological references, its title giving an example on its own. Indeed, the iambic hexameter poem represents a revisitation of the history of the Olympians. Moreover, the work presents different registers, depending on the context of the scene depicted. Among these, the conspicuous presence of Swiss-German dialectal elements is to be remarked (Highet 1952). As pointed out by Gilbert Highet, the story of the Greek gods is told 'with a strangely enlarged view of the universe as background. We do not meet the Olympians first as divine children. [...] No, they are immortals, and so they are never born. We first see them lying in the underworld, sleeping a sleep which seems to have had no beginning. Like veins of gold a thousand miles deep in the earth, they could slumber unseen in the dark forever' (ibid. 341). Indeed, also the old Kronos and the inhabitants of his kingdom, after being defeated, do not really die but fall in an everlasting sleep in the underworld. In Spitteler's re-elaboration, the real ruler, above gods, earth, and underworld, is Ananke, representing destiny and necessity, namely 'the constrained constraint [der gezwungene Zwang]' (Spitteler 1900/1906: *Erster Gesang*). However, the Olympians are all depicted with their popular characteristics, and, although rethought in its deepest meaning, the story does not contradict its tradition. In *Prometheus and Epimetheus* too, mythological echoes are easy to be tracked, as the title suggests this time too. It is indeed another revisitation of the Greek tradition, namely of the popular legend of the two brothers Prometheus and Epimetheus. Some of Spitteler's characters are the same as in the original myth, for example, the brothers themselves and Pandora. At the same time, however, further characters appear, whose features reveal other references to the ancient Greeks or to mythology more broadly. For instance, one of the God's three children is called 'Mythos', whilst his daughter's name is 'Doxa'; moreover, Prometheus's 'soul' is referred to as 'Sophia', and the subtitle of the book is *Ein Gleichnis*, thus suggesting a certain Christian inspiration. Indeed, Christian and Gnostic references are to be found throughout (Highet 1949: 529). Even more than this, Spitteler deserves to be acknowledged for his ability to transform the original myth and enrich it through Platonic, Gnostic, and Neo-Platonic elements, in a way that recalls Goethe's, Herder's, Byron's, and Shelley's re-elaboration of the same myth (Kluth 1918: 25–28). Similarly to *Faust*, the story begins with a conflict between two non-human potencies: God is sick and intends to protect his beloved people from the continuous threats of his archenemy's Behemoth. Also in this case, a messenger comes down to earth. This time, however, the messenger is an angel who informs Prometheus about God's will. Lastly, God's last child bears the name of 'Messias'. At the end of the story, however, it will be Myth to ascend to God's throne. This latter element can be compared to Prometheus's constantly challenging the Gods which, as observed by Fritz Buri, can be regarded as Spitteler's attempt to counterbalance the hero-model generated by the figure of 'Christ' (Buri 1945: 30–40).

To conclude this first discourse, *Zarathustra* mythological and biblical references have been partly discussed already, and even more will be added in the following chapters. Thus there is no need to repeat or anticipate anything here, except from recalling their relevant presence. After all, Nietzsche himself referred to his work as a 'fifth "gospel"' [*fünftes 'Evangelium'*], as he wrote to his editor Ernst Schmeitzer from Rapallo, on 13 February 1883 (eKGWB: letter n. 375). Similarly, in a letter to his sister Elisabeth and his brother in law Bernahrd Förster from Sils Maria, dating 29 July 1885, he speaks of his 'profound gospel' [tiefsinnigen Evangelium] (ekGWB: letter n. 614). Also in *Nachlaß*, Zarathustra is sometimes addressed as a 'gospel' (NF 6[4] 1886; summer 1886–spring 1887, KSA 12: 234). Sossio Giametta has intensively dealt not only with Nietzsche's usage and meaning of the very phrase 'fifth "gospel"' in relation to *Zarathustra*'s anti-Christian function but also with the strong, albeit hidden, fascination that Hölderlin arguably exerted over Nietzsche's poetry. In particular, although Nietzsche and Hölderlin promote antithetical ultimate ideas, *Zarathustra* can be reasonably understood as inspired by Hölderlin's *Empedokles* not only in regard to the many recurrent topics and images of the book, but also because of the similar experience that the two authors went through (the most significant one being the 'cosmic revelation' experienced by both Nietzsche and Hölderlin in Switzerland, in Sils Maria and Hauptwyl respectively) (Giametta 1988, 2006, 2009).

What was called a 'return to mythology' is majorly visible through the frequent utilisation of recurrent symbolical patterns in all of the works mentioned above. Such images as the sun or the journey (often associated with a wanderer); the ideas of sacrifice and transition, as well as death, are features recurring in all of the 'visionary' works. In both *Zarathustra* and *Faust II*, the invocation to the sun occurs significantly; in *Prometheus*, Spitteler regularly refers to the sun, its daily path and seasons, whenever a new discourse has to be introduced. Another recurrent motif concerns, as said, travelling, often in *solitude*. To begin with, Faust travels from one place to another throughout the evolving of the story, and Hyperion calls himself a voluntary exiled—he has indeed traveled non-stop from Greece to Sicily, then to Germany and finally back to Greece. Moreover, the entire first part of Vischer's *Auch Einer* describes the accidental meeting between the protagonist, the writer 'A. E.', and a man who will unexpectedly become his heir, during a journey on a train—the novel's subtitle is 'A travel acquaintance' [Eine Reisebekanntschaft]; in the *Pfahldorfgeschichte*, as expected from any proper myth, a few moments of hero's travels and solitude are depicted. Furthermore, in *Prometheus and Epimetheus*, as well as in *Olympian Spring*, several episodes describe journeys and wanderings (in *Prometheus*, Pandoras being sent on earth is likely to represent the most significant example). Lastly, Zarathustra consistently travels from his cave on the mountains to cities, islands, and woods, waiting for his 'teaching' to be understood. Consequently, the protagonists of most of these works come across similar landscapes, such as mountains—meant as symbols of wisdom, as opposed to the vulgarising of the 'city'—forests, deserts—which remind one of biblical imagination, more generally. Furthermore, all of these 'visionary' works share the frequent utilisation of natural motifs, such as plants and wild animals.

Besides, in all of these texts, magic or supernatural creatures appear quite frequently, not rarely coming from the underworld. Still in this perspective, the transposition of the feminine element onto a supernatural level lies at the core of all of these works. *Faust* embodies the continuous quest for the perfect feminine symbol: Gretchen in the first part, Helena and the mothers in the second. Hyperion falls in love with Diotima, who gives him motivation and strength to leave his country and fight; her loss will cause him unbearable pain. In *Olympian Spring*, the ability to decipher the 'book of stone' with the 'rules of destiny' is only given to the prophetess Sybil (Spitteler 1900/1906: *Erster Gesang*); in *Prometheus and Epimetheus*, Prometheus's feminine 'soul' is the reason why he refuses the angel's proposal and gives up his kingdom on behalf of his brother. In the *Pfahldorfgeschichte*, the adoration of the goddess Selinur is at the centre of any other action; besides, it is to be recalled that the 'druid' Alpin, the hero of the story, is in love with a maiden, Sigune, who lives with her father and takes care of her siblings. Nietzsche—as anticipated—defines the figure of Ariadne as the essential element to balance and complete Dionysus and his solitude.

2.2 'Visionary' Authors

2.2.1 Theology

All of the 'visionary' authors appear to enjoy playing with names, pseudonyms, and false identities: Spitteler published *Prometheus* under the name of Carl Felix Tandem; Vischer used the pseudonym of Deutobold Symbolizetti to publish his first edition of *Faust III* (1862), namely a parody of Goethe's masterpiece, then republished in 1886; Hölderlin used the name Scardanelli to write from the tower in Tübingen, at the time of his mental illness; Goethe pretended he was called Johann Philipp Möller during his travel to Italy (1786); Nietzsche, as is well-known, loved to play with his identity by creating a tension between himself and his role as a writer, and *Ecce Homo* is surely the best literary example; he also—wrongly—boasted Polish roots for his surname, Niëtzky or Nietzky (NF 21[2], Summer 1882, KSA 9: 681; eKGWB: letter n. 324, 28 July 1862 to Raimund Granier, from Gorenzen). Besides, other features might be considered, which hold these authors together. First of all, they all seem to show interest in theology. With the only exception of Goethe, all of these 'visionary' authors were enrolled in the Faculty of Theology, even though, in most cases, they dropped out after a short time. However, Goethe too was deeply interested in the subject, as will be further explored below.

Johann Christian Friedrich Hölderlin (1770–1843) was raised and educated in Swabia. He attended the religious schools of Denkendorf, Maulbronn, and the famous *Stift* in Tübingen, where he studied theology, philosophy, and philology. His family boasted a religious tradition, especially from the maternal side (his grandfather was a pietist parson); he was therefore expected to become a theologian as well. However, in 1793, Hölderlin decided to become a private preceptor, supported by Friedrich Schiller. Such a profession did not seem to be his design either, so he moved to Thuringia and studied philosophy in Jena in 1795. He spent there only one year, but during that time, he could enjoy Fichte's lectures and deepen his relationship with Schiller. In the following year, he settled down in Frankfurt, where he was assigned the role of a private teacher; however, due to an affair with the lady of the house where he was working, he was not allowed to keep such a job for a long time. After this experience, Hölderlin tried to succeed as a writer while working as a private teacher, until madness burst into his life irreversibly (Castellari 2002: 15–21).[2] Although Hölderlin abandoned the faculty of Theology, he never ceased to be engaged in theological issues, taking on a position often defined as 'pantheistic'. As remarked by a few scholars, the poet came across a strong Spinozian tradition as early as his day in Tübingen. In addition to this, Hegel's philosophy has possibly impacted Hölderlin's pantheistic view, predominantly characterised by dialectical thinking: as part of nature, man can be regarded as divine, but because of his experiencing the wound of life—through the uniqueness of the moment—he perceives the distance between himself and nature, and suffers accordingly. It can be argued that the divine wholeness finds its resolution in the dynamic process of life and its flowing through time. In the first moment of this dialectical process, through the experience of fleetness, the individual feels the suffering, solitude, and otherness in the world, so he or she can relate to the divine only in terms of unreachability. Right before the separation, however, man, the world, and the divine appear united in a state of perfection, for such suffering encourages one to be withdrawn and meditative, to the point of auto-reflection. This is the second moment of the dialectical process at the core of Hölderlin's pantheism. At this stage, man can acknowledge the divine both in nature and within. Finally, in the last moment, man can reunite with such a divine in a different way and on a different level. Poetry seems to be the perfect medium for such a purpose, since it recreates the same process and leads to experience the same feeling of divine unity. Greek myth, in particular, appears to be the most effective instrument for a representation of the perfect union of human and the divine; it also represents an everlasting model, inspiring, and effective throughout different epochs (Gottschalk 1943: 54–67). Hölderlin's dialectical pantheism, lastly, can be recognised within *Hyperion* itself (Craig 1996: 162–172).

Friedrich Theodor Vischer (1807–1887) came from a tradition of evangelic theologians and his father, a parson in Württemberg—who passed away when the author was only seven years old—was a representative of Rationalistic Theology. It is most likely due to his family's financial situation that Vischer decided to study theology in Tübingen. Differently from his friend David Friedrich Strauß—who will later happen to be the unfortunate target of Nietzsche's first *Untimely Meditation* (*David Strauß. The Confessor and the Writer* [*David Strauß. Der Bekenner und der Schriftsteller*]; 1873)—Vischer did not seem to be particularly involved in religious debates; at least not as much as he was concerned with aesthetics. Nonetheless, he accomplished his study in 1832 and worked for the Lutheran church of his region. His passion for philosophy and philology led him to habilitate for teaching both subjects as well. In 1834, Vischer started to teach and, in 1844, achieved a full professorship. During his inaugural lecture though, his anti-pietistic theologian position caused him a two-year suspension. As suggested by Ulrich Köpf, to understand Vischer's relation to theology, three directions are to be investigated, that is, a 'biographical-psychological', a 'scientific' and a 'historic' one. In regard to the 'biographical-psychological' investigation, all of the aforementioned aspects of Vischer's relation to his family are to be considered; the 'scientific' analysis, instead, has to be understood as related to his philosophical position—apparently determined by a strong Hegelian resonance, in which the only significant aspect of religion is its relation to the absolute (dogmas and rigidity are denied—religion representing the first step of the 'Spirit', followed by beauty and philosophy). The last possible approach to the issue of Vischer and religion, namely the 'historic' perspective, concerns Vischer's relation to his contemporaries, in particular his criticism to New Pietism. Vischer and Strauß were taught by Ferdinan Christian Baur about the importance of a *mythological* reading of the New Testament and of a similar approach to the Bible overall; Strauß grounded his *Life of Jesus* [*Das Leben Jesu*] (1835/1836) on such a teaching indeed. Vischer, above all, blames contemporary Pietism for not being able to approach religion from a 'modern' or 'mythic' perspective; and for being too radical in his religious attitude, presumably hiding a lack of faith. In so doing, Vischer stresses the contradictions within the movement, as well as their radical positions, such as extreme rationalism, or supernaturalism. Vischer's understanding of religion can be arguably regarded as in the same tradition of Hegel's 'speculative theology', in which contemporary men and women can reach his or her past through a mythological approach to the Scriptures (Köpf 2011).[3]

Nietzsche (1844–1900) could be proud of his Lutheran roots from both his maternal and his paternal side. He attended the religious school of *Schulpforta*, and then began to study Theology and Philology in Bonn in 1864. Only a few months later, he first abandoned Theology, then changed university and moved to Leipzig. Since this issue will be discussed further on, only a few significant elements are to be brought out in this section. First of all, as many scholars have pointed out, Nietzsche's reflection can hardly be separated from his Christian education. Karl Schlechta, for instance, defines *Zarathustra* as a 'secularised hell' [säkularisierte Hölle], interpreting Nietzsche's philosophy as only possible within the framework of Christian categories—whose values appear indeed complementary to *Zarathustra*. According to his understanding, the only result emerging from *Zarathustra* would be a triumph of resignation and discomfort (Schlectha 1954: 66). Recently, Julian Young expressed himself against more traditional positions which regarded Nietzsche as an atheist, such as those of Kaufmann, Bäumler, or Bertram, and proposed an alternative reading, which emphasises Schopenhauer's fascination on Nietzsche, and considers the latter as a 'religious reformer' belonging to the German 'Volkisch' tradition of his time (Young 2006: 2; see Santaniello 2007). A meticulous investigation of Nietzsche and his religious education has been undertaken by Joahnn Figl, in his *Nietzsche und die Religionen*. The scholar analyses Nietzsche's knowledge on religion from his years in *Naumburger Gymnasium* and *Schulpforta* onwards. Interestingly, along with Christian, pre-Christian, and Western non-Christian religions, Nietzsche appears to have had a wide knowledge of Indian and Eastern religions as well, started already in his earliest education in *Pforta* (Figl 2007: 35–38), and then mediated by readings, among which is Emerson (ibid.: 130–131). Finally, Peter Köster's collection of articles *Kontroversen um Nietzsche: Untersuchungen zur theologischen Rezeption* deserves to be recalled. Majorly stressed by the author is the impossibility of any theological reading of Nietzsche not intending to 'revaluate' their own fundamentals. Nietzsche's greatest merit, indeed, would be having highlighted the auto-contradiction present in any theological reflection. In his investigation, the author seriously discusses and questions the most traditionally shared opinions on Nietzsche and Christianity, showing, instead, a certain radicalism in Nietzsche's understanding of theology (Köster 2003; Liebscher 2005). Such irremediable auto-contradiction was the core of Franz Overbeck's speculation in his book *Über die Christlichkeit unserer heutigen Theologie* (1873), published contemporarily to Nietzsche's first *Untimely Meditation* (Overback 1873; Pellegrino 2005). Nietzsche and Overbeck shared a house in Basel, where they both were teaching, and remained friends until the very end of Nietzsche's conscious life.

Carl Friedrich Georg Spitteler (1845–1924) had also been seriously engaged with theological issues since his youngest years, especially due to his frequent visits to the Widmann family. Widmann, the father of Carl's friend Josef Viktor ('Peppi') and Anna (Spitteler's first love), was initially a Jesuit monk strongly influenced by Strauß' *Life of Jesus*, who then converted to Protestantism. After moving to Liestal, he eventually started his career as a parson (Faesi 1933: 14–17). During his years as a young student, Spitteler lived with his aunt, far from the rest of his family; thus he spent much of his time in the household of his friend Josef Viktor. In particular, as reported by his biographers, Spitteler loved to be entertained by long theological discussion with Widmann, who also prepared him for his confirmation. Such a figure is likely to have played a significant role in Spitteler's decisions, to the point that he is even mentioned in the curriculum presented before Spitteler's theology final exam in 1871. In the same document, however, Spitteler also refers to a certain sense of 'inner emptying' [innere Entleerung] that he felt after his first communion, due to the 'pause occurring in the external ecclesiastical life'. Private classes of 'Herr Prf. Widmann' would help Spitteler 'restrain' such a feeling, but could do nothing for it to be 'deterred' (Buri 1945: 9–10). A similar sense of 'emptying' was experienced by Spitteler also at the time of choosing his university career. Precisely such a conflict with traditional Protestantism led him to the study of theology, among whose issues Spitteler was mainly concerned with the question of man's relation to God and the divine. Already in the 233 theses written in May 1862, Spitteler was setting his goal in showing weak points of the Christian doctrine. First of all, he wanted to contrast the concept of 'human dignity' [Würde des Menschen] with the feeling of inferiority preached by the Church. To this end, the divine element present in man through *incarnation* was emphasised, and the qualities of opposition and exteriority traditionally attributed to the Christian concept of God were contradicted. Second, the understanding of 'Sin' [Sünde] was investigated and criticised, to which the idea of 'mistake' [Fehler] was counterposed, and the concept of 'repentance' [Reue] was substituted with the possibility of 'improving' [verbessern]. Man and the divine had to be understood as parts of the same wholeness, to which sin could still belong, but in a different perspective: 'God wants sin; else he would be miserable'. Although Spitteler had been dreaming of becoming a poet since he was 16, and then attempted a jurisprudential career to follow his father's example (a state officer), such a determination in re-examining Christianity pushed him to study theology in Zurich during the period 1865–1870. After having completed his study, he moved to Russia and Finland and worked as a private preceptor. In 1879, Spitteler returned to Switzerland and devoted himself to primary education and journalism (ibid.: 11–29; Faesi 1933: 21–28).[4]

Johann Wolfgang Goethe (1749–1831) dedicated much of his time to theological studies in his youngest years, although his university plan involved the study of law. As it was for Spitteler, also Goethe's father was indeed a state officer and planned for his son a similar career. At the age of 16, Goethe joined the faculty of Jurisprudence at University of Leipzig—culture-wise more stimulating than his hometown Frankfurt am Main. However, the three years he spent there were not pleasant for him, and culminated with a sudden—and relatively obscure—return to Frankfurt, where he remained for a while. Goethe's psychological discomfort did not seem to disappear, until he met Susanna Klettenberg, a friend of his mother, and approached Gnosticism and alchemy. The lady belonged to a semi-Moravian sect, and professed a form of Christianity in which a certain tendency to Pietism was blended with 'introspective mysticism' of occultism, Neo-Platonism, and Hermeticism (Williams 1998: 1–13).

Thus, Goethe started to face authors such as Nostradamus, Paracelsus, Agrippa von Nettesheim, Böhme, Van Helmont, and Welling. In such readings, he was hoping to find alternatives to the traditional sciences, as well as to fulfil his need for introspection. Thanks to his own medical doctor, he even experimented with some alchemic products on himself and recovered in a short time. In 1770, he completed his study of law in Strasbourg. However, Goethe's relation to religion had even deeper roots, as well as even deeper consequences. It can be dated back to 1755, when the Lisbon earthquake took place and upset his imagination of a creative God, protector of his own creatures. Besides, still in his childhood, Goethe read the Bible, as well as the sacred epic poem by Klopstoc, *Der Messias* (1748–1773). Several scholars have dealt with the issue of Goethe and religion, and different aspects have been brought out: often his keen and deep propensity to religious reflection emerged; other times, the merely aesthetic meaning of religious *feeling* was stressed above all. What is common to all these studies, however, is Goethe's peculiar dedication to religious issues and debates.[5] In particular, Goethe openly called himself a 'pantheist'. So in a letter to Jacobi, dating 6 January 1813, he writes:

> As a poet and artist I am polytheist, pantheist instead as a naturalist, and the one just as decidedly as the other. When I need a God for my personality, as a moral human being, then I do not have to worry either. Heaven and earth are such a wide realm, that can only be grasped by uniting the organs of all beings.

Several times, indeed, he even displayed a predilection for Spinoza—whose thinking he first came across in 1773—by making use of sections from his *Ethics* (1667), in order to ground his argument on nature. Moreover, Goethe was also fascinated by Kant, and engaged in complex philosophical debates with Fichte, Schelling, and Hegel. Regardless of the question of Spinoza's philosophy as an actual representation of pantheism, Goethe significantly recognised the philosopher as such and used his thought to identify his own reflection in a precise philosophical-religious tradition (Lange 2011). Lastly, the wideness of Goethe's knowledge on religion is not to be forgotten: as a child, he was educated as a Lutheran; in Leipzig, he came across Pietism; in Italy he got to know Catholicism; thanks to Susanna Klettenberg, he became passionate about Gnosticism and alchemy. To this all, Goethe's interest in Eastern religions and Hebraism is to be added, the latter being known by him since his childhood (Simm 2000). Particularly in his earliest writings, Goethe questioned the Christian understanding of Providence, as well as Christ's role as the actual founder of Christianity: according to him, Christianity was originally to be understood as a political institution. In his view, the idea of the divine could only take place in a representation of the world meant as harmony and wholeness. If Goethe's early poem *Prometheus* (1772–1774/1789) can be doubtless read in this way (Weber 2009), a similar but more mature understanding can be found in *Faust* as well. On 3 January 1830, Goethe wrote to Eckermann: 'Faust is something incommensurable, and any attempt to bring it closer to the understanding is vain. Also, it is to be considered that the first part is the result of a somewhat dark state of the individual. But this very darkness tempts men, and they struggle with it, as with all unsolvable problems'.

2.2.2 Basel and Its Environment

As anticipated, Nietzsche taught Philology at *Pädagogium* and University of Basel. The former was the same school where Spitteler studied in his teens, and that a few years later Jung too would attend. One of the most influential figures in Basel was Jacob Burckhardt; he was a colleague of Nietzsche's, as well as a former teacher of Spitteler's at *Pädagogium*. Another major figure in that environment was Johan Jacob Bachofen. At the time of Jung's adolescence, Burckhardt and Bachofen were quite old but still lived in Basel; Jung even reported to have seen them walk on Basel streets (MDR: 111). Since its foundation in 1454, the University of Basel has always boasted a certain academic freedom, coming to represent an important model of independence for other institutions (e.g. for University of Bologna). By defining itself as a melting pot of different cultures—above all French and Italian—it has always shown up as cosmopolitan and supranational. Following post-Napoleonic geographic and political readjustments, Basel was to pick between two possible models: either that of French *grandes Écoles*—more oriented towards professional skills—or the Humboldtian one, whose only purpose was its students' *Bildung*. The latter was chosen as a model, and in 1820, a few reformations took place, aiming, above all, at breaking off from the narrowness of academic environment, and opening up to Basel citizenship. Accordingly, a few hours of professorship contracts were to be dedicated to public lectures, and professors had to teach additional classes or seminars at *Pädagogium*. Figures such as Burckhardt or Bachofen played their major parts in this context (Schorske 1994; Bonjour 1960).[6]

According to Lionel Gossman and his monograph *Basel in the Age of Burckhardt* (2000), both Bachofen and Burckhardt came from families settled in Basel since the sixteenth century, both belonging to the upper class, and both oriented to giving religious education to their children. Johan Jacob Bachofen (1815–1887) was brought up as a Calvinist, thanks to Burckhardt's father, who was a parson and prepared him for his Confirmation. The parson had also published a *Lehrbuch des christlichen Religionsunterrichts für die kirchen des Kantos Basel*, officially approved, whereby a different type of Calvinism came across as strongly influenced by Illuminism and Pietism. As opposed to traditional Calvinism, in such a *Lehrbuch*, the doctrine of predestination was said to have less value, whereas man's *divine* nature was stressed, man being 'the noblest part of Creation'. Bachofen attended the most prestigious schools in Basel quite successfully, culminating with *Pädagogium* (1831–1834), where he could study both the humanities and sciences. At the end of his period there, he decided to deepen his knowledge of Latin and Greek at the University of Basel, where he stayed until 1835. Although there is no evidence that he attended De Wette's theology classes, it can be stated that this name played a major role in Bachofen's future myth conception. De Wette, indeed, was a friend of Creuzer's and shared with him the opinion that Old and partly New Testaments had to be read *symbolically*, so that the Scriptures could maintain a certain impact on their readers even in the modern or contemporary age, and despite dogmas. In fact, once freed from historical facticity, the Bible could achieve a *mythological* meaning. Bachofen then moved to Berlin, where he stayed until 1837, and studied Laws, although he decided that his curriculum should focus on a more historical approach. Among his teachers, names such as Ranke, Böckh, Lachmann, and Savigny are to be recalled. His doctoral dissertation was written in Basel in 1838, but immediately afterwards, he left once more and spent one year in Paris and two in England; both travels represented significant experiences for his personal education. On his way back, Bachofen decided not to carry on his family trade tradition; he would therefore start an academic career—in 1841 he was indeed assigned the chair of Roman Law in Basel. After only three years, however, he decided to give up his position, due to the scandal provoked by the liberal journal *Neue Basler Zeitung*, where it was reported that several professorships were assigned to too young persons. He was not a direct target of such criticism; nevertheless, he made the decision to retire and become a private preceptor, still maintaining a close relationship with Basel University, where he kept delivering expert advice. Even though with no official role, Bachofen remained around the academic environment of Basel throughout his life; Nietzsche himself was said to visit his house on a regular basis, although there is no certain evidence that he had ever met Johan Jacob Bachofen (Gossman 2000: 111–127). From Bachofen's teaching, Nietzsche arguably drew part of his dichotomy between Apollinean and Dionysian in the *Birth of Tragedy*. In *Das Mutterrecht* (1861) and *Das lykische Volk und seine Bedeutung für die Entwicklung des Altertums* (1862), Bachofen distinguished for the first time between these two categories, in order to highlight the 'matriarchal' and obscure elements of the most ancient societies, as counterposed to the rational understanding implicit in the modern idea of 'state'. Still the same distinction was then applied to Rome in *Die Sage von Tanaquil* (1870), in which Rome was interpreted as the intersection between West and East, ancient and modern, matriarchal and patriarchal, nature and law. Lastly, as a result of a few anthropological and ethnological studies (*Antiquarische Briefe*, I, 1880, II, 1886), Bachofen was able to let his theory focus more on the 'matriarchal' organisation of pre-patriarchal societies. He thus dedicated much of his time to the analysis of funeral lamps (*Römische Grablampen nebst einigen anderen Grabdenkmälern vorzugsweise einiger Sammlung … mit Ausführungen zu einzeln Theilen der Römischen Gräbsymbolik*, published by his descendants in 1912) and primitive religions. According to Gossman, Creuzer's influence on this aspect can be considered relevant: Bachofen read Creuzer's *Symbolik und Mythologie der alten Völker* (1819–1823) quite in-depth, and shared with it the dualistic view of erotism-spirituality, which corresponded to his own distinction between interiority and exteriority, personal history, and history of humanity. What gained significance above all, was the attention to the *symbol*, meant as the linkage between ancients and moderns, civility and generations, through which the study of history could succeed. Indeed, our interest in History appears to be kept alive by our quest for traces of the past, permeating the present and giving it meaning. Such an interest in symbology also justifies Bachofen's attention to the 'Dionysian' and the darkest sides of ancient societies. Equally, it might have affected his elitist view on writing, which excludes the idea of being shared with a general audience. Writing, however, appears, at the same time, to be constantly misinterpreted by its readers, due to the unavoidability of filtering contents through one's own interests or expertises (ibid.: 140–153).[7] At the beginning of *Symbol and Myth* (in *An Essay on Ancient Mortuary Symbolism*, 1859), Bachofen states: 'Myth is the exegesis of the symbol. It unfolds in a series of outwardly connected actions what the symbol embodies in a unity'. In the following paragraph, he writes:

> Human language is too feeble to convey all the thoughts aroused by the alternation of life and death and the sublime hopes of the initiate. Only the symbol and the related myth can meet this higher degree. The symbol awakens intimations; speech can only explain. The symbol plucks all the string of the human spirit at once; speech is compelled to take up a single thought at time. The symbol strikes its roots in the most secret depths of the soul; language skims over the surface of the understanding like a soft breeze. The symbol aims inward; language outward. Only the symbol can combine the most disparate elements into a unitary expression. [...] Words make the infinite finite, symbols carry the spirit beyond the finite world of becoming into the realm of infinite being. Intimating the ineffable, they are mysterious as all religion by its very nature must be [...]. Therein lies the mysterious dignity of the symbol, which so eminently enhances the solemnity of the ancient tombs. Therein lies the spell of the mythical representations, which show us the great deeds of the primordial age in the muted light of distant melancholy recollection, and that is what lends them the aura of consecration characteristic of the ancient necropolises. (Bachofen 1967: 48–50)

The same view on writing was also shared by Carl Jacob Christoph Burckhardt (1818–1897), intimate friend of Bachofen's since their childhood. As partly anticipated, his father was a successful clergyman, nominated *Antistes* of the Swiss Reformed Church, who had studied in Heidelberg and had Creuzer as a teacher. The young Jacob attended the same schools as Bachofen, and had the same teachers, in addition to Luigi Picchioni, teacher of Italian, once active member of *Carboneria*, whom Burckhardt felt particularly close to: Burckhardt's second edition of *The Civilisation of the Renascence in Italy* [*Die Kultur der Renaissance in Italien*] (1860) was indeed dedicated to Luigi Picchioni. After having completed his studies at *Pädagogium*, Burckhardt moved to Neuchâtel to learn French for a while; there he realised how problematic it would turn out to find a job in Basel, other than following the tradition of his family—his grandfather was a clergyman as well. So Burckhardt too was about to start his university career with the study of Theology. When he was still in Neuchâtel, however, Burckhardt had also come across Charles-Henri Godet, an expert on the classics and preceptor of several members of aristocracy across Europe, from whom he had learnt much. By the time of his first year at Basel University, Burckhardt was able to speak Italian and French fluently and had some knowledge of English; he had studied drawing and composed music for poems by Goethe and Schiller, written a few poems himself, and collected *exerpta* from classic texts and commentaries. He kept a keen interest for Greek and Latin (he also knew Hebrew fundamentals) throughout his life. Although he attended the faculty of Theology, Burckhardt kept taking Greek classes with Wilhelm Vischer, and deepening his passion for history and the German language thanks to Wackernagel; both Wilhelm Vischer and Wackernagel played an important role in his moulding. The former teacher's role was crucial in transmitting to him the idea of human insufficiency before the Providence, that is, the unavoidability of fate; the latter passed to him the notion of a development in literary genres, which follows the development of man's attitude to history from beliefs to critical ability. Lastly, Burckhardt was also impressed by De Wette—from whom he learnt the impoverishment of religion in relation to the increasing modern (i.e. rational and critical) speculation—and Hagenbach, who taught him about the history of Medieval Church. His father had been a pupil of De Wette's as well, particularly impressed with his different approach to the Bible, according to which the figure of 'Christ' could be interpreted as a *myth*. At nearly the end of his university career, Burckhardt decided to abandon the study of Theology and attend the faculty of History in Berlin, where also Bachofen had attended some classes, a few years earlier. He also spent some time studying with Welcker, then in Bonn, before going to Paris, from where he finally returned to Basel in 1843. Burckhardt became Professor of History of Art, but could not feel comfortable in Basel's narrow environment; thus he spent much time in Berlin, as well as in those lands which would be shortly after called 'Italy', and which the scholar felt particularly attracted to, especially due to their historical-cultural testimony. In 1848, Burckhardt steadily established himself in Basel, and alternated his lectures between University and *Pädagogium* (Gossman 2000: 204–235). What differentiates his approach to history from his contemporaries'—but brings it closer to Ranke's—is his understanding of mankind as a whole and of history as the history of its evolution. Different parts of the 'organism' of mankind corresponding to different cultures, the relationship between cultures deserves much of one's attention; therefore, *cultural* history, rather than political, had to be privileged; since its actual subject is *man*. In this sense, culture is regarded as immortal, for the trace of interactions among men have existed over the centuries. Religion or State are two important elements to be investigated, as human relationships originate in these (ibid.: 249–261). In the introduction to *Considerations of Universal History* [*Weltgeschichtliche Betrachtungen*] (1860–1873), it is stated, for instance: 'only through symbols can knowledge set one free from a past' (Burckhardt 1868–1873: 8; translation of Burckhardt's writings is my own throughout). Later on, Burckhardt will focus more on threatening situations for a human community, and will give attention to the 'great men', but he will never cease to consider the study of the past which is helpful in understanding of the present as well as of the future. In 1880, in the preface to the second edition of *The Age of Constantin The Great* [*Die Zeit Constantins des Großen*] (1853/1880), Burckhardt writes, indeed: 'the scale and the essential cultural-historical tendency [should] not be changed or removed by reinforcing political and biographical details'. Lastly, similarly to Bachofen and Creuzer, Burckhardt's understanding of the Greek society comes across as radically different from the predominant theories of the time. In particular, Burckhardt stresses the pagan element of ancient societies, and shows their discordance with Christianity. As it was with Bachofen, Burckhardt also highlights the darkest and hidden element of the ancient Greeks, and, similarly to Nietzsche, the strong link between paganism and death, in contradiction with what is traditionally expected. Religions and myths are regarded as symbolic lenses through which two different epochs could be connected, once stripped bare of their contingent elements, so that they could finally reveal a universal message. In this regard, Burckhardt's *Griechische Kulturgeschichte* (1898–1902) is to be remarked. Here, the Ancients are depicted as not happy, and their paganism appears anything but the joyful image prevailing among contemporary representations (Gossman 2000: 269–279; see Burckhardt 1898–1902, vol. 1: 13–54).

Quoting from Gossman, Bishop highlights a strong Goethean echo, lying at the core of both Bachofen's and Burckhardt's theories, which can be then reconnected to Jung himself. Goethe's distinction between 'analysis' and 'synthesis' could be regarded as representing the same distinction between 'causal' and 'symbolic' introduced by Bachofen—and then largely recalled by Jung—in 'a paper read to the Basel Historical Society on 15 December 1864 entitled "The Basic Laws of the Development of Nations and of Historiography"'. According to Bachofen, a causal explanation finds its roots and purpose on determined temporal sequences, furnishing interpretations grounding on 'what preceded [events] and what followed'; this method represents Goethe's understanding of 'analytical'. A 'symbolic' explanation, instead, '"supposes a view of the whole", explaining events "as the manifestation of the whole in the part", and, being synthetic, involves "powers of imagination, insight, and sympathetic understanding that far exceed the methods of analysis"'. Bishop also observes: 'Bachofen's empiricism implied "a kind of Goethean attentiveness to the object world with a view to discovering its internal laws, as opposed to the Kantian and Enlightenment effort to grasp the world" by means of comparison, examination, distinction, abstraction, deduction, and demonstration'. Quite similarly, Bishop spots Goethean elements in Burckhardt's understanding of 'imagination' in his lectures. First, Burckhardt utilises the 'Goethean term "Anschauung"'; second, he stresses the importance of imagination in reconstructing the history of past civilities. According to Bishop, such an active role of imagination and 'contemplation' allows one to overcome a merely aesthetic approach to the ancient world. Such an approach is what will mostly characterise Jung's depth psychology (Bishop 2012: 50–53).

As argued above, Bachofen and Burckhardt had seriously engaged with Creuzer's understanding of symbol; as it is well-known, Creuzer was also a friend of Goethe's. Goethe wrote in *Maxime und Reflexionen* (1809–1829):

> Word and image are correlates, constantly looking for each other, as we become sufficiently aware through metaphors and allegories. So, what was said or sung inwardly to the ear had to be likewise presented to the eye all along. And so in childish days we see word and image in a continuous balance; in the book of the law and in the order of salvation, in the Bible and in the primer. When something was spoken that could not be pictured—[something was] pictured that could not be spoken—, then it was all right; but one made mistakes quite often and spoke, instead to picture, and thence arose the doubly evil monstrosity of symbolical mysticism. (Goethe 1949, vol. 9: 617)

Furthermore, as already said, Hölderlin was in contact with Schiller, who introduced him to Goethe. The first impression of Hölderlin's official visit to Goethe is described by the latter with these words:

> Yesterday Hölderlin was also here; he looked somewhat subdued and peaky, but he is really amiable and both modest and anxious. He engaged with several subjects in a way that bespoke your school, he appropriated a few main ideas very well, so that he could easily recall things too. I especially

> suggested that he write short poems and that he choose for each of them an interesting subject to human beings. He seemed to still have some tendencies to the Middle Ages, in which I could not encourage him. (Goethe 1949, vol. 20: 404; Goethe to Schiller, letter dating 23 August 1797)[8]

However, the two had already accidentally met in 1794. Hölderlin was spending some time in Schiller's place, and a 'taciturn stranger' called in to see Schiller, who was eager to give him a copy of the journal *Thalia*, where Hölderlin's *Fragment of Hyperion* and *Das Schicksal* were published. For some reason, however, the young poet misheard the name pronounced at the time of the official introduction, and did not exhibit particular reverence; instead, he came across as quite 'indifferent'. Only at night could he hear by someone that Goethe had come over that day. This is arguably the reason why, also in the following year, when both writers met again for the second time, Goethe adopted a somewhat formal attitude. Nevertheless, Hölderlin had a totally positive impression of that second meeting, as reported in the letters he sent to Neuffer and Hegel. According to Eudo C. Mason, Goethe's cordial attitude might be attributed to his respect for his friend Schiller, without being able to really forget his very first meeting with Hölderlin: indeed, anytime Goethe had to mention Hölderlin, he would never express positive judgements on him. Besides, as the scholar points out, Hölderlin's relationship with Schiller had such an impact on Hölderlin that he seemed to suffer from Schiller's severity throughout their correspondence (which lasted until 1801). Hölderlin's veneration and respect for both Schiller and Goethe never vanished, to the point that he asked for a copy of his own translation of Sophocles's dramas being sent to both in 1804; likely in the hope to please Goethe (Mason 1975: 9–21). Although the debate on Goethe's actual influential role on Hölderlin's writings is still open, it is arguable to admit, still with Mason, that 'similarities' do exist, between Hölderlin's mature works and Goethe's, especially concerning *Faust ein Fragment* (1790) (ibid.: 31–33, 82–83). Among these, Manson highlights the importance of the Faustian *Erdgeist* for the evolving of Hölderlin's *Hyperion*. In particular, he recognises too deep a difference between Hölderlin's utilisation of Greek mythology and the allegoric meaning with which his contemporaries made use of the myth; such utilisation—at the same time—appears as far from his contemporaries as it seems close to Goethe. Although Hölderlin fell into madness before *Faust I* was published (1808), Mason does not exclude the possibility that Hölderlin had previously come across the manuscript in Schiller's house, even. Nonetheless, according to the scholar, a major assonance with *Faust* might be found in *Empedocles* (1793–1800), whereas *Hyperion* appears to resemble *Werther* (1774/1787). These last considerations, however, have to remain on a hypothetical level, due to their lack of effective evidence (ibid.: 95–113). Moreover, as already said, relevant differences also occur between Goethe and Hölderlin's styles (Feldman 1972).

Vischer too spent some time in Switzerland, precisely in Zurich, from 1855 to 1866. He also had a short correspondence with Burckhardt, who sent him four letters in the period 1854–1867. The tone of these letters is friendly and colloquial, and the topics generally concern Burckhardt's research and travels. Among these letters, unfortunately, only the first one has kept Vischer's answer (Leyh 1936/1937).[9] In the last months of his life, Vischer composed an essay entirely dedicated to symbols (*Das Symbol*, 1887). Its contents appear in harmony with Burckhardt's ideas, as well as with the peculiar utilisation of symbols discussed above in relation to Goethe and Hölderlin. What he majorly criticised was the limitless use that his contemporaries were making of symbols without a proper reflection. What is mostly stressed is the ungraspable yet immediate essence of symbols if compared with ideas: as opposed to ideas, symbols are indeed intuited through images, thus they do not need any kind of mediation to become manifest; at the same time, however, they seem to maintain a certain distance from the subject, which makes it impossible to completely identify with them. The process of a symbolic experience evolves together with humanity: in a first stage, represented by myth and magic, man tends to identify with symbols; then his reflectivity increases, and symbols are meant as allegories; finally, man gains the ability to reflect on, and relates to, symbols in a more detached way. However, the first step does not imply a negative process; on the contrary, it aids reflection to grasp ideas better: the religious symbol of Maria's virginity, for instance, makes it easy to represent and comprehend the idea of 'pure femininity' [reine Weiblichkeit] (Vischer 1844, vol. 4: 420–456. See Bausinger 2011; Richter 2011: 271–272).

As Anticipated, Burckhardt was Spitteler's History teacher at *Pädagogium* (1861–1863); furthermore, Spitteler also attended some of his lectures during his first years at Basel University. As argued by some scholars, Burckhardt's inspiration might appear in the dynamical conception of Spitteler's cosmology in *Prometheus*, as well as in his choice to make use of *epos* to better represent and spread such a dynamic. Through this, indeed, the link between past and present seems to emerge violently

(Faesi 1933: 12; Buri 1945: 21; Theisohn 2001: 93–94; Meissner 1912: 6–7).[10] There is no evidence of a possible mediation from Bachofen, however. Nonetheless, it is important to recall Philip Theisohn's opinion, according to which the necessity of a dualism grounding the myth of *Prometheus*—that is to say, the couple of brothers, two elements complementary and indispensable—can be interpreted as a reflection of Bachofen's matriarchal-patriarchal division (Theisohn 2001: 113–114).

As a final remark, it might be of interest to recall that Nietzsche and Spitteler got to know each other through a complicated correspondence, dominated by misunderstandings on both sides. At the time of Nietzsche's professorship in Basel, Spitteler was completing his education abroad; however, rumours on a talented young professor of Philology reached him. According to what he reports, after he published *Prometheus* anonymously, a few acquaintances of his—among whom a few former students of Nietzsche's—insisted that the book be sent to the philosopher. As it is easy to imagine, Spitteler never gave his permission, but when *Zarathustra* came out three years later, he suspected that Nietzsche might have read his text and drawn some inspiration from it. Whether or not this is true, in summer 1887, Nietzsche took an interest in Spitteler's work—possibly through the mediation of Widmann, copyeditor of the journal *Bund*—and promised to help him with the publication of his *Aesthetica*. Shortly afterwards, Spitteler was invited by the German writer Ferdinand Avenarius, living in Dresden at the time, to collaborate on his project *Kunstwart*, another journal. A few months later, Widmann asked him to review some of Nietzsche's works, which caused him to feel uncomfortable, lacking proper philosophical skills. Arguably for this reason, Spitteler did not seem to put enough effort in writing his reviews. Moreover, he ignored that he owed Avenarius's proposal to Nietzsche, and even felt mocked by the philosopher, who had offered him help and never got back to him so far. No wonder Nietzsche did not respond well to these first reviews. On 10 February 1888, after having read the first reviews by Spitteler, Nietzsche wrote to him from Nice and showed his disappointment. In a draft, he even called himself 'indignant' (eKGWB: letter n. 987). In the version he sent him, he wrote:

> Herr Spitteler has a fine and pleasant mind; unfortunately, as it appears to me, in this case the task itself lays too far away and outside his usual prospects, more than he would have even regarded it. He talks and sees nothing as Aesthetica: my issues are bluntly withheld,—including myself. There is no a single essential point mentioned which characterises me. And lastly it lacks of form, too. (ibid.: letter n. 988)

However, Nietzsche contacted him again in spring 1888, still showing interest in his *Aesthetica*; in autumn, Spitteler came across *The Case of Wagner* [*Der Fall Wagner*] (1888), and decided to review it for the journal *Bund* (Spitteler 1908: 12–40). This time, Nietzsche's reaction was positive, to the point that he even planned to meet Spitteler in Switzerland; although the meeting, eventually, never took place. If one wanted to make a more general statement, it should be noted that, throughout their correspondence, Nietzsche adopted an ambivalent attitude towards Spitteler: the opinion on his writing skills was never questioned, and, even if disappointed with his reviews and behaviour, he never put an end to his search for a publisher for Spitteler's *Aesthetica* (draft of a letter to Hermann Credner on 25 February 1888; eKGWB: letter n. 999). When he eventually succeeded, that is to say, when Credner agreed to publish Spitteler's work, Nietzsche wrote to Köselitz: 'I *succeeded* in something at which you will laugh: I provided that *Spitteler* (unpleasant remembrance), unrequested, but in the knowledge that otherwise nobody does anything for him, with an *editor* for a thick volume Aesthetica [...] Sp<itteler> has been careful not to thank me' (ibid.: letter n. 1000). The whole misunderstanding between these two authors was brought about by a proximity between *Prometheus* and *Zarathustra*, which many of their contemporaries also perceived. One of the most significant testimonies is represented by Meissner's comparison between *Prometheus* and *Zarathustra*. According to the scholar, despite a few similar stylistic elements, a substantial difference exists in Nietzsche's and Spitteler's purposes. The former would aim at spreading a message translatable into concepts, therefore he would make use of a poetical language regardless of his purpose; the latter—the 'poet' Spitteler—could not help but use poetry, for the richness of his contents could no way be forced into philosophical concepts (Meissner 1912: 27–31; a similar comparison is also portrayed by Kluth 1918: 98–99).

In regard to his relationship with his contemporaries, Spitteler did not take part in debates, preferring to remain silent. The first time he expressed his opinion was in fact in 1908, 20 years later, when he realised it was about time to let everyone know about his business with Nietzsche, in a short text called *My Relationships with Nietzsche* [Meine Beziheungen zu Nietzsche]: 'Now I am breaking my silence because I am convinced, because I can no longer keep quiet, because it is necessary to protect my face' (Spitteler 1908: 6).[11]

2.2.3 Liber Novus *as Jung's 'Visionary' Experience*

As pointed out in the introduction, Jung's feeling of proximity to Nietzsche's and Goethe's *prophetical* experiences makes it possible to regard *Liber Novus* as Jung's 'visionary' work. This seems also to be confirmed through its style and contents, as well as through descriptions or phrases used by Jung while referring to his *Liber Novus* experience, as previously argued. One episode is particularly remarkable. In October 1913, Jung describes the emotional state following his fantasies by stating: 'It left me exhausted and confused. And I thought my mind had gone crazy. From then on the anxiety toward the terrible event that stood directly before us kept coming back' (RB I: 231). Even though such a state is an atypical one in comparison to Jung's normal attitude to his fantasies, the experience of 'anxiety' deserves to be noticed. As anticipated, his *Faust* and *Zarathustra* experiences are depicted as bringing about a similar anxiety in Jung, to the point that he 'was forced to reflect on' himself (MDR: 102). Also, as will be investigated in the next chapters more closely, similarly to 'visionary' works, *Liber Novus* places itself as a prophetical experience. Furthermore, as in all of the 'visionary' works, representations of transition, death, and sacrifice are quite recurrent motifs in *Liber Novus*; similarly, abundant references to biblical and mythological symbology occur prominently. As will be argued in the next sections, some of *Liber Novus* main episodes concern the 'sacrifice of the hero', the 'death' and the 'rebirth' of 'God', and the whole story represents a transition, namely the process leading to the realisation of the 'self'. Even more, mythology doubtless plays one of the main roles also in regard to its psychological origin and effects. In a letter to J. A. Gilbert dated 20 December 1929, Jung discusses his method in terms of 'mythology' indeed:

> I found sometimes, that it is of great help in handling such a case, to encourage them, to express their peculiar contents either in the form of writing or of drawing and painting. There are so many incomprehensible intuitions in such cases, phantasy fragments that rise from the unconscious, for which there is almost no suitable language. I let my patients find their own symbolic expressions, their "mythology". (Jung's Family Archives. In Shamdasani 2009, RB: 216)

As anticipated, Paul Bishop has brought out the importance of Weimar Classicism and German Idealism for Jung and *Liber Novus*, and has also stressed the role of Vischer among Jung's possible sources of inspiration

(Bishop 2012: 354). Surely is much of *Auch Einer* in *Liber Novus*, as well as of *Faust II*, which Jung had always felt attracted to, even though he had not found the courage to interpret it seriously, until he came across alchemy. According to Jung's understanding, what characterises *Faust II*, is indeed the possibility of transcending the personal layer of the unconscious, and reaching the 'prophetical' ability to talk about unknown things (Jung 1949). Similarly, traces of Spitteler and Hölderlin are quite easy to be found in *Liber Novus*. As will be investigated in the following chapters, Nietzsche's presence is equally—if not even more—recurrent.

Furthermore, it is not to disregard the fact that Jung grew up and studied in Basel and came across figures such as Burckhardt, Overbeck (SNZ I: 635; 25 October 1935), Elisabeth Förster-Nietzsche, Lou von Salomè (Bishop 1995: 276–281),[12] and Spitteler himself (to whom he sent his *Psychological Types*). On Burckhardt, Jung will recall: 'I wish I could show you the old man Jacob Burckhardt as I saw him practically every day, walking near the Cathedral coming from the University library' (SNZ II: 862; 26 February 1936). From him, he also claimed to have borrowed the idea of 'original images' [Urbilder]. Besides, Jung had a strong interest in theology as well, and came from a tradition of parsons: 'In my mother's family there were six parsons, and on my father's side not only was my father a parson but two of my uncles also' (MDR: 42). Throughout his life, Jung strongly engaged in debates with characters such as Victor White, Martin Buber, Richard Wilhelm, D. T. Suzuki, showing a keen interest not only in Christianity, but also in all of the Western and Eastern religions. Lastly, Jung spent much of his time dealing with Gnosticism (see Ribi 2013), Greek and Egypt mythology, as well as with alchemy, extending such an interest to ancient religions, equal to his interest in the modern ones.[13]

Notes

1. As James L. Jarrett points out in a footnote, Jung is likely to refer to Spitteler's reaction to his *Psychological Types*. The writer had indeed responded to Jung's analysis by stating that his characters were merely fictional figures and did not symbolise anything more.
2. In Tübingen, Hölderlin studied with Hegel e Schelling, with whom he remained in contact throughout his life.
3. Vischer took position in the debate twice: *Dr. Strauß und die Wirtemberger* (1838) and *Über allerhand Verlegenheiten bei Besetzung einer dogmatischen Leherstelle un der gegenwärtigen Zeit* (1839) (*Hallischen Jahrbüchern für deutsche Wissenschaft und Kunst*).

4. After the death of his mother-in-law (1893), Spitteler no longer needed to work and decided to invest his full time in literature. Already as a young student, Spitteler had composed a short poem, *Der Ketzer*, centred on the same necessity of redefining the relationship between human and the divine.
5. A few scholars have dealt with Goethe and religion. Goethe's relationship with Gnosticism has been fully explored by Stefan Hajduk, who has also proposed an interpretation of *Faust* based on Gnostic ideals and images (Hajduk 2010). *Faust* has also been analysed within the context of the religious debate contemporary to Goethe (Smith 2011) and Goethe's overall engagement with religion has been explored in depth in a collection of essays edited by Hans-Joachim Simm (2000). Moreover, Goethe's understanding of Christianity in a wider aesthetic perspective has been also analysed (Thielicke 1982), as well as his ambivalent relation to Catholicism (Kock 1999).
6. It might be of interest to recall that C. G. Jung's grandfather was in charge of reforming the faculty of Medicine.
7. Creuzer's *Symbolik und Mythologie der alten Völker* (1822) has been fully explored in relation to the development of a symbolic approach to myth and religion, as well as its impact on cultural history more broadly (Gödde 2010; Blok 1994; Howald 1926).
8. In his answer, Schiller cannot help but to reveal a certain enthusiasm while describing Hölderlin, so that he even compares him to Schlegel by calling him a 'poetical genius' (Schiller to Goethe, 7 September 1797; ibid.: 418). Hölderlin, on the other hand, was being quite docile towards Schiller and his teachings (see Hölderlin's letter to Schiller on August 1797; Hölderlin 1922: 167–170).
9. In a letter dating 14 January 1866, Schiller is also mentioned.
10. Schopenhauer seems also to have played a part in Spitteler's cosmology. On a precise analysis of Spitteler's relationship with Burckhardt, see Stauffacher (1973: 165–178); on Spitteler's reception of Schopenhauer, see Mockrauer-Bähr (1965); Aler (1965); Rommel (1965); Lo Cicero (1964).
11. Interestingly, in the same lines, Spitteler also mentions his keeping quiet regarding his attitude towards 'Keller, Mayer, Jacob Burckhardt and Böcklin'.
12. As Bishop also points out, Jung met Ludwig Binswanger, the nephew of Otto Binswanger, professor of Psychiatry in Jena and director of asylum at the time of Nietzsche's admission.
13. It is not to be forgotten that a Gnostic codex found in Nag Hammadi (Egypt) was named after Jung ('Jung Codex'). G. Fowden (1986) has shown an actual link between Hermeticism and Egyptian tradition.

References

Aeppli, Ernst. 1922. *Spittelers Imago: eine Analyse*. Frauenfeld and Leipzig: Huber.

Ajouri, Philip. 2011. Vischer als Literathurhistoriker und Literathurkritiker. In *Friedrich Theodor Vischer. Leben – Werk – Wirkung*, ed. Barbara Potthast and Alexander Reck, 99–118. Heidelberg: Universitätsverlag Winter GmbH.

Aler, Jan. 1965. Dichterglossen. Carl Spitteler liest die *Parerga und Paralipomena*. *Schopenhauer-Jahrbuch* 46 (1965): 45–66.

Althaus, Thomas. 2011. Von den Stockwerken des Lebens und von der Tücke des Objekts. Friedrich Theodor Vischers Roman *Auch Einer* und sein Held als Phraseur. In *Friedrich Theodor Vischer. Leben – Werk – Wirkung*, ed. Barbara Potthast and Alexander Reck, 169–190. Heidelberg: Universitätsverlag Winter GmbH.

Bachofen, Johan Jakob. 1948–1967. *Gesammelte Werke*. Edited by Karl Meuli, Max Burckhardt, José Dörig, Johannes Dörmann, and Karl Meuli. Basel: Schwabe.

———. 1967. *Mutterrecht und Urreligion*, A Selection Edited by Rudolf Marx, Translated from the German by Ralph Manheim. In *Myth, Religion, And Mother Right*. Selected Writings of J. J. Bachofen, with a Preface by George Boas and an Introduction by Joseph Campbell. London: Routledge & Kegan Paul.

Bausinger, Hermann. 2011. Zwischen Dilettantismus und Wissenschaft: Friedrich Theodor Vischer. In *Friedrich Theodor Vischer. Leben – Werk – Wirkung*, ed. Barbara Potthast and Alexander Reck, 1–14. Heidelberg: Universitätsverlag Winter GmbH.

Beck, Adolf, and Paul Raabe, eds. 1970. *Hölderlin. Eine Chronik in Text und Bild*. Frankfurt: Insel.

Bishop, Paul. 1995. Jung's Annotation of Nietzsche's Works: An Analysis. *Nietzsche-Studien* 24: 271–314.

———. 2012. Jung's *Red Book* and Its Relation to Aspects of German Idealism. *The Journal of Analytical Psychology* 57: 335–353.

Blok, Josine H. 1994. Quests for a Scientific Mythology: F. Creuzer and K.O. Muller on History and Myth. *History and Theory* 33 (4, December): 26–51.

Bonjour, Edgar. 1960. Zur Gründungsgeschichte der Universität Basel. *Schweizerische Zeitschrift für Geschichte* 10: 59–80.

Burckhardt, Carl Jacob Christoph. 1868–1873. *Weltgeschichtliche Betrachtungen*. Edited by Jacob Oeri. Berlin and Stuttgart: Verlag von W. Spemann, 1905.

———. 1898–1902. *Griechische Kulturgeschichte*. 5th ed. Edited by Albert Oeri. Berlin and Stuttgart: Verlag von W. Spemann, 1908.

———. 1955–1959. *Gesammelte Werke*. Edited by Bernd Roeck, Christine Tauber, and Martin Warnke. Basel: Schwabe.

Buri, Fritz. 1945. *Prometheus und Christus. Grösse und Grenzen von Car Spittelers religiöser Weltanschauung*. Bern: A. Francke AG.
Castellari, Marco. 2002. *Hyperion nello specchio della critica*. Milan: Cooperativa Universitaria Editrice Milanese.
Craig, Edward. 1996. *The Metaphysic of the Romantic Era*. Oxford: Oxford Scholarship Online, 2003.
Creuzer, George Friedrich. 1822. *Symbolik und Mythologie der alten Völker*. Leipzig and Darmstadt: Leske.
Emery, George Edward. 1990. Hölderlin and His Biographers. *The Journal of English and Germanic Philology* 89 (January): 51–86.
Faesi, Robert. 1933. *Spittelers Weg und Werk*. Frauenfeld and Leipzig: Von Huber & Co. Aktiengesellschaft.
Feldman, Burton. 1972. *The Rise of Modern Mythology, 1680–1860*. Bloomington: Indiana University Press.
Figl, Johann. 2007. *Nietzsche und die Religionen. Transkulturelle Perspektive seines Bildungs- und Denkweges*. Berlin and New York: De Gruyter.
Fowden, Garth. 1986. *The Egyptian Hermes. A Historical Approach to the Late Pagan Mind*. Princeton, NJ: Princeton University Press.
Gerber, Stefan. 2011. 'Meine Bildung ist mir wurst'. Friedrich Theodor Vischer und die zeitgenössichen Bildungsinstitutionen. In *Friedrich Theodor Vischer. Leben – Werk – Wirkung*, ed. Barbara Potthast and Alexander Reck, 15–35. Heidelberg: Universitätsverlag Winter GmbH.
Giametta, Sossio. 1988. Lo *Zarathustra* di Nietzsche come quinto evangelio, I. In *Criterio: nuova serie filosofica 7*, vol. 1: 48–62.
———. 2006. *Commento allo 'Zarathustra'*. Milan: Mondadori.
———. 2009. *Introduzione a Nietzsche: opera per opera*. Milan: Bur.
Gödde, Susanne. 2010. '... das Unendliche im Endlichen gebären...': Verfahren des Bedeutens in Creuzers Symboltheorie. *Flaubert: Revue Critique et Génétique* (4). http://flaubert.revues.org/1214.
Goethe, Johann Wolfgang. 1772/1808–1832. *Faust*. Stuttgart and Tübingen, 1835. English Translation. http://www.wisdomportal.com/PoetryAnthology/Goethe-Anthology.html.
———. 1949. *Gedenkeausgabe der Werke, Briefe und Gespräche*. 27 vols. Edited by Ernst Beutler. Zurich: Artemis-Verlag.
Gossman, Lionel. 2000. *Basel in the Age of Burckhardt. A Study in Unseasonable Ideas*. Chicago and London: University of Chicago Press.
Gottschalk, Hans. 1943. *Das Mythische in der Dichtung Hölderlins*. Stuttgart: Cotta.
Habicht, Werner. 2011. Friedrich Theodor Vischer und die deutsche Shakespeare-Rezeption im 19. Jahrhundert. In *Friedrich Theodor Vischer. Leben – Werk – Wirkung*, ed. Barbara Potthast and Alexander Reck, 119–135. Heidelberg: Universitätsverlag Winter GmbH.

Hajduk, Stefan. 2010. Goethes Gnostiker: Fausts vergessener Nihilismus und sein Streben nach Erlösungswissen. *Goethe Yearbook* 17: 89–118.

Highet, Gilbert. 1949. *The Classical Tradition: Greek and Roman Influences on Western Literature*. Oxford and New York: Oxford University Press, 1976.

———. 1952. A Neglected Masterpiece: 'Olympian Spring'. *The Antioch Review* 12 (3, Autumn): 338–346.

Hofmann, Peter. 2002. *Goethes Theologie*. Paderborn: Ferdinand Schöningh Verlag.

Hölderlin, Johann Christian Friedrich. 1922. *Briefe*. Weimar: Lichtenstein Verlag.

———. 1946–. *Sämtliche Werke*. 6 vols. Stuttgart: W. Kohlhammer Verlag.

———. 1990. *Hyperion and Selected Poems*. Edited by Eric L. Santner. New York: Continuum.

Hörisch, Jochen. 2002. Religiöse Abrüstung: Goethes Konversions-Theologie. In *Spuren, Signaturen, Spiegelungen: Zur GoetheRezeption in Europa*, ed. Bernhard Beutler and Anke Bosse, 31–44. Böhlau: Köln, Weimar and Vienna.

Howald, Ernst. 1926. *Der Kampf um Creuzers Symbolik: eine Auswahl von Dokumenten*. Tübingen: J.C.B. Mohr P. Siebeck.

Jung, Carl Gustav. 1921. *Psychological Types*. Collected Works of C. G. Jung. Vol. 6.

———. 1922/1931. *On the Relation of Analytical Psychology to Poetry*. Collective Works of C. G. Jung. Vol. 15, §§ 97–132.

———. 1925. *Introduction to Jungian Psychology, Notes of the Seminar on Analytical Psychology Given in 1925*. Rev. ed. Edited by Sonu Shamdasani. Princeton: Princeton University Press, 2012.

———. 1930/1950. *Psychology and Literature*. Collected Works of C. G. Jung. Vol. 15, §§ 133–162.

———. 1949. Faust und die Alchemie. Vortrag im Psychologischen Club, Zürich, vom 8. Oktober 1949. In *Goethes Faust. Eine tiefenpsychologische Studie über den Mythos des modernen Menschen*, ed. Irene Gerber-Münch. Küsnacht: Verlag Stiftung für Jung'sche Psychologie, 1997.

———. 1989. *Nietzsche's Zarathustra: Notes of the Seminar Given in 1934–9*. 2nd ed. Edited by James L. Jarrett in two parts. London: Routledge, 1994.

Jung, Carl Gustav, and Aniela Jaffé. 1962. *Memories, Dreams, Reflections by Carl Gustav Jung*. Recorded and Edited by Aniela Jaffé. New York: Vintage Books, 1989.

Kieser, Franz. 1606. *Cabala Chymica*. Mühlhausen.

Kirchner, Werner. 1949. *Der Hochverratsprozeß gegen Sinclair. Ein Beitrag zum Leben Hölderlins*. Marburg: Simon Verlag.

Klopstoc, Friedrich Gottlieb. 1748–1773. Der Messias. Halle: Hemmerde.

Kluth, Otto. 1918. *Carl Spitteler et les sources de son génie épique. Un essai*. Geneva: Imprimerie Sonor.

Kock, Erich. 1999. Fasziniert und verärgert. Das widersprüchliche Verhältnis des Dichters zum Katholizismus. *Rheinischer Merkur* 23: 16–25.

Köpf, Ulrich. 2011. Friedrich Theodor Vischer Verhältnis zu Theologie und Kirche. In *Friedrich Theodor Vischer. Leben – Werk – Wirkung*, ed. Barbara Potthast and Alexander Reck, 67–78. Heidelberg: Universitätsverlag Winter GmbH.

Köster, Peter. 2003. *Kontroversen um Nietzsche: Untersuchungen zur theologischen Rezeption*. Zurich: Theologischer Verlag.

Lange, Horst. 2004. Goethes Theologie, Review of Peter Hofman *Goethes Theologie* (2002). *Goethe Yearbook* 12 (1): 285–288.

———. 2011. Goethe and Spinoza: A Reconsideration. *Goethe Yearbook* 18: 11–34.

Lefebvre, Jean-Pierre. 1990. *Hölderlin: journal de Bordeaux (1er janvier–14 juin 1802)*. Bordeaux: Blake.

Leyh, Georg, ed. 1936/1937. *Vier Briefe Jacob Burckhardts an Friedrich Theodor Vischer*. Hamburg: Corona.

Liebscher, Martin. 2005. Controversies around Nietzsche: Studies on Theological Reception by Peter Köster. Review of Peter Köster. *Kontroversen um Nietzsche: Untersuchungen zur theologischen Rezeption. The Journal of Nietzsche Studies* 29: 71–74.

Lo Cicero, Vincent. 1964. A Reappraisal of Spitteler's View of Schopenhauer. *The Germanic Review* 39: 37–49.

Mason, Eudo C. 1975. *Hölderlin and Goethe*. Bern and Frankfurt am Main: Lang.

Meissner, Carl. 1912. *Carl Spitteler: zur Einfühlung in sein Schaffen; mit einem Anhange: Eugenia: eine Dichtung*. Jena: Diederichs.

Michel, Wilhelm. 1940. *Das Leben Friedrich Hölderlins*. Bremen: Schünemann.

Mockrauer-Bähr, Johanna. 1965. Spittelers Randglossen zu den *Parerga und Paralipomena*. *Schopenhauer-Jahrbuch* 46: 18–44.

Nietzsche, Friedrich Wilhelm. 1883–1885. *Thus Spoke Zarathustra*. 2nd ed. Translated by R. J. Hollingdale. New York: Penguin Classics, 1969.

———. 1899–1911. *Kleinoktav-Gesamtausgabe*. Leipzig: Naumann und Kröner.

———. 1930 [1883–1885]. *Thus Spake Zarathustra*. Translated by Thomas Common. New York: The Modern Library.

———. 1967–. *Kritische Gesamtausgabe der Werke Nietzsches*. Edited by Giorgio Colli and Mazzino Montinari. Berlin and New York: De Gruyter.

———. 1980–. *Kritische Studienausgabe*. Edited by Giorgio Colli and Mazzino Montinari. Berlin and New York: De Gruyter.

———. 2009–. *Digital Critical Edition*. Edited by P. D'Iorio.

Overbeck, Franz Camille. 1873. Über die Christlichkeit unserer heutigen Theologie. In *Werke und Nachlass Schriften bis 1873*, vol. 1. Stuttgart and Weimar: Metzler, 1994.

Pellegrino, Antonia. 2005. *La città piena di idoli: Franz Overbeck e la crisi della teologia scientifica*. Pisa: ETS.

Potthast, Barbara, and Alexander Reck. 2011. Vischers Tendenzen und die Tendenzen der Karikatur. In *Friedrich Theodor Vischer. Leben – Werk – Wirkung*, 207–229. Heidelberg: Universitätsverlag Winter GmbH.

Reck, Alexander. 2007. *Friedrich Theodor Vischer – Parodien auf Goethes 'Faust'*. Heidelberg: Winter.

Renan, Ernest. 1863. *Vie de Jésus*. Paris: Nelson/Colman Lévy.

Ribi, Alfred. 2013. *The Search for Roots. C. G. Jung and the Tradition of Gnosis*. Forward by Lance S. Owens. Los Angeles and Salt Lake City: Gnosis Archive Books.

Richter, Sandra. 2011. Die 'Gunst des Zufalls'. Vischers äesthetische Schriften als transhistorische Dokumente der Wissenschaft vom Schönen. In *Friedrich Theodor Vischer. Leben – Werk – Wirkung*, ed. Barbara Potthast and Alexander Reck, 261–275. Heidelberg: Universitätsverlag Winter GmbH.

Rommel, Otto. 1965. Schopenhauer und der 'Olympische Frühling'. *In Schopenhauer-Jahrbuch* 46: 67–65.

Santaniello, Weaver. 2007. Nietzsche's Philosophy of Religion. *Ars Disputandi* 7 (1): 136–138.

Schlechta, Karl. 1954. *Nietzsches grosser Mittag*. Klostermann: Frankfurt am Main.

Scholz, Rüdiger. 1983. *Goethes 'Faust' in der wissenschaftlichen Interpretation von Schelling und Hegel bis heute*. Rheinfelden: Schäuble.

Schorske, Carl E. 1994. Formation civique et culture savant à Bâle: Bachofen et Burckhardt. *Histoire de l'education* 62: 15–30.

Shamdasani, Sonu. 2009. 'Introduction' and 'Footnotes'. In *The Red Book: Liber Novus*, ed. C.G. Jung. Edited and Introduced by Sonu Shamdasani, Translated by Mark Kyburz, John Peck, and Sonu Shamdasani. New York and London: W. W. Norton & Company.

Simm, Hans-Joachim, ed. 2000. *Goethe und die Religion. Aus seinen Werken, Briefen, Tagenbüchern und Gesprächen*. Frankfurt am Main: Inseln.

Smith, John H. 2011. Die Gretchenfrage: Goethe and Philosophies of Religion around 1800. *Goethe Yearbook* 18: 183–204.

Spinoza, Baruch. 1773. *The Ethics*. Translated from the Latin by R. H. M. Elwes. Project Gutemberg, 2009.

Spitteler, Carl. 1881. *Prometheus und Epimetheus. Ein Gleichnis*. Jena: Eugen Diederichs, 1906.

———. 1900/1906. *Olympischer Frühling*. Jena: Eugen Diederichs, 1910.

———. 1906. *Imago*. Jena: Eugen Diederichs, 1922.

———. 1908. *Meine Beziehungen zu Nietzsche*. Munich: Süddeutsche Monatshefte G.m.b.H.

Stadler, Peter. 2001. Review of Lionel Gossman, *Basel in the Age of Burckhardt* (2000). *Historische Zeitschrift* 272 (3): 786–788.

Stauffacher, Werner. 1973. *Carl Spitteler. Biographie*. Zurich: Artemis.

Stocker, Peter. 2011. Friedrich Theodor Vischer, Gottfried Keller und die Dialektik des Satirischen. In *Friedrich Theodor Vischer. Leben – Werk – Wirkung*, ed. Barbara Potthast and Alexander Reck, 153–168. Heidelberg: Universitätsverlag Winter GmbH.

Strauß, David Friedrich. 1835–1836. *Das Leben Jesu*. Tübingen: Osiander.

Theisohn, Philipp. 2001. *Totalität des Mangels. Carl Spitteler und die Geburt des modernen Epos aus der Anschauung*. Würzburg: Königshausen & Neumann.

Thielicke, Helmut. 1982. *Goethe und das Christentum*. Munich: Piper Verlag.

Vischer, Friedrich Theodor. 1844–. *Kritische Gänge*. 6 vols. Edited by Robert Vischer. Tübingen: Fues.

———. 1862/1886. *Faust. Der Tragödie drittel Teil*. Stuttgart: Reclam, 1978.

———. 1878. *Auch Einer. Eine Reisebekanntschaft*. Leipzig: Heffe & Becker Verlag.

Wackwitz, Stephan. 1997. *Friedrich Hölderlin*. Weimar: Metzler.

Weber, Christian. 2009. Goethes Prometheus: Kritik der poetischen Einbildungskraft. *Goethe Yearbook* 16: 101–134.

Williams, John R. 1998. *The Life of Goethe: A Critical Biography*. Oxford: Blackwell Publishers.

Witkop, Gregor, ed. 1993. *Hölderlin. Der Pflegsohn. Texte und Dokumente 1806–1843 mit den neu entdeckten Nürtinger Pflegschaftsakten*. Stuttgart: Metzler.

Young, Julian. 2006. *Nietzsche's Philosophy of Religion*. New York: Cambridge University Press.

CHAPTER 3

Nietzsche in *Liber Novus*

Then suddenly the spirit seized me and carried me to a desert country in which I read Zarathustra. (SNZ I: 259)

3.1 Nietzsche and the Style of *Liber Novus*

3.1.1 Introductory Remarks

As pointed out, Jung never published a work called 'The Red Book'. Surely significant visions happened to him, and doubtless, he kept reflecting on that material for decades; nevertheless, what was first published in 2009 is not part of Jung's planned *Collected Works*. What this means in the context of this study, is that Jung's strong Nietzschean inspiration is not easy to be traced and investigated, and several variables have to be taken into account. The complexity of the style of *Liber Novus* on the one hand, and of Nietzsche's inspirational role on it on the other, can be summarised, first of all, by remarking that an accurate reading of *Liber Novus* offers two layers: visions and style. On the first level, one finds Jung's direct experiences with his inner world, that is visions, voices heard from his innermost being, encounters with unusual characters, or paradoxical happenings. All this happened to Jung in a precise and relatively short lapse of time, namely from 1913 to 1916, with the gap of one year from summer 1914 to summer 1915. Beside the 'raw material' of such an experience, *Liber Novus* is

G. Domenici, *Jung's Nietzsche*,
https://doi.org/10.1007/978-3-030-17670-9_3

also characterised by comments, paintings, or drawings; the text is written in folio and in Gothic type, in several drafts and versions, and chapter initial letters are quite often painted in miniature. Jung's fantasies, in fact, are re-elaborated, commented, and represented through images. This latter part of his work kept Jung busy for quite a long time, that is, pretty much consistently until 1928, and occasionally until 1959 (when the 'Epilogue' was written). Nietzsche occurs quite prominently in both layers.

In visions, Nietzsche appears as a proper character during the asylum episode; sometimes a sentence or phrase from *Zarathustra* is pronounced; other times characters, situations, or motifs remind one of *Zarathustra*, as well as of concepts or ideas expressed by Nietzsche elsewhere. In nearly all of these cases, Nietzsche's appearance happened after January 1914, that is to say, a few months before Jung's second *Zarathustra* reading, which took place in winter 1914–1915. However, from September 1915 onwards, Nietzsche becomes one of the main targets of the conversations between Jung's 'I' and Philemon, although his presence often remains implicit. Not only this, Nietzsche also represents a deliberate choice of Jung's while re-elaborating his work. At the moment of picking a model for the style of *Liber Novus*, he recognises in Nietzsche one of the closest cases to his own experience, even though *Zarathustra* seems to him 'too strongly consciously' and aesthetically elaborated (March 1918, Private possession, Stephen Martin; letter to J. B. Lang, cited in Shamdasani 2009, RB: 207). This second layer shows a different way of reading Nietzsche's presence concerning Jung's retrospective comments on his previous fantasies. Sometimes Nietzsche remains hidden and can be only guessed through revisitations of Zarathustrian phrases or similar stylistic choices, as well as through numerous citations from the Bible or mythological literature (both German and Greek), which play a significant role in his writings too. Other times, instead, Nietzsche and his philosophy appear more clearly. This level is as helpful as the former to reconstruct and analyse Jung's interpretation of Nietzsche, since it permits to individuate those elements—in both a purely philosophical and a merely stylistic way—which Jung reckoned important and usable as valid prototypes.

However, Nietzsche's inspirational role on *Liber Novus* goes beyond such—more or less explicit—references to his writings and reaches an even deeper level of engagement of Jung's. Indeed, differently from Schopenhauer, Kant, or Plato, it is not Nietzsche's *philosophy* that interests Jung but his *personality*: Nietzsche, as the 'visionary' author of *Zarathustra* (CW 15: §§ 139–141), is taken by Jung as a model to represent the same kind of experience Jung himself is going through in his *Liber Novus*. By reading markings and annotations on Jung's own copy of Nietzsche's texts, it is possible to furnish more evidence of Nietzsche's effective presence, especially concerning those references that might sound too generic. Not rarely, indeed, alongside *Zarathustra* passages, Jung wrote down sentences or remarks referring to his own *Liber Novus*. In some cases, thanks to these annotations, it is also possible to integrate other comments on Nietzsche in Jung's voluntarily published works, whose interpretation sounds slightly obscure, thus making them clearer: using *Liber Novus* as a source definitely sheds some light on the development of Jung's interpretation of Nietzsche.

If the question as to why Jung sometimes refers to Nietzsche when recalling biblical symbols, rather than taking such symbols directly from their original source might be raised at this point, the answer can be found in the significance of *Liber Novus* to Jung. A certain slowness, dedication, and secrecy let one figure out *Liber Novus* as the mirror of a real confrontation experience in Jung's life. Citing Nietzsche, one could argue that it represents a sort of 'transvaluation' of Jung's old 'idols', oriented to getting rid of their all too strong influence or fascination, and proposing a new and more personal thinking, independent from them, yet inspired by their teachings. In this sense, what emerges from Nietzsche's presence in *Liber Novus* is the idea of folly as a consequence of the 'death of God': by refusing the possibility of a rebirth of God, one inevitably falls into madness. Jung's confrontation with Nietzsche is thus aimed at proving him wrong on the one hand, and, consequently, saving himself from the fear of mental illness on the other. No wonder one of the strongest and recurrent motifs of such a psychological fight is indeed the Bible: by evoking the same biblical quotations, Jung tries to 'transvalue' Nietzsche's own 'transvaluation', advocating a return to a specific form of Christianity.

The following parts of this chapter will be divided into two sections. In the first section, Nietzsche's implicit presence in both visions and consciously chosen metaphors will be investigated. Second all of the explicit references to Nietzsche in *Liber Novus* will be explored. In the first part, three groups of symbolic constellations will be analysed, which seem relevant to an exhaustive comprehension of both *Liber Novus* and *Zarathustra*: desert and lion; poisonous serpents and dwarf; sun, sunset, and Eastern wisdom. It is not to deny that such symbolic constellations can be recurrent in other pieces of literary, biblical, or philosophical production too; however, the way these have been used by Jung unavoidably alludes to

Nietzsche. In some of these cases, Jung's annotations on his own *Zarathustra* copy present clear references to *Liber Novus*; other times, Nietzsche's presence can be traced back by consulting Jung's published works and confronting his interpretation of such Zarathustrian symbols with the way similar images recur in *Liber Novus*. Most of these references, however, belong to layer 2, that is, they are to be found in Jung's retrospective reflections or re-elaborations. The second part of this chapter, instead, focuses on how Jung's direct confrontation with Nietzsche can be read and understood in *Liber Novus*. To this end, all of those references which openly allude to the German philosopher (not rarely quotes or crypto-quotes from his writings) will be analysed, along with Nietzsche's role as a character. These topics have been grouped into three categories too: folly as the other side of life; mocking, teaching, and imitating; the 'death' and 'rebirth' of God. Also in this case, such allusions recur more frequently in layer 2, even though one of the most significant fantasies (layer 1) of *Liber Novus* is represented by the meeting with Nietzsche and the conversation with the librarian on the significance of Nietzsche for the most urgent contemporary religious issues.

It might be eventually noted that, as remarked, what has just been called 'Nietzsche's explicit presence' manifests itself mainly in the last eight chapters of *Liber Secundus*, and culminates in *Scrutinies*, turning into a sort of proper response to *Zarathustra*, as well as to other texts which Jung has been having a confrontation with. Here, indeed, layers 1 and 2 are strongly entwined, and Jung switches from fantasies to comments or reflections consistently. However, this very last part has been set aside—besides a few remarkable passages—as it will play one of the main roles in the next chapter—this section from *Liber Novus* representing one of the most significant sources for a comparison between *Liber Novus* and Jung's seminar on Nietzsche's *Zarathustra*.

3.2 Similar Symbology: Nietzsche's Hidden Presence

3.2.1 Desert, Lion, and Transformation

The very first *Liber Novus* chapter, 'The Way of What is to Come', begins with four biblical quotations, drawn from Isaiah 53: 1–4, Isaiah 9:6; John 1:4; Isaiah 35:8 respectively. The last of such quotations is worth being recalled. It reads:

> Isaiah said: The wilderness and the solitary place shall be glad for them; and the desert shall rejoice, and blossom as the rose. It shall blossom abundantly, and rejoice even with joy and singing… Then the eyes of the blind shall be opened, and the ears of the deaf shall be unstopped. Then shall the lame man leap as a hart, and the tongue of the dumb sing: for in the wilderness shall waters break out, and streams in the desert. And the parched ground shall become a pool, and the thirsty land springs of water: in the habitation of dragons, where each lay, shall be grass with reeds and rushes. And an highway shall be there, and a way, and it shall be called way of holiness; the unclean shall not pass over it; but it shall be for those: the wayfaring men, though fools, shall not err therein. (Isaiah, 35:1–8) (RB I, 1: 229)[1]

A few lines below, the desert symbol is used by the 'spirit of the depths', to illustrate the idea of sacrifice as a necessary condition of renewal:

> But the spirit of the depths said: "No one can or should halt sacrifice. Sacrifice is not destruction, sacrifice is the foundation stone of what is to come. Have you not had monasteries? Have not countless thousands gone into the desert? You should carry the monastery in yourself. *The desert is within you* [Die Wüste ist in euch]. The desert calls you and draws you back, and if you were fettered to the world of this time with iron, the call of the desert would break all chains. Truly; I prepare you for solitude". (ibid.: 230; italics added)

In the chapter from *Zarathustra* 'Among the Daughters of the Desert', Nietzsche writes: 'the desert grows: woe to him who harbours desert!' [Die Wüste wächst: weh Dem, der Wüsten birgt] (Za IV, 16, KSA 4: 380; translation modified). In *Symbols of Transformation*, Jung quotes from Nietzsche's *Dithyrambs of Dionysus* version of the same poem in order to show Nietzsche's intuition of the ancient 'mysterious truth' about the link between life and death, mythologically symbolised through the image of 'the sinister mother who secretly lays a poisonous serpent in [the hero's] path to undo him'. Exactly as the mother, every source of life also contains the seeds of death within itself (CW 5: §§ 596–597; translation modified. Nietzsche's citation was present already in the 1912 edition: WSL: 362). Jung recalls Nietzsche's words:

> Here I sit,
> Or rather,
> Here I am swallowed down

By the smallest oasis.
Yawning it opened
Its lovely lips—
[…]
All hail to that whale
If he provides thus
For his guest's welfare!
[…]

Hail to his belly,
If it is
Such a lovely oasis belly!
[…]

The desert grows; woe to him who hides deserts!
Stone grinds on stone, the desert gulps and strangles.
Monstrous Death, glowing under his tan,
Stares and chews … his life is his chewing…
O man burnt out by lust, do not forget:
You are the stone, the desert, the death's head! (DD 2, 'Among the Daughters of the Desert', KSA 6: 383–387; Jung quotes without brackets)

Returning to *Liber Novus*, what follows the passage quoted above, is Jung's 'I''s decision to go to the 'desert of' his 'own self' and experience the state of loneliness that the spirit of the depth has announced. The vision dated 28 November 1913 starts with these words:

> Sixth night. My soul leads me into the desert, into the desert of my own self. I did not think that my soul is a desert, a barren, hot desert, dusty and without drink. […] Why is my self a desert? Have I lived too much outside of myself in men and events? Why did I avoid my self? Was I not dear to myself? But I have avoided the place of my soul. I was my thoughts, after I was no longer events and other men. But I was not my self, confronted with my thoughts. I should also rise up above my thoughts to my own self. My journey goes there, and that is why it leads away from men and events into solitude [Einsamkeit]. Is it solitude, to be with oneself? Solitude is true only when the self is a desert. (RB I, 4, 'The Desert': 235–236)

The 'desert' metaphor represents a peculiar biblical motif, quite recurrent in the literature as well, in order to allude to the dangers of solitude. But solitude also appears as an essential element towards inner enrichment and renewal. Jesus was tempted by Satan in the desert; Flaubert describes

St Anthony temptations in the Egyptian desert (Flaubert 1849)[2]; the incessant quest of the 'wanderer' in the fourth part of *Zarathustra* stopped for a while when he found his oasis in the desert with the dancing girls: Suleika and Dudu. In the solitude of his own desert, Jung's 'I' encounters significant figures, some of them representing old prophets or saints, such as Elijah (with his daughter, Salome), and the 'anchorite' Ammonius. This latter deserves attention in the first place, as he plays an important role in the discourse on desert, inner transformation and Jung's confrontation with Nietzsche. In the chapter 'The Remains of Earlier Temples'—where the allusion might be to the temple of Jerusalem—while commenting on his vision dated 5 January 1914, Jung realises the necessity of combining his human and animal elements; that is to say, of becoming 'a man again who carried within himself the conflict between a longing for the world and a longing for the spirit'. His purpose is to become 'conscious of your self', namely to attain a complete independence from the external world and its influence on his own decisions. Such independence is symbolised by the image of the *lion*, and compared to its opposite 'chamaleonesque' nature:

> After all the rebirths you still remain the lion crawling on the earth, the ΧΑΜΑΙ ΛΕΩΝ [Chameleon], a caricature, one prone to changing colors, a crawling shimmering lizard, but precisely not a lion, whose nature is related to the sun, who draws his power from within himself who does not crawl around in the protective colors of the environment, and who does not defend himself by going into hiding. (RB II, 7: 276–277)

After this dialogue, towards the end of the episode, Jung will decide to 'wander to the far East'. The opposition lion-chameleon is again a biblical one, recalling the dichotomy Christ-Jude (John 5:5). Albeit not fully explicit, this utilisation of the lion symbol also evokes Nietzschean elements, which are worth mentioning. To begin with, what happens in 'The Remains of Earlier Temples' follows Jung's second meeting with two important characters who are now completely transformed: The Red One—who has been the protagonist of the very first *Liber Secundus* chapter—and Ammonius, whom Jung's 'I' has just encountered as an 'anchorite'. Both characters recount Jung's 'I'—how they met in Italy for the first time and decided to travel together. The Red One, who had first appeared as 'the devil', has now learnt how to dance and has become religious. However, in the first meeting that they had ('The Red One', 26 December 1913), it was Jung's 'I' emphasising the role of dancing in religion in the first place:

> I know how to dance. Yes, would we could do it by dancing! Dancing goes with the mating season. I know that there are those who are always in heat, and those who also want to dance for their Gods. Some are ridiculous and others enact Antiquity, instead of honestly admitting their utter incapacity for such expression. (RB II, 1: 260)

Nietzsche writes in *Zarathustra* ('Of Reading and Writing'): 'I should believe only in a God who understood how to dance' [Ich würde nur an einen Gott glauben, der zu tanzen verstünde] (Za I, 7, KSA 4: 49). Jung underlined the word 'dance' in his own copy (Nietzsche 1899–1911), available at Jung's personal library in Küsnacht [Zurich], and drew a double mark alongside, together with an 'x' sign referring to an annotation written below: 'too much devil' [zuviel Teufel]. At the end of the chapter, another passage connected to dancing is marked: 'Now I am nimble, now I fly, now I see myself under myself, now a God dances within me' [Jetzt bin ich leicht, jetzt fliege ich, jetzt sehe ich mich unter mir, jetzt tanzt ein Gott durch mich] (ibid., KSA 4: 50). The last sentence is fully underlined, the word 'God' presents even a double underlining, while a vertical mark accompanies the text. As written above, after the first conversation with The Red One, Jung has recognised him as 'the devil' (more precisely, he has recognised him as his 'own devil'). *Zarathustra* chapter 'Of Reading and Writing', therefore, is quite likely to be connected to The Red One in Jung's mind, and 'The Remains of Earlier Temples' arguably presents the same link too.

In this respect, moreover, it is to be considered that Jung changed the title of that chapter from the *Handwritten Draft* to the *Corrected Draft* by substituting 'Sixth Adventure' with 'Degenerate Ideals', thus stressing the closeness to Nietzsche's fight against idols and ideals. Another probable allusion to Nietzsche in 'The Remains of Earlier Temples', furthermore, concerns a reference to the mythological Greek Hyperboreans, figures that do not belong to *Zarathustra* but occur a couple of times in other texts of Nietzsche's (known by Jung), referring to 'free spirits'. So Jung's 'I' says to Ammonius: 'But my dear friends, what's wrong with you? I'm the Hyperborean stranger, who visited you, Oh Ammonius, in the desert', to which Ammonius replies: 'I recognize you, you supreme devil. My downfall began with you' (RB II, 7: 275). In the aphorism 265 from *The Wanderer and His Shadow*, at the end of *Human, All Too Human*, II (1879), Nietzsche compares children's happiness to that of the Hyperboreans: exactly like these figures, children live on earth and can only figure out an earthy life, with no notion of heaven or fear of Christian judgement (MA II, WS 265, KSA 2: 666–667). At the beginning of *The Anti-Christ*, Nietzsche writes: 'We are Hyperboreans', meaning that he has finally found the way to reach an ancient happiness again, and to overcome modernity (AC 1, KSA 6: 169). Several other mentions, moreover, occur in *Nachlaß* as well (1873, 29 [125], KSA 7: 688; 1886–1887, 5 [46], KSA 12: 200; 6 [26], KSA 12: 246; 1887–1888 11 [118], KSA 13: 56; 1888, 14 [77], KSA 13: 256; 14 [156], KSA 13: 341; 15 [118], KSA 13: 477; 18 [17], KSA 13: 537; 19 [4], KSA 13: 543). Since, as just stated, one of such references happens in *The Anti-Christ* and this *Liber Novus* dialogue refers to paganism and the dualism between Christ and Antichrist, it is not to be excluded that Jung is here alluding to Nietzsche again.

Finally, another reference to the necessity of learning how to dance appears in *Zarathustra* chapter 'Of the Higher Man' too: 'You Higher Men, the worst thing about you is: none of you has learned to dance as a man ought to dance—to dance beyond yourselves!' (Za IV, 13, KSA 4: 358). Also in this case, it is double-marked in Jung's text, and 'to dance beyond yourselves' is even underlined. The relationship dance-devil is also highlighted in the *Prologue* of *Zarathustra*, where Jung underlined the word 'devil' several times. In particular, referring to the episode of Zarathustra's encounter with the 'old man' after the death of 'ropedancer', in relation to being hungry, Jung annotated: '[he] should devour the devil' [sollte den Teufel fressen].

Returning to the lion symbol, it is important to remark that at the end of Jung's German version of *Zarathustra*, a meaningful inscription—quite surely written in a later period—reads:

> In fact now [one should try] to really live the gained knowledge on human nature and not only to think of it. From that a battle with the lions would arise and from its overcoming the Puer Aeternus, namely the child would arise. That already means illness, though.[3]

Facing the lions represents a necessary step towards that transformation process which Jung will later call *individuation*—the lions symbolising the natural repulsion against the instincts taking place within each individual. Initially, such a repulsion causes individuals to fight against their own instincts; however, instincts are to be accepted and incorporated within one's own personality, if one intends to 'individuate'. Only once the fight against the lions has been faced is it possible to achieve a different and wider view of oneself, on the one hand, and on human nature, more broadly, on the other. This all implies, however, another unavoidable confrontation: illness. Indeed, confronting the lions also means facing madness, and the risk of losing oneself in it. According to Jung, that is precisely what happened to Nietzsche, who, already scared by their presence, refused to fight with the lions. In Jung's German version of *Zarathustra*, 'Among the Daughters of the Desert' displays several underlinings and marks, among which, near the lines 'Ah! / Roar Once Again, / Roar morally! / Roar like a moral lion / Before the daughters of the desert!' [Ha! / Noch Ein Mal brüllen, / Moralisch brüllen! / Als moralischer Löwe / Vor den Töchtern der Wüste brüllen!] (Za IV, 16, KSA 4: 384–385), a meaningful inscription reads: 'Morals has devoured the other leg' [Die Moral hat das andere Bein gefressen]. These lines are entirely underlined and supported by a vertical mark along the text in Jung's own copy. Moreover, just two stanzas above, the phrase 'Angry, blonde-maned / Lion-monster?' [Grimme[n] gelbe[n] blondgelockte[n] Löwen-Unthiere?] is underlined and displays a pencil inscription: 'S[ee]. Below' [S. unten], where Jung probably refers to the aforementioned passage and his own comment (KSA 4: 384). As I have showed elsewhere, Jung's understanding of Nietzsche's symbol of the lion in its relation to the desert follows a parallel evolution to Jung's own understanding of Nietzsche. For this reason, this image can be considered one of the key-symbols to understand Jung's confrontation with Nietzsche. In fact, if compared with the English version used by Jung during his seminar available at Jung's personal library in Küsnacht, the same preoccupation concerning the relation between the girl's leg, the lion, and Nietzsche's morality emerges quite clearly, although Jung has never been able to interpret 'Among the Daughters of the Desert' in the seminar, possibly due to the irruption of World War II. 'Oh, pity for that loveliest other leg!' (Nietzsche 1930: 306) is underlined; in the German text, this and the previous lines—'She has lost it! / It has gone! / Gone forever! / That other leg!' [Sie hat es verloren! / Es ist dahin! / Auf ewig dahin! / Das andre Bein!]—are accompanied by a vertical sign, and the sentence 'Sie hat es verloren' is even underlined. In the context of the seminar, however, it is not just Nietzsche's personal morality that was unable to defeat Nietzsche's instincts but that of Germany, and possibly Europe, for which Zarathustra serves as a prophetical mirror (Domenici 2015). Lastly, in the essay *On the Psychology of the Unconscious* (1917–1943), Jung refers to the lion appearing at the end of *Zarathustra*, in order to demonstrate Nietzsche's incapability to effectively accept his instincts, in spite of what is promoted by his philosophy:

> He talked of yeah-saying and lived the nay. His loathing for man, for the human animal that lived by instinct, was too great. Despite everything, he could not swallow the toad he so often dreamed of and which he feared had to be swallowed. The roaring of Zarathustrian lion drove back into the cavern of the unconscious all the "higher" men who were clamouring to live. (CW 7: § 37)

The same image of the roaring lion also occurs in *The Transcendent Function* (1916/1958), this time referred to the 'ugliest man' (CW 8: § 162). The reference to Nietzsche's toad dream also occurs in *Transformation and Symbols of the Libido* (CW 5: § 47, footnote 1; WSL: 36, footnote 1). In this dream, Nietzsche's hand becomes transparent and a toad sits on it; instead of being repulsed by the animal, Nietzsche's instinct is to swallow it, and so he does. Both Jung's annotation and the quoted passage do not refer to 'Among the Daughters of the Desert' solely, but also to *Zarathustra* chapter 'Of the Three Metamorphoses'. Here the transformation process begins with the necessity to enter the 'dirty water' and 'not to disdain cold frogs and hot toads' [kalte Frösche und heisse Kröten nicht von sich weisen]. This is followed by a travel within 'the loneliest [einsamsten] desert' of oneself, where one stops carrying the weight of old values (like the *camel*) and becomes *lion*, that is to say, one becomes 'lord in his own desert' [Herr sein in seiner eigenen Wüste]. The lion is only a transition element though; for it can just fight and rebel against the dragon—symbol of pre-established values—but is not yet capable to 'create new values'. Such a task belongs to the last result of the third metamorphose, namely the *child*, symbol of 'innocence and forgetfulness, a new beginning' (Za I, 1, KSA 4: 29–31; italics added). In Jung's *Zarathustra* copy, the words 'camel', 'lion', 'child', 'desert', 'be lord [Herr]' are underlined (needless to say, they all belong to biblical terminology). Beside the plural 'lions' referred to by Jung, versus the singular 'lion' from *Zarathustra*, the main apparent difference between Jung's psychological reading and Nietzsche's idea lies in the fact that according to the former, one should face the lions; according to the latter, the spirit must become lion itself. However, fighting against the lions means, first of all, recognising them as a part of oneself, meaning that, according to Jung too, one should identify with the lions, although Nietzsche's lion fights against the dragon of morals, whereas Jung's lions represent morals itself. But there is more: according to Jung, after identifying with the lions, one should go beyond them by distantiating from one's own *morals*, exactly like the lion-spirit of 'Of the Three Metamorphoses' ought to transform into 'child' after beating the 'dragon'. Following Jung's interpretation, despite the *Zarathustra* message, Nietzsche could not interrupt his identification with those moral lions that roared against the lowest human instincts, as he was never able to accept and incorporate his instincts. Hence, he was never able to transform into the 'Puer Aeternus', the 'child'.

Referring to *Liber Novus* again, what follows 'The Remains of Earlier Temples' is the meeting with Izdubar narrated in the chapter 'First Day' (8 January 1914). Later on, while reflecting on this fantasy, Jung will write: 'if we are surrounded by night, our brother stands in the fullness of the light, doing his great deeds, tearing up the lion and killing the dragon' (RB II, 8: 280–281). The reference to Nietzsche is quite arguable, also thinking of other motifs recurring in the chapter, such as the image of God as 'sick' or strictly depending on human imagination, or of some allusions to light and darkness that can recall *Zarathustra*'s 'The Night Song'. As will be expanded in the second half of this chapter, Nietzsche's presence in the Izdubar episode can be considered explicit, indeed (see Sects. 3.3.2 and 3.3.3). So, 'I cannot reach the blinding power of the sun, just as he, the Powerful One, cannot reach the ever-fruitful womb of darkness' does not sound far away from Nietzsche's words: 'Light am I: ah, that I were night! But this is my solitude, that I am girded round with light. / I, that I were dark and obscure! How would I suck at the breast of light!' (Za II, 9, 'The Night Song', KSA 4: 136). Another reference to the same motif was already present in 'The Remains of Earlier Temples': 'I want to exist from my own force, like the sun which gives light and does not suck light' (RB II, 7: 277), and will be exhaustively discussed in the last section of the first part of this chapter (see Sect. 3.2.3). Quite interestingly, however, and as a demonstration of how close the pieces of 'visionary' works analysed in Chap. 2 are—not only to one another but also to *Liber Novus*—a similar image also occurs in *Auch Einer*, in regard to the 'unknown god'. So, Vischer writes: 'But not, not! Not dark, dull power he is, he is bright, candid, quite candid. *Light is he*, he shines through everything and in everything, everything being translucent' [Aber nein, nein! Nicht dunkle, dumpfe Macht ist er, er ist hell, offen, ganz offen. *Licht ist er*, er scheint durch alles und in alles, da ist alles durchsichtig]. And again, a people 'from far lands towards the sunset', namely the 'Gaels', is said to believe in a God 'to venerate in the quiet, mysterious wood': 'But this God is a dark God and an *abyss* [*Abgrund*]'. Lastly, there are 'other men coming from even further from a wide island in deep water [...]. They believe he is the sun too, and speak of him: "***Light is his way and his wheel, sunshine his chariot*** [***Licht ist sein weg und sein Rad, Sonnenschein sein Wagen***], and with the ghosts" swaying [Geisterschwingen] he floats above the waters, big is he in earth and seas, the biggest in all worlds' (Vischer 1878: 196–197; italics added).

Furthermore, the same figure of the *toad* occurs sometimes in *Liber Novus*. In 'The Magician', for instance, the newborn God is a 'son of frogs'. Remarkably, the same image of the 'king of toads' [Froschkönig] also occurs in Spitteler's *Imago* (Spitteler 1906: 62).[4] The birth of this 'new God' symbolises the culmination of a transformation path which recalls the three metamorphoses in *Zarathustra*. Since the symbol of the toad is a key element of Jung's seminar on *Zarathustra*, this topic will be exhausted in the second part of Chap. 4 (see Sect. 4.3.2). However, a couple of elements need to be highlighted here too. To begin with, some lines above the description of the frog-God, the same old reference to the desert appears again in Jung's reflection:

> The word has become heavy for me, and it barely wrestles itself free of the soul. Bronze doors have shut. Fires have burned out and sunk into ashes. Wells have been drained and where there were seas there is dry land. My tower stands in the desert. Happy is he who can be a hermit in his own desert. He survives. (RB II, 21, § 189 [6], *Draft*: 327)

Moreover, in the same chapter a reference to the 'Basilisk egg' occurs, that was already featured in 'Second Day': a close connection between 'second Day' and 'The Magician' is then surely arguable. The same image also appears in one of Nietzsche's poems, *Glory and Eternity* [*Ruhm und Ewigkeit*], which Jung cites in *Transformations and Symbols of the Libido*, in order to show the importance of introversion for one's psychological rebirth: 'How long already have you sat on your misfortune? / Give heed, lest you hatch me / An egg, / A basilisk egg / From your long travail' (DD 8, KSA 6: 402). Jung comments: 'The hero is himself the serpent, himself the sacrificer and the sacrificed' (CW 5: §§ 592–593; WSL: 358; translation modified), which is a further—this time implicit—allusion to another dithyramb by Nietzsche, *Amidst Birds of Prey* [*Zwischen Raubvögeln*]:

> Hunted by yourself,
> Your own prey,

> Bored into yourself.
> Now—Solitary, only yourself for company,
> Twain in the knowledge you possess,
> In the midst of one century of suspect memories,
> Tired from every injury,
> Frozen by every ice,
> Neck / strangled by the rope-noose that you tied, your own auto-knower!
> Your own auto-hangman! (DD 4, KSA 6:391)

This latter is also quoted by Jung in both the 1912 and 1952 editions of *Transformations and Symbols of the Libido*. In 'Descent into Hell in the Future', it occurs again: 'I myself am a murderer and murdered, sacrificer and sacrificed' (RB I, 5: 239). In *After the catastrophe* (1945), Jung will explain the self-sacrificer-sacrificed concept in terms of Germany's 'collective guilt', and will draw on *Zarathustra* chapter 'Of the Pale Criminal' to justify his position: as Nietzsche's 'pale criminal'—who 'shows all the signs of hysteria'—'will stoop to every kind of self-deception if only he can escape the sight of himself', so the German collective psychology is incapable of acknowledging its own inferiority and cannot help but to project such inferiority onto other peoples, turning them into public enemies (CW 10: § 417; see also Bishop 1995a: 315–322, 1999).

Being able to 'be a hermit in his own desert' is the criterion for succeeding in the confrontation with oneself and bringing to completion such a transformation process. But this is not simple at all, and, while commenting on his vision described in the chapter 'The Way of the Cross' (27 January 1914), Jung shows the possibility of failure by referring to *Zarathustra* again:

> He who goes to himself climbs down. Pathetic and ridiculous forms appeared to the greatest prophet who came before this time, and these were the forms of his own essence. He did not accept them, but exorcized them before others. Ultimately; however, he was forced to celebrate a Last Supper [Abendmahl] with his own poverty and to accept these forms of his own essence out of compassion [Mitleid], which is precisely that acceptance of the lowest in us. But this enraged the mighty lion, who chased down the lost and restored it to the darkness of the depths [Da aber empörte sich der Löwe seiner Macht und scheuchte das Verlorene und Wiedergebrachte in das Dunkel der Tiefe zurück]. And like all those with power, the one with the great name wanted to erupt from the womb of the mountain like the sun [sonnengleich aus dem Schoße der Berge hervorbrechen]. But what

> happened to him? His way led him before the crucified and he began to rage. He raged against the man of mockery [Mann des Spottes] and pain because the power of his own essence forced him to follow precisely this way as Christ had done before us. Yet he loudly proclaimed his power and greatness. No one speaks louder of his power and greatness than he from whom the earth disappears under his feet. Ultimately the lowest in him got to him, his incapacity; and this crucified his spirit, so that, as he himself had predicted, his soul died before his body [seine Seele eher starb als sein Körper]. (RB II, 20: 310)[5]

Compassion [Mitleid] is precisely Zarathustra's 'last sin' (Za IV, 2, 'The Cry of Distress', KSA 4: 301): in the last part of the book, in fact, his love for men prevents him from really despising the lowest ones and causes all of his teaching attempts to fail. After sharing his 'Last Supper' [Das Abendmahl] with the higher men (Za IV, 11, KSA 4: 353–355), Zarathustra discovers his guests celebrating a pagan religious ceremony and venerating an ass.[6] In that very moment, he realises that people are not ready for his wisdom yet. The following day, as narrated in the chapter 'The Sign', he wakes up 'like a morning sun emerging from behind dark mountains' [wie eine Morgensonne, die aus dunklen Bergen kommt] and finds a roaring 'mighty [starke(n)] lion' outside his cave, whose presence and tenderness let him realise that the time for his teaching has finally come:

> "*Compassion* [*Mitleid*]*! Compassion with the Higher Man!* He cried out, and his countenance was transformed into brass. Very well! That—has had its time!
>
> My suffering [Leid] and my compassion—what for them! Am I striving for *Happiness*? I am striving for my *works*!
>
> Very well! The lion came, my children are near, Zarathustra has become ripe, my hour has come:—
>
> This is my morning, my day begins: *rise up now, rise up, great noontide* [grosser Mittag]!"
>
> Thus spoke Zarathustra and left his cave, glowing and strong, like a morning sun emerging from behind dark mountains. (Za IV, 19, KSA 4: 405–408; translation modified)

In Jung's personal text, the first three quoted lines are nearly completely underlined and alongside, the following inscription is visible: 'the lion of morality chases human nature away' [der Moral Löwe scheucht das Menschliche weiter Weg]. There are a couple of other reading marks in the first part of the chapter; the sentence 'But I still lack my rightful men' [Aber noch fehlen mir meine rechten Menschen] is underlined and, in the following page, the words 'moralistic roaring lion' [moralischer Brülllowe] are written in pencil. Ultimately, it can be noted that, exactly as at the end of *Zarathustra* the protagonist finds a lion outside his cave, so *Liber Secundus* ends with the figure of a God emerging 'from the water [...] with a swirling lion mane' (RB II, 21, 'The Magician': 329).

The solitude question raised by Jung at the very beginning of his experience, along with his response to it, can also explain his later understanding of Nietzsche's 'Among the Daughters of the Desert'. Jung's words 'Why did I avoid my self? Was I not dear to myself? But I have avoided the place of my soul' (RB I, 4, 'The Desert': 235–236) do not sound too far away from the words expressed by Nietzsche not only in 'Among the Daughters of the Desert' but also in another chapter of *Zarathustra*. Indeed, in 'Of the Virtuous', Zarathustra cries out: 'Your virtue is your dearest self. The ring's thirst is in you! To attain itself again—to that end every ring struggles and turns itself' (Za II, 5, KSA 4: 121; translation modified). In Jung's own *Zarathustra* copy, the sentence presents a vertical mark along the text and the words 'ring's thirst is in you' are underlined. While commenting on his previous vision ('On the Service of the Soul', 15 November 1913), Jung had expressed himself this way: 'If your virtues hinder you from salvation, discard them, since they have become evil to you. The slave to virtue finds the way as little as the slave to vices' (RB I, 3: 235). This sentence reminds one of another significant *Zarathustra* phrase, pronounced by the protagonist of the chapter 'Of the Chairs of Virtue': 'And even when one has all the virtues, there is still one thing to remember: to send even these virtues to sleep at the proper time' (Za I, 2, KSA 4: 33). This all suggests that, in his 1914 reading of *Zarathustra*, Jung associates Nietzsche's experience with his own. In this sense, according to Jung's later annotations on 'Among the Daughters of the Desert', it is arguable that Nietzsche's 'self' appears to Jung as 'a desert' and it is therefore unavoidable, for the philosopher, to be devoured by his own solitude. Roaring at the girls means indeed to rebel against the possibility of a confrontation with one's strangeness, that is, remaining stuck in the aridity of one's own *thoughts*, instead of trying to deeply *experience* them. By accepting to face his own strangeness in *Liber Novus*, Jung has also accepted to measure the desert of his own self in order to verify his capability to survive such a strength. Nietzsche, by contrast, appears to have succumbed. As already established, in the second part of the book, the philosopher will incarnate Jung's encounter with madness, indeed. Towards the end of his *Liber Novus* experience, namely in *Scrutinies*, Jung tells his soul: 'The solitude of this acceptance terrifies me. I dread the madness that befalls the solitary', to which she replies: 'As you already know, I have long predicted solitude for you. You need not be afraid of madness. What I predict is valid' (RB *Scrutinies*, § 2: 336). At the same time, Jung also appears as trying to prove the importance of such a confrontation by showing Nietzsche's personal breakdown caused by his refusal. This is shown quite clearly through the allusion to the ropedancer's tragic fate at the end of the last quoted sentence from 'The Way of the Cross': 'his soul died before his body'. In the *Prologue*, Zarathustra says to the dying ropedancer: 'Your soul will be death even before your body: therefore fear nothing more!' [Deine Seele wird noch schneller todt sein als dein Leib: fürchte nun Nichts mehr!]. The whole sentence is underlined in Jung's *Zarathustra* and cited again in the essay *On the Psychology of the Unconscious*, exactly some lines above the aforementioned lion, in order to interpret that passage as a prophecy on Nietzsche's own destiny, brought about by the contradiction between his teaching and his life (CW 7: § 36).

To conclude this part, it is relevant to note that, in *Symbols of Transformation*, Jung deals with the Christian meaning of the lion symbol exhaustively (CW 5: §§ 524–526). As he observes, the lion symbolises both 'the tribe of Judah' in the Old Testament and the devil in the New Testament. However, it is the connection with the role of 'Christ'as a hero that interests Jung the most. In this sense, the lion represents an equivalent symbol to the 'bull' for the Mithraic Mysteries, where 'the cult-hero has to fight the bull; in the "transitus" he carries it into the cave, where he kills it'. So, 'the struggle in Christ's soul in Gethsemane [...]; then the "transitus", the carrying of the cross, when he takes on his shoulder the symbol of the deadly mother and in so doing carries himself to the grave [...] all these images express the same fundamental thought: that Christ is a divinity who is eaten in the Lord's Supper'. Moreover, the lion is discussed in relation to its antagonism with the serpent symbol in the Mithraic monuments. In such peculiar monuments, as Jung reports, 'we often come across a strange symbol: a krater (mixing bowl) with a serpent coiled round it, and a lion facing the serpent like an antagonist'. As Jung remarks, the lion and the serpent appear to be 'fighting for the krater', which 'symbolizes the maternal vessel of rebirth', while the serpent represents 'fear and resistance', and 'the lion raging desire' (ibid.: § 671). Finally, in several passages, Jung stresses the zodiacal meaning of the lion, namely that of ***domicilium solis***, 'the fierce heat of midsummer' (ibid.: § 600, footnote; see also §§ 176; 425). These three connotations attributed to the lion—the Christian, the mythological, and the zodiacal one—were already present at the time of *Wandlungen und Symbole der Libido* (1912) and can be therefore directly reconnected to the meaning of the lion in *Liber Nous.*

3.2.2 Poisonous Serpents, Riddles, Dwarfs

In a vision dated 12 December 1913, recollected in *Liber Novus* under the name of 'Descent into Hell in the Future', Jung's 'I' is in a cave, flooded by dark water. On the opposite side, he sees a red stone that he knows he 'must reach', despite the fear he is feeling and the 'frightful noise of shrieking voices' pervading the cave. Finally, he takes the stone and finds another 'dark opening in the rock', from which he can hear 'underground waters' flow, and can see 'the bloody head of a man on the dark stream' with 'a large black scarab floating past on the dark stream'. He carries on with the description:

> In the deepest reach of the stream shines a red sun, radiating through the dark water. There I see—and a terror seizes me—small serpents on the dark rock walls, striving toward the depths, where the sun shines. A thousand serpents crowd around, veiling the sun. Deep night falls. A red stream of blood, thick red blood springs up, surging for a long time, then ebbing. I am seized by fear. What did I see? (RB I, 5: 237)

Serpents are important symbols for the development of *Liber Novus.* Commenting on the vision, Jung calls himself 'victim of [his] thinking', realising that it is now time to give up his one-sided scientific 'knowledge'. In the desert, Jung's 'I' has indeed experienced 'madness' upon himself, which has led him to a more complete form of 'knowledge', with 'a thousand voices, an army roaring like lions'. Such a 'knowledge' opens up to the counterpart of 'science', namely the *soul.* Jung's 'I' prays to his soul with these words: 'protect me from the serpent of judgment, which only appears to be a healing serpent, yet in your depths is infernal and agonizing death' (ibid.: 238; italic added). The 'serpent of judgment', because of serpents' misleading nature, hides behind Asclepius's 'healing serpent', symbol of a wild and natural wisdom, far away from science and rationality. In this sense, the serpent also deceives those who believe to reach it. This is exactly what is happening to Jung, who, in 1952, will write in *Symbols of*

Transformation: 'serpent dreams always indicate a discrepancy between the attitude of the conscious mind and instinct, the serpent being a personification of the threatening aspect of that conflict' (CW 5: § 615; translation modified. On Jung's specific interpretation of Aesculapius cult and the coiled serpent as its symbol, see CW 5: §§ 577–579). As stated, at the end of *Liber Primus*, Jung's 'I' comes across the characters of Elijah and Salome. Elijah is an old man, namely the biblical prophet of the same name, and Salome, a blind girl, is apparently his daughter, although Jung's 'I' realises she should rather be Herod's daughter. The former is said to represent *forethinking* [Vordenken]; the latter *pleasure* [Lust], and it is also revealed that she loves Jung's 'I'. The serpent is defined in terms of 'a third principle', necessary to keep these both principles united; for it is that *earthly* [erdhaft] element indeed, which is 'a stranger to both principles although it is associated with both'. It 'has the weight of the earth in itself but also its changeability and germination from which everything that becomes emerges', and through its connection with *longing* [Sehnsucht], it reminds one of life and reunifies the opposites (RB I, 9, 'Mysterium Encounter': 247; italics added). In fact, this figures have a double meaning, that is to say, beside their healing power, serpents also preserve the destructive force of their poison. This is well symbolised through the appearance of the white serpent as a second element, necessary to resolve the event at the end of the episode (RB I, 11, 'Resolution': 251; 25 December 1913).

As a motif, serpents occur many times in *Liber Novus*, with both their healing and destructive attributions. As these qualities are mainly derived from the Bible, those scenes where serpents are depicted as dangerous present some elements that can be easily found in Nietzsche as well. As a very general statement, it can be interesting to notice that the serpent is sometimes compared with a *bridge* [Brücke] connecting the opposites. With the same metaphor, the *Übermensch* is introduced in *Zarathustra* more than once. Moreover, just as a comparison, the following example can be given:

> Elijah climbs down from the stone [vom Steine herunter], his form becomes smaller in descending, and finally becomes dwarflike [zwerghaft], unlike himself.
>
> I ask: "Who are you?"
>
> "I am Mime, and I will show you the wellsprings. The collected light becomes water and flows in many springs from the summit into the valleys

of the earth." He then dives down into a crevice. I follow him down into a dark cave. I hear the rippling of a spring. I hear the voice of the dwarf [Zwerg] from below: "Here are my wells, whoever drinks from them becomes wise." (ibid.)

Here the main allusion is certainly to Wagner's *Ring*, the dwarf himself claiming to be Mime; however, a few similarities with the episode narrated in *Zarathustra* chapter 'Of the Vision and the Riddle'—whereby the 'eternal return' is notoriously announced in *Zarathustra*—can be also recalled, despite the contextual difference of the two episodes. In the scene depicted by Nietzsche, in particular, Zarathustra faces the 'Spirit of Gravity' through a verbal fight with a dwarf (representing the heaviness of the 'spirit of gravity'). This latter addresses Zarathustra as 'stone of wisdom' [Stein der Weisheit], and adds: 'You have thrown yourself thus high, but every stone that is thrown must—fall! Condemned by yourself and to your own stone-throwing. O Zarathustra, far indeed have you thrown your stone, but it will fall back upon *you*!' (Za III, 2, KSA 4: 198). The whole passage is accompanied by a couple of vertical lines in Jung's own copy. Furthermore, since Wagner represents an important model for Nietzsche—besides occurring a couple of times in *Liber Novus* as well[7]—among the sources of Nietzsche's allusion, *The Ring of the Nibelungs* has not to be excluded categorically.

Returning to *Liber Novus*, in his comment on the Elijah vision, Jung compares the risk of becoming one-sided to an 'ugly dwarf who lives in a dark cave like an unborn in the womb', and forethinking to 'a dwarfish cleverness, false and of the night' (RB I, 11: 253). Again, *Zarathustra*'s dwarf says: 'All truth is crooked, time itself is a circle' (ZA III, 2, KSA 4: 200). Once more, the first part is underlined by Jung. More generally, a couple of further similarities with Nietzsche's episode are also present in the contents of Jung's fantasy. Jung's 'I' tells Elijah: 'You pose dreadful riddles' [du gibst mir grausame Rätsel auf], while the atmosphere becomes 'gloomy and doubtful' [düster und zweifelhaft] (RB I, 9, 'Mysterium Encounter': 246). This seems to remind one of the beginning of 'Of the Vision and the Riddle [Räthsel]', where the vision is introduced through a 'deadly-grey twilight' [leichenfarbne Dämmerung], in which the protagonist walks 'gloomily and sternly with compressed lips' [düster und hart, mit gepressten Lippen] (Za III, 2, KSA 4: 198). Jung's immediately following vision starts, then, with an allusion to a 'crater' [Krater] (RB I, 10, 'Instruction': 248). Again, the 'Blissful Islands' from where Zarathustra is leaving on board of a ship—a place which has been certainly well-known to Jung—are characterised by the presence of a 'volcano' [Feuerberg] (Za II, 18, 'Of Great Events' KSA 4: 167). As discussed, Jung has referred to that chapter in his doctoral thesis as an example of *cryptomnesia* (CW 1: §§ 140–142 and 180–184. See Bishop 1993, 1995b: 280). In his own copy, the chapter presents some reading marks and annotations.

Besides the similar tone of these two episodes, as pointed out at the beginning of this section, what seems to really link Nietzsche with the serpent symbol in *Liber Novus*, is its poisoning aspect. Towards the end of Zarathustra's vision from 'Of the Vision and the Riddle', indeed, a serpent appears, to symbolise the darkest aspect of the 'eternal return', as well as its necessity to be accepted. As was the case with the lion chasing the instincts away, the bite of the poisonous serpents in *Zarathustra* is one of Jung's favourite metaphors to explain Nietzsche's inflation in his published writings. However, such a metaphor remains partly unexplained, without considering the same image in *Liber Novus*. To this end, the chapters 'First Day' and 'The Magician' from *Liber Novus* need to be compared with 'Of the Vision and the Riddle' on the one hand, and with the aphorism 113 from *The Gay Science* on the other hand. In 'First Day', Izdubar, who comes from the East and knows nothing of western culture, compares science to poison and adds: 'You call poison truth? Is poison truth? Or is truth poison? Do not our astrologers and priests also speak the truth? And yet theirs does not act like poison ' (RB II, 8, 'First Day': 278; 8 January 1914). In *The Gay Science* 113, 'On the Doctrine of Poisons' [Zu Lehre von den Giften], Nietzsche expresses the same analogy between scientific thinking and poison. According to him, the former is originated by the union of different impulses which, each of them being unilateral, act exactly like poisons on the whole organism of life. In fact, they prevent the organism from realising how important it would be to achieve cooperation of science with 'artistic energies' and 'practical wisdom of life' (FW 113, KSA 3: 473–474). Furthermore, again during the same *Liber Novus* dialogue, Jung explains that because of the importance given to science in western culture, western man remains 'dwarfish' [zwerghaft]. And, again:

> I: "Now you perhaps see that we had no choice. We had to swallow the poison of science. Otherwise we would have met the same fate as you have: we'd be completely lamed, if we encountered it unsuspecting and unprepared. This poison is so insurmountably strong that everyone, even the

> strongest, and even the eternal Gods, perish because of it. If our life is dear to us, we prefer to sacrifice a piece of our life force rather than abandon ourselves to certain death." (RB II, 8: 279)

According to Jung's 'I' in his dialogue with Izdubar, science is not only poisonous but also to be swallowed; similarly, it can be anticipated, the serpent in the shepherd's mouth described by Nietzsche at the end of 'Of the Vision and the Riddle' has to be bitten. Moreover, the ability of killing 'the eternal Gods' through the poison of science can be taken as a possible example of another allusion to Nietzsche. However, another passage is to be emphasised and appears in Jung's retrospective reflection on the same vision:

> So the path [Pfad] of my life led me beyond the rejected opposites, united in smooth and—alas!—extremely painful sides of the way which lay before me. I stepped on them but they burned and froze my soles. And thus I reached the other side. But the poison of the serpent, whose head you crush, enters you through the wound in your heel; and thus the serpent becomes more dangerous than it was before. Since whatever I reject is nevertheless in my nature. I thought it was without, and so I believed that I could destroy it. But it resides in me and has only assumed a passing outer form and stepped toward me. I destroyed its form and believed that I was a conqueror. But I have not yet overcome myself. (ibid.)

Remarkably, a similar phrase also appears in another comment by Jung, written in the chapter 'The Magician':

> I continue on my way; accompanied by a finely polished piece of steel, hardened in ten fires, stowed safely in my robe. Secretly; I wear chain mail under my coat. Overnight I became fond of serpents, and I solved their riddle. I sit down next to them on the hot stones lying by the wayside. I know how to catch them cunningly and cruelly; those cold devils that prick the heel of the unsuspecting. (RB II, 21: 317)

The meeting with the dwarf happens to Zarathustra on a mountain 'path' [Pfad]. The same path will then be used to exemplify the traditional view of time, and to introduce the idea of the eternal return: a 'gateway' [Thorweg], which represents the present 'moment' [Augenblick], divides the 'long lane' [lange Gasse] into two paths, symbolising both sides of eternity, namely, past and future. To acknowledge the eternal return means to stop considering time as a continuative line, and to start giving value and responsibility to the moment. For what is happening right now, not only has already happened infinite times in the past, but has still to be eternally *repeated*. In order not only to admit that possibility but also to accept it, Zarathustra's vision continues with another scene, in which a shepherd has 'a heavy, black serpent' hanging from his mouth, causing him convulsions and torment. As mentioned, the only solution for him to be safe is to bite the serpent's head and tear it off. The serpent symbolises the heaviest and darkest side of Nietzsche's 'abysmal though', that is, the 'disgust' [Ekel] at life; but once such a thought is accepted, it frees one, offering them a *lighter* perspective. In exactly this sense, the shepherd turns himself into 'a transformed being, surrounded with light, *laughing*' [ein Verwandelter, ein Umleuchterer, welcher *lachte*] (Za III, 2, KSA 4: 199–202; translation modified).

In 1952, Jung comments on this *Zarathustra* episode comparing the episode to 'the Sabazios mysteries', where 'the serpent god [...] crawls into the mouth of the celebrant'. Nietzsche would represent such celebrant ('the ποιμήν or ποιμάνδρης, the shepherd of souls and preacher'), and the unconscious function of the serpent would be that of stopping Nietzsche 'from talking too much, and secondly to make him ἔνθεος—"enthused", "filled with God" '. However, 'the serpent had already bitten fast, but fear was swifter and more violent: it bit off the serpent's head and spat it out'. So, Jung concludes:

> *If you want the serpent to bruise your heel you have only to tread on its head.* The shepherd laughed on getting rid of the serpent—a wild *hysterical laughter*, because he had dished the compensation from the unconscious. He could now reckon without his host, and with the well-known consequences: *one has only to read the passages in Zarathustra where Nietzsche speaks of laughing and laughter.* Unfortunately, everything happened afterwards just as if the whole German nation had paid heed to Nietzsche's sermon.
>
> The unconscious insinuates itself in the form of a serpent if the conscious mind is afraid of the compensating tendency of the unconscious, as is generally the case in regression. But if the compensation is accepted in principle, there is no regression, and the unconscious can be met half-way through introversion. It must be admitted, however, that the problem as it presented itself to Nietzsche was insoluble, for *nobody could expect the shepherd to swallow down a serpent under such circumstances.* We are confronted here with one of those fatal cases, by no means uncommon, where the compensation appears in a form that cannot be accepted and could only be overcome by something that is equally impossible for the patient. (CW 5: §§ 586–587; translation modified; italics added)

In the first edition of *Wandlungen und Symbole der Libido*, which preceded the Izdubar fantasy of a couple of years, the reference to Nietzsche's chapter was already present, but Jung's analysis stopped at the stage of introversion: the serpent represented the libido's withdrawal process, and through that, it became a symbol of rebirth (WSL: 355–356). Furthermore, both in 1912 and in 1952, Jung stresses the 'serpent's poison' [Schlangengift] from Nietzsche's poem 'Amidst birds of Prey' (DD, KSA 6: 391) in relation to the separation from the 'mother' and the process of creation. In 1912, the motif of the 'birth out of oneself' [Geburt aus sich selber] was Jung's main concern (WSL: 290), while in 1952, the issue is understood in terms of 'individuation process'. Before introducing the quotation, Jung states: 'At this stage the mother-symbol no longer connects back to the beginnings, but points towards the unconscious as the creative matrix of the future. "Entry into the mother" then means establishing a relationship between the ego and the unconscious [...]' (CW 5: § 459). Then these following lines by Nietzsche are cited:

> Why hast thou enticed thyself
> Into the old serpent's Paradise?
> Why hast thou stolen
> Into thyself, thyself?
>
> A sick man now,
> Sick of the serpent's poison;
> A captive now
> Who drew the hardest lot:
> Bent double
> Working in thine own pit,
> Encaved within thyself,
> Burrowing into thyself,
> Heavy-handed,
> Stiff,
> A corpse—
> Piled with a hundred burdens,
> Loaded to death with thyself,
> A knower!
> Self-knower!
> The wise Zarathustra!
> Thou sought the heaviest burden
> And found yourself. (KSA 6: 391)

Jung's overall understanding of the poem, however, remains the same in both editions: 'Sunk in his own depths, he is like one buried in the earth; a dead man who has crawled back into the mother' (CW 5: § 460; WSL: 291). Returning to the 1952 version and the comment on 'Of the Vision and the Riddle', beside the idea of Nietzsche's impossibility to compensate, as 'the problem [...] was insoluble', two more details are worth mentioning. The first one being Jung's emphasising the shepherd's 'hysterical laughter' and laughing as it generally appears in *Zarathustra*. Interestingly, one of Jung's marginalia to the chapter 'The Ass Festival' (ZA IV, 18, KSA 4: 390–394) reads: 'laughing kills' [Lachen tötet]. The second detail to be noticed is Jung connecting the serpent bite to the *heel*. As I have demonstrated elsewhere, the reference to the heel in Jung's comments on 'Of the Vision and the Riddle' in *Symbols of Transformation* can be explained only if such a comment is related to Jung's seminar on *Zarathustra* on the one hand and to 'First Day' and 'The Magician' on the other, since no heels are mentioned by Nietzsche in 'Of the Vision and the Riddle' (Domenici 2018). As will be shown in the next chapter, on 11 December 1935, Jung makes use of a similar phrase in his analysis of the *Zarathustra* section 'Of the Adder's Bite': 'To be caught by the heel is the usual fate of a man. Crush the head of the serpent and it will bite you in the heel'. He also points out that 'the same motif comes again later', referring to 'Of the Vision and the Riddle', indeed (SNZ I: 755–756).

Focusing back on the encounter with Elijah and Salome, something more must be added. If a link is to be found between Jung's and Nietzsche's stress on the poisoning aspect of serpents, the importance of its acceptance deserves to be equally remarked, as the precondition for personal development. Also in this case, the analogy with Nietzsche and Zarathustra appears to be helpful. Exactly as the shepherd in *Zarathustra* was surrounded by light and laughed as 'no human' had ever done before, after which Jung realised and accepted the double nature of serpents—that is after the reconciliation of forethinking and feeling (as Jung retrospectively comments)—'Elijah transforms into a huge flame of white light' (RB I, 11, 'Resolution': 252). Quite surprisingly, the *Corrected Draft* version reads: 'the forethinking in me had the form of an old prophet, which showed that it was pre-Christian, and transformed itself into a principle that *no longer appeared in a human form*, but in the absolute form of a *pure white light*' (ibid.: 255, footnote 240; italics added). If the lion was interpreted by Jung as a resistance against human instincts, the serpent represents its counterpart, the instincts indeed, and if it is necessary to face the roaring lion of morality, it is also essential to 'swallow down' the serpent, without biting off its head: 'In the mystery man himself becomes the two principles, the lion and the serpent' (ibid.: 254). Moreover, as already argued, in *Symbols of Transformation*, Jung stresses the antagonism between serpents and lions in the Mithraic mysteries (CW 5: § 425). Only if these two aspects are combined can the instincts be effectively integrated within oneself, leading to a more complete awareness of one's own (human) nature. Finally, again with the same meaning, it is important to recall that Atmavictu—who will later provide Jung's 'I' with teaching and guidance—is also said to be a serpent.

3.2.3 Sun, Sunset, and Eastern Wisdom

In 'Descent into Hell in the Future', Jung's 'I' decides to give up what was defined as a one-sided scientific knowledge, and to 'be stunned' again. He makes his decision by pronouncing these words: 'I want to go down cleansed into your depths [Ich möchte als Reiner in deine Tiefe steigen] with white garments and not rush in like some thief, seizing whatever I can and fleeing breathlessly' (RB I, 5: 238). In quite a similar way, Zarathustra expresses the necessity of his sunset [Untergang]: 'To that end I must descend into the depths [Dazu muss ich in die Tiefe steigen]: as you do at Evening, when you go behind the sea and bring light to the underworld, you overaboundant star! Like you [the sun] I must *go down* [untergehen]' (Za I, *Prologue* 1, KSA 4: 11; translation modified). 'To that end I must descend into the depth', 'light to the underworld', *go down* are underlined in Jung's personal copy. Referring to his soul, just compared to the sun, Jung's 'I' wonders: 'How shall I ever walk under your sun if I do not drink the bitter draught of slumber to the lees?' [wenn ich nicht den bitteren Schlummertrank trinke, und bis zur Neige leere] (RB I, 5: 238). And so Zarathustra to the sun: 'Bless the cup that wants to overflow, that the waters may flow golden from him and bear the reflection of the joy over all the world! Behold! This cup wants to be empty again, and Zarathustra wants to be man again' [Segne den Becher, welcher überfliessen will, dass das Wasser golden aus ihm fliesse und überallhin den Abglanz deiner Wonne trage! Siehe! Dieser Becher will wieder leer werden, und Zarathustra will wieder Mensch werden] (KSA 4: 11). In Jung's personal copy, the last sentence is underlined.

The sun, often together with images such as the ripening or the vessel, is one of the most recurrent symbols in both works. From a broader point of view, the sun is a predominant symbol in mythological literature, especially in ancient Greece and Egypt, where the link between its path and seasons, also in terms of zodiac, was majorly stressed (Creuzer 1822: 297). The stress on the sun path in relation to the seasons is an important element in *Zarathustra*. In the chapter 'On the Mount of Olives' (Za III, 6, KSA 4: 218–221), for instance, winter is personified as an 'ill guest'. Explicit references to the mythological tradition are easy to be found in *Liber Novus* too, as well as in several other writings of Jung's, where he explicitly refers to myths in order to show the sun-zodiac connection. In particular, the mythological connotation of the sun is one of the most important and recurrent elements in *Symbols of Transformation*. It is thus arguable that Nietzsche and Jung might have drawn their images from similar sources. However, a few elements offer details for a closer comparison and deserve to be recalled, concerning Nietzsche's and Jung's utilisation of the sun path in regard to the figures of wisdom in *Zarathustra* and *Liber Novus* respectively.

The first encounter with the 'anchorite' Ammonius takes place in the desert, far from men and society, where the old man has been living for ten years, precisely like Zarathustra on his mountain top. Both Zarathustra and Ammonius, in their characterisation, are strongly associated with the sun and its path. Ammonius tells Jung's 'I' indeed: 'You found the tracks of my daily walks at daybreak and sunset' (RB II, 4, 'The Anchorite': 268). As already pointed out, Zarathustra identifies with the sun at the very beginning of the *Prologue*, and in several other passages the same phenomenon comes about quite clearly. Furthermore, not only does he want to donate his knowledge to men as the sun brings 'light to the underworld' at the time of sunset, but he also wakes up at or just before daybreak and expresses his deepest sadness at night, that is, in all those moments of the sun's absence. In a similar way, Jung's 'anchorite' exclaims:

> But I see that the sun has gone down. Soon it will be completely dark. Night is the time of silence. I want to show you your place for the night. I need the morning for my work, but after midday you can come to me again if you like. Then we will continue our conversation. (RB II, 4: 269)

The analogy with the sun does not concern Zarathustra only, but can be extended to all of those figures in Nietzsche's text presenting traditional wisdom features. Still in the *Prologue*, immediately after making the decision to go to the people, Zarathustra comes across an old Christian hermit, an 'old man, who has left his holy hut to look for roots in the forest'. He abandoned his old life because he 'loved mankind all too much'. Now he is living in the 'desert' [Einöde], where he can 'make songs and sing them', in order to 'praise God'. Unlike the protagonist, he does not in fact love men anymore (Za I, *Prologue* 2, KSA 4: 12–13). In Jung's *Zarathustra*, this chapter presents several underlinings and marks. In a similar manner, Jung comments on his meeting with the anchorite by saying that 'the solitary lives in endless desert full of awesome beauty' and 'loves the desert above all': 'no cloudiness of the sky, no haze or mist is allowed to be around him, otherwise he cannot look at the distant manifold in the whole' (RB II, 4: 269). Another significant Zarathustrian character with qualities that recall Ammonius is the other 'old man' in the woods, whom the protagonist asks for help while carrying the ropedancer's corpse on his shoulders and moving away from the town. Zarathustra realises he is hungry and his new host offers him 'bread and wine'. He lives far from men as well, and willingly provides food and drinks for 'whoever knocks' at his door, including animals or, as in this case, 'corpses' (Za I, *Prologue* 8, KSA 4: 24–25). Jung drew several underlinings, marks, and annotations in his copy; both in the previous and in this chapter, the words 'old man' are underlined. In a way that recalls the same hospitality, Ammonius gently tells Jung's 'I': 'Here is your place and your supper. Sleep well, and do not forget your morning prayer, when the sun rises' (RB II, 4: 269). Such attention to morning prayers and sunrise also reminds one again of Zarathustra himself and his identification with the sun.

What happens the day after is narrated by Jung in the following chapter, 'Dies II' (1 January 1914). The story begins with an allusion to the sun, that 'reddens the East', and continues with the description of a dream:

> It seems to me as if I had seen this white horse on the Eastern sky over the rising sun. The horse spoke to me: What did it say? It said: "Hail him who is in darkness since the day is over him." There were four white horses, each with golden wings. They led the carriage of the sun, on which Helios stood with flaring mane. I stood down in the gorge, astonished and frightened. A thousand black serpents crawled swiftly into their holes. Helios ascended, rolling upward toward the wide paths of the sky: I knelt down, raised my hands suppliantly, and called: "Give us your light, you are flame-curled,

> entwined, crucified and revived; give us your light, your light!" This cry woke me. Didn't Ammonius say yesterday evening: "Do not forget to say your morning prayer when the sun rises." I thought that perhaps he secretly worships the sun. (RB II, 5, 'Dies II': 270)

Taking Ammonius's advice, Jung's 'I' tries to pray to the sun. Thereby, he suddenly realises he lacks proper words, and truly experiences the desert; this means, Jung's 'I' grasps the meaning of being in the desert: in a state of solitude and aridity, the boundaries between oneself and objects fail to be clearly defined. On the one hand, things and animals 'appear animated', but, on the other hand, the desert, in its desolation, 'seems absolutely to demand prayers', and Jung's 'I' is himself tempted to pray to a black scarab, as well as to the earth. The desert makes one lose the sense of time, too. In fact, after formulating such considerations, Jung's 'I' realises that it is already noontime, and the sun is shining high in the sky (ibid.: 271). At the same time, and as a consequence, he also understands Ammonius's nature, as well as his necessity of escaping men, which the anchorite can figure out only in terms of devil temptations. This is all about Ammonius's personal story: he used to be an Egyptian scholar, then converted to Christianity and was involved in interpreting gospels from the standpoint of their future meaning, that is to say, from what 'is yet to come'. Because of his isolation, he has been stuck for quite a long time though, and no new interpretation seems to come to his mind. He would need more of human contacts, but when Jung tries to make him aware of it, Ammonius, seized by uncontrollable rage, takes him for the devil. In the desert, one could argue, the anchorite is seeking absolute certainty, eternal truth, and divine essence, and by so doing, he is avoiding humanity and instincts. However, these cannot be avoided, and a certain form of *paganism*, hidden behind such a devotion to the sun, reveals such an impossibility to avoid humanity and instincts (ibid.: 272).

In his retrospective interpretation of the episode, Jung states:

> How can I pray to the sun, that rises far in the East over the desert? Why should I pray to it? I drink the sun within me, so why should I pray to it? But the desert, the desert in me demands prayers, since the desert wants to satisfy itself with what is alive. I want to beg God for it, the sun, or one of the other immortals.

> I beg because I am empty and am a beggar. In the day of this world, I forget that I drank the sun and am drunk from its active light and singeing power. But I stepped into the shadows of the earth, and saw that I am naked and have nothing to cover my poverty. No sooner do you touch the earth than your inner life is over; it flees from you into things. (ibid.)

The stylistic choice of phrases such as 'drunk fire' [Feuer getrunken], 'drunk from its active light and singeing power' [trunken bin von wirkendem Lichte und sengender Kraft], 'I drank the sun within me' [Ich trank ja die Sonne in mich], or 'suckle from the sun' [an der Sonne saugt], inevitably evokes a very frequent motif in Nietzsche's 'The Night Song', chapter also recalled through the emptiness-fullness paradox. Nietzsche writes:

> Light were I: ah, that I were night! But this is my solitude, that I am girded round with light.
>
> I, that I were dark and obscure! How would I suck at the breast of light! [Ach, dass ich dunkel wäre und nächtig! Wie wollte ich an den Brüsten des Lichts saugen!]
>
> And I should bless you, little sparkling stars and glow-worms above!—and be happy in your gifts of light.
>
> But I live in my own light, I drink back into myself the flames that break from me [Aber ich lebe in meinem eignen Lichte, ich trinke die Flammen in mich zurück, die aus mir brechen].
>
> I do not know the joy of the receiver; and I have often dreamed that stealing must be more blessed than receiving [Ich kenne das Glück des Nehmenden nicht; und oft träumte mir davon, dass Stehlen noch seliger sein müsse, als Nehmen]. (Za II, 9, KSA 4: 136)

At the end of the *Liber Novus* chapter here considered, Jung seems to answer the desert question raised at the beginning of his adventure with his fantasies. He describes and interprets what is happening to Ammonius with these words:

> The solitary fled the world; he closed his eyes, plugged his ears and buried himself in a cave within himself but it was no use. The desert sucked him dry, the stones spoke his thoughts, the cave echoed his feelings, and so he himself became desert, stone, and cave. And it was all emptiness and desert, and helplessness and barrenness, since he did not shine and remained a son of the earth who sucked a book dry and was sucked empty by the desert. He was desire and not splendor, completely earth and not sun.

> Consequently he was in the desert as a clever saint who very well knew that otherwise he was no different from the other sons of the earth. If he would have drunk of himself he would have drunk fire. (RB II, 5: 273)

Once again, Nietzsche's phrases 'the desert is within you' and 'the desert gulps and strangles' can be compared with the image of the desert that 'sucked [the anchorite] dry'. Moreover, the reference to the cave seems to recall Zarathustra's dwelling, and the allusion to drinking fire from oneself seems to disclose the same 'Night Song' motif just mentioned. At the very end of the chapter, Jung comments:

> And therefore what happened to every desirous solitary also happened to him: the devil came to him with smooth tongue and clear reasoning and knew the right word at the right moment. He lured him to his desire. I had to appear to him as the devil, since I had accepted my darkness. I ate the earth and I drank the sun, and I became a greening tree that stands alone and grows. (ibid.)

He seems here to distance himself not only from the anchorite, but also from any 'solitary' prisoner in their own desert. By admitting to have 'accepted the darkness', he moves away from Zarathustra's impossibility of receiving anything outside himself, and, therefore, he also seems to distantiate from Nietzsche. Jung's response to the desert issue lies in his acceptance of both 'earth' and 'sun', that is, human and divine, devil and anchorite. Returning to the literal question, 'Is it solitude to be with one self?', one could now argue that Jung interpreted his experience in retrospect, as if his self was no longer a desert, and therefore there was no longer solitude in remaining alone.

The last point emerging from the encounter with Ammonius is the reference to the East, regarded as both the source of daylight and a symbol for a different kind of wisdom. Such alternative wisdom represents the counterpart to the Western tradition: coming from the East, the sun brings light to the West. Even if may be trivial, it is not to forget that the historical figure of Zarathustra comes from the East too, and is the well-known founder of a religion based on a distinction between good and evil, represented by light and darkness, which implies a consequent sun worship. The relationship between East and West is further brought out in *Liber Novus* during the Izdubar episode. As already seen, this figure comes from the East and ignores Western culture. Jung's 'I' claims to have 'set out to the East, to the land of the rising sun, to seek the light that we lack'. Western light is in fact unsatisfying; it is helpful to 'measure how fruitful this light is. But if you come from such a dark land, then beware of such an overpowering light. You could go blind just as we all are somewhat blind'. Jung explains, reflecting on this fantasy:

> I wandered toward the South and found the unbearable heat of solitude with myself. I wandered toward the North and found the cold death from which all the world dies. I withdrew to my Western land, where the men are rich in knowing and doing, and I began to suffer from the sun's empty darkness. And I threw everything from me and wandered toward the East, where the light rises daily. I went to the East like a child. I did not ask, I simply waited. (RB II, 8, 'First Day': 279)

The East appears as a symbol for the possibility of a new—and yet unknown—condition, in which the old 'poisoning' western knowledge can be finally overcome, as well as the aridity of the solitude within oneself, and the deadly coldness of the war. All of the 'saint' figures just seen share a state of solitude and isolation from mankind, as well as a certain feeling of discomfort towards the solidity of western knowledge and tradition. Lastly, sketching out further similarities with the wisdom-representing characters from *Zarathustra*, as the saint in the forest does not know that God is dead, so Izdubar has been told that in the western world 'even the Gods die' (RB II, 8: 279), but he cannot understand what this really means. Henceforth Nietzsche's presence will be central until the end of *Liber Novus* experience, in both visions and style. In the chapter 'Death'—which separates the two encounters with Ammonius—the already mentioned reference to the Zarathustrian idea of a 'brotherhood' between vices and virtues appears again (RB II, 6: 274).[8] In the next chapter, 'On the Remains of Earlier Temples', as already argued, several and meaningful allusions to *Zarathustra* will take place. Ultimately, it is not to forget that even the last step towards wisdom and rebirth, required by the Dead in *Septem Sermones*, is pronounced by someone coming from the East: 'You will go to men as one veiled. Your light shines at night. Your solar nature departs from you and your stellar nature begins' (RB *Scrutinies*, 13: 355). The allusion to a 'solar nature', as well as to a 'will to go to men', might be read again in relation to Zarathustra's features.

3.3 Nietzsche's Explicit Presence: Overcoming Rationalism

3.3.1 *Folly as the Other Side of Life*

In the first dialogue with Ammonius, the idea of God as a god 'of words' and *logos*, attributed to Greek-speaking Jewish philosopher Philo of Alexandria, is discussed.[9] The anchorite has 'unlearned' it and now he is living in the desert, in the hope to achieve a deeper view. At the time he was still 'rhetorician and philosopher' in Alexandria and taught his students, he 'even believed' in the 'reality' of words, as well as 'that we possessed the divine and had committed it to words'. Influenced both by Jewish and Greek philosophy, he used to confer words 'divine potency'. As already stated, at the time of his encounter with Jung, he was trying to give gospels a symbolic reading, indeed, connected to the future and the meaning of 'what is to come'. Through Ammonius, Jung seems to experience, for the first time, the necessity to go beyond *rationality* in order to give religion a new comprehension, that is to say, to 'comprehend the darkness'. Indeed, the logos represents reason; but what Jung realises here is the necessity of *divinising* man. This is brought out by Ammonius quite clearly, namely in his re-interpretation of John's gospel against the predominant reading of Alexandria's Philo. According to such a re-interpretation, it is not the logos elevating 'the lower to the higher spirit' but John bringing the 'meaning of the [logos] down to man'. In reply, Jung's 'I' asks Ammonius whether 'the human stands higher than the [logos]', to which Ammonius responds: 'if the human God had not become important above everything, he would not have appeared as the son in the flesh, but in the [logos]' (RB II, 4, 'The Anchorite': 268–270).[10]

To 'comprehend the darkness' means to accept human being as a totality, that is to say, to recognise one's 'evil' side as a normal and necessary part of one's nature. After the rebirth of the god—that Jung retrospectively identifies with Izdubar—this process of acceptance begins to happen, according to Jung's later understanding of his fantasies. In this new state, Jung's 'I' undergoes a few peculiar experiences: first he goes to Hell (RB II, 12, 'hell': 288–290), then he is forced to commit a dreadful sacrifice by eating the liver of a dead young girl (RB II, 13, 'The Sacrificial Murder': 290–291). The next step towards a full confrontation with what could be defined as the *Shadow* of the traditional idea of divinity, is represented by the encounter with *folly*. Again, Nietzsche plays a crucial role in this context. This time, however, the philosopher is not hidden behind implicit allusions; on the contrary, not only is Nietzsche now explicitly mentioned, but he even appears as a proper character. In the chapter 'Divine Folly', Jung describes a vision in which he enters a library and asks for Thomas à Kempis's *The Imitation of Christ* (*Imitatio Christi*), which sounds to the librarian like an unusual request, Jung's 'I' being neither theologist nor religious. He justifies his choice: 'there are actually moments in life where science also leaves us empty and sick. In such moments a book like Thomas's means very much to me since it is written from the soul'. There seems to be a point in one's life when religion is put aside, nevertheless a certain need seems to remain. According to the librarian, traditional religions do not appear able to satisfy this necessity though, because of their 'lack of a true and proper sense of actuality'. Nietzsche, like Goethe's *Faust*, appears to have written 'a more than veritable book of prayer'. However, Jung's 'I' finds 'Nietzsche's truth [...] too agitated and provocative—; it's good for those who are yet to be set free'. Next to this kind of men, are 'those who are forced into a corner'; such men seem to need 'a depressive truth', instead, 'which makes man smaller and more inward'. As Jung's 'I' notices, 'Nietzsche speaks to those who need more freedom, not to those who clash strongly with life, who bleed from wounds, and who hold fast to actualities'. Those people are conferred a 'precious feeling of superiority', as the librarian points out. However, Jung's 'I' claims to 'know men who need inferiority; not superiority'—'inferiority' meaning 'resignation, a word that one used to hear a lot of, but seldom anymore'. At this point, the librarian cannot help but to remark that such a concept sounds very Christian, to which Jung's 'I' replies: 'As I said, there seem to be all sorts of things in Christianity that maybe one would do well to keep. Nietzsche is too oppositional. Like everything healthy and long-lasting, truth unfortunately adheres more to the middle way, which we unjustly abhor' (RB II, 14, 'Divine Folly': 293).

Here the reference to Nietzsche must be contextualised in a wider perspective concerning the deeper confrontation with 'Christ' as a model, which will be dealt with in the next section of this chapter (see Sect. 3.3.2). He still appears as 'our natural model', even when we fight against him or try to deny his power. If one imitates, instead of truly living, then it is no longer possible for the divine to live within oneself. Imitating 'Christ' dos not mean emulating; rather, it means comprehending his life and following his example, becoming—in this sense—'Christ' oneself. 'Christ' was independent, and to learn from him means to attain a similar independence.

However, sometimes one confuses Christianity with emulation, and, therefore, does not 'succeed in uniting Christ with prophets of this time. The one demands bearing, the other discarding; the one commands submission, the other the will' (ibid.). Schopenhauer and Nietzsche are most likely to be those prophets indeed, Jung is referring to. In order to comprehend the meaning of his own life and reconcile these voices with his Christian feeling, Jung's 'I' realises that what he needs is an 'acceptance of the other', that is, 'a descent into the opposite, from seriousness into the laughable, from suffering into the cheerful, from the beautiful into the ugly, from the pure into the impure' (ibid.). After such a reflection, Jung's vision continues and shows his 'I' entering another room—which he soon discovers being a kitchen—starting to read and falling asleep after a while.

What happens now is quite an impressive dream, in which the protagonist finds himself in an asylum, where two doctors are diagnosing his situation as a case of 'religious paranoia': 'nowadays, the imitation of Christ leads to the madhouse'. He is now ready to discover and accept madness in himself. This is important not only at the level of personal development, but also in terms of social improvements. For this side of life seems to be forgotten or ignored and no longer integrated; but in fact it still keeps a divine aspect, which not only cannot be disregarded, but can be even considered as its strongest element:

> The problem of madness is profound. Divine madness—a higher form of the irrationality of the life streaming through us—at any rate a madness that cannot be integrated into present-day society—but how? What if the form of society were integrated into madness? At this point things grow dark, and there is no end in sight. (RB II, 15, 'Nox Secunda': 295)

To Jung, this means accepting the other side of religion, namely what is refused and condemned by modern Christianity, but was highly praised by original Christianity. By so doing—so Jung interprets his vision—all *the dead*, namely all those who cannot find their place in a Christian living, could be finally redeemed. The number of dead has now become higher than that of living, i.e. of those who can be considered saved by 'Christ' and his teaching. It is very much significant that, in the *Draft* version of the chapter, Jung implicitly refers to Nietzsche as a 'prophet' who, on the one hand, has tried to defend and reevaluate the rights of the dead, and on the other hand, has been driven mad by being 'their blind spokesman' (Shamdasani 2009, ibid.: 297). But the dead are also part of Jung himself, therefore he needs to be 'alone with the dead', in order to accept the lowest and 'the chaos' within, meaning his own madness (ibid.: 297–298). Jung's vision culminates with the encounter with a fool who believes to be Nietzsche, dated 18 January 1914. Jung's 'I' is still in the madhouse, and the patient who is sleeping in a bed next to his own suddenly stands up, stares at him and cries out: 'Something worse happened to me, it's five years now that I've been here. [...] But I am Nietzsche, only rebaptized, I am also Christ, the Savior, and appointed to save the world, but they won't let me' (RB II, 16, 'Nox Tertia': 298). So, the dialogue continues:

> I: "Who won't let you?"
> The fool: "The devil. We are in Hell. But of course, you haven't noticed it yet. I didn't realize until the second year of my time here that the director is the devil."
> I: "You mean the professor? That sounds incredible."
> The fool: "You're an ignoramus. I was supposed to marry the mother of God long ago. But the professor, that devil, has her in his power. Every evening when the sun goes down he gets her with child. In the morning before sunrise she gives birth to it. Then all the devils come together and kill the child in a gruesome manner. I distinctly hear his cries."
> I: "But what you have told me is pure mythology."
> The fool: "You're crazy and understand nothing of it. You belong in the madhouse. My God, why does my family always shut me in with crazy people? I'm supposed to save the world, I'm the Savior!".

Remarkably, the following sentence from the fifth paragraph of *Zarathustra*, *Prologue* was marked by Jung in his own copy: 'No herdsman and no one herd. Everyone wants the same thing, everyone is the same: whoever thinks otherwise goes voluntarily into the madhouse [Irrenhaus]' (Za I, *Prologue* 5, KSA 4: 20). Returning to *Liber Novus*, after his speech, the fool returns to his usual apathetic state, leaving Jung's 'I' alone and with a new vision. Now he sees a red sun rising above the horizon line, with a cross from which an undefinable animal-shaped figure (serpent, bull, or an ass) is hanging. Looking at the symbol more carefully, Jung's 'I' wonders whether that may not represent himself, as Christ crucified, who is actually hanging down from the cross and wearing a crown of thorns: 'The sun of martyrdom has arisen and is pouring bloody rays over the sea'. The higher the sun rises, the hotter it 'burns down white on a blue sea [blaues Meere]', whose 'salty smell' reminds Jung's 'I' of a 'charitable and quiet summer'. Suddenly, a wave 'breaks on the sand with a dull thunder and returns incessantly [immer erneut kehrt sie wieder], twelve times, the strokes of the world clock [die Glockenschlägen der Weltuhr]—the twelfth hour is complete. And now silence enters. No noise, no breeze. Everything is rigid [starr] and deathly still [totenstill]' (RB II, 16: 299).

Nietzsche as a character has already gone, but his presence seems to linger throughout the rest of the chapter. First of all, a similarity of motifs with *Zarathustra* chapter 'The Intoxicated Song' is to be recalled, concerning the height, the sea, and the 'midnight-bell'. 'The Intoxicated Song' reads this way:

> Zarathustra [...] stood there like one intoxicated: his eyes grew dim, his tongue stammered, his feet tottered. And who could divine what thoughts passed over Zarathustra 's soul?
>
> But it seemed that his soul fell back and fled before him, and was in remote distances and as if "upon a high ridge", as it is written, "wandering like a heavy cloud between past and future" [Ersichtlich aber wich sein Geist zurück und floh voraus und war in weiten Fernen und gleichsam 'auf hohem Joche', wie geschrieben steht, zwischen zwei Meeren,—zwischen Vergangenem und Zukünftigem als schwere Wolke wandelnd]. (Za IV, 19, KSA 4: 397–398)

A few lines below:

> And at once it grew still and mysterious all around; from the depths, however, there slowly arose the sound of a bell [der Klang einer Glocke]. Zarathustra listened to it, as the Higher Man did; then he laid a finger to his lips a second time and said again "*Come! Come! Midnight is coming on!*" and his voice had altered. But still he did not move from his place: then he grew yet more still and mysterious, and everything listened, even the ass and Zarathustra's animals of honour, the eagle and the serpent, likewise Zarathustra's cave and the great, cool moon and the night itself. Zarathustra, however, laid his hands to his lips for the third time and said:
>
> *Come! Come! Come! Let us walk now! The hour has come! Let us walk into the night!* (ibid.)

And again:

> You Higher Man, midnight is coming on: so I will say something in your ear, as secretly, as fearfully, as warmly as that midnight-bell [Mitternachts-Glocke] tells it to me, which has experienced more than man: which has already counted your fathers' painful heartbeats—ah! ah! how it sights! How in dreams it laughs! the ancient deep, deep midnight! (ibid.)

Jung surely took interest in this chapter, and understood it as an introspective experience of Nietzsche's, similar to his own *Liber Novus*. The following passage—towards the end of the chapter—is indeed put in brackets by Jung, who annotates, at the end of the page: 'he discovered joy in himself through the union with his underworld' [er hat die Lust in sich entdeckt durch die Vereinigung mit seiner Unterwelt].:

> All joy wants eternity of all things, wants honey, wants dregs, wants intoxicated midnight, wants graves, wants the consolation of graveside tears, wants gilded sunsets,
>
> *what* does joy not want! It is thirstier, warmer, hungrier, more fearful, more secret than all woe, it wants *itself*; it bites into *itself*, the will of the ring wrestles within it,
>
> it wants love, it wants hatred, it is superabundant, it gives, throws away, begs for someone to take it, thanks him who takes, it would like to be hated. (ibid., KSA 4: 402–403)

The midnight-bell motif is a predominant element in 'The Intoxicated Song', exactly as the 12 strokes that bring Jung's fantasy to a state of completion and perfection. However, if Nietzsche's bell recurs throughout Zarathustra's song—whose rhythm is literally defined by its strokes—Jung's 12 strokes appear only once, and are responsible for revealing such a state of completion and perfection to Jung's 'I', who is now left alone in his beatitude. Moreover, whereas the symbol of the sun seems to guide Jung's vision, in Nietzsche it is the moon, together with the depth which it represents, to inspire Zarathustra's 'song'. However, according to Zarathustra, 'midnight is also noonday', and the perfect noontide is a recurrent theme not only in another *Zarathustra* chapter, 'At Noontide', but also in *Human, All Too Human*, I (1878) and II (1879).

In 'At Noontide', the same motif of 'death rigidity' occurs, reminding one of the ending of Jung's fantasy with 'Nox Tertia'. Zarathustra is going through a vine and finds himself attracted by the 'golden grapes', therefore he stops. But even stronger than this attraction, it seems to be his 'desire [...] to lie down beside the tree at the hour of perfect noon and sleep'. While falling asleep, he says to himself:

> Soft! Soft! Has the world not become perfect? What has happened to me?
>
> As a delicate breeze, unseen, dances upon the smooth sea [getäfeltem Meere], light, light as a feather: thus—does sleep dance upon me.

My eyes it does not close, my soul it leaves awake. It is light, truly as light as a feather. (Za IV, 10, 'At Noontide', KSA 4: 342–343)

Then Zarathustra compares his soul to a 'ship' which 'leans against the earth, weary of long voyages and uncertain seas'. In such state of blissfulness he wonders, just before waking up: 'has the world not become perfect?' (ibid., KSA 4: 344). In Jung's copy, this chapter presents some underlinings and several markings, one of which being along the passage referring to the ship and the sea indeed. In the entire chapter, the same motif of eternity and perfection returns overwhelmingly, as well as a certain correspondence between noontide and midnight. Furthermore, both motifs of the perfect noontide and of the bell strokes recur in other writings of Nietzsche's. At the end of the aphorism 638 of *Human, All Too Human*, the conclusive one, Nietzsche compares the purity of new, future, philosophers, to 'the day between the tenth and the twelfth bell-stroke' [der Tag zwischen dem zehnten und zwölften Glockenschlage] (MA I 638, KSA 2: 363). And in the aphorism 308 of *The Wanderer and His Shadow*, from *Human, All Too Human, II,* entitled 'At Noontide' [Am Mittag], Nietzsche seems to anticipate several of the motifs which will characterise the *Zarathustra* chapter of the same name. Among these, while referring to a 'sleeping Pan', a 'death with waking eyes' [Tod mit wachen Augen] is mentioned: in the state of eternity and perfection, the god is one and the same with nature and does not seem to want anything more (MA II, WS 308, KSA 2: 690). None of the above chapters from Jung's library, unfortunately, present markings at all. However, both *Human, All Too Human*, I and II display several reading marks and annotations throughout.

Other Nietzschean themes can be found again in the same *Liber Novus* chapter, through phrases such as 'to accept the lowest in you', as well as a reference to chaos, all belonging to Jung's retrospective interpretation of what happened to him. In particular, the following sentence deserves to be marked: 'But the lowest in you is also the eye of the evil that stares at you and looks at you coldly and sucks your light down into the dark abyss' [Das Geringste in dir ist aber auch das Augen des Bösen, das dich starr und kalt anblickt und dein Licht in den finstren Abgrund hinuntersaugt] (RB II, 16: 300). Besides a resemblance with the famous aphorism 146 from *Beyond Good and Evil* (1886), 'Whoever fights monsters should make sure that in the process he does not become a monster himself. And if you stare long enough into an abyss, the abyss will stare back into you [Und wenn du lange in einen Abgrund blickst, blickt der Abgrund auch in dich hinhein]' (JGB 146, KSA 5: 98; my own translation), a certain similarity is worth recalling between this comment and *Zarathustra*. Not only does the main theme of 'The Night Song' reappear here; a similar expression also occurs again at the end of 'At Noontide', where Nietzsche makes Zarathustra pronounce these words:

> Oh sky above me [...] are you watching me? Are you listening to my strange soul?
>
> When will you drink this drop of dew that has fallen upon on earthy things—when will you drink this strange soul
>
> —when, well of eternity! Serene and terribly noontide abyss [Mittags-Abgrund]! When will you drink my soul back into yourself? [wann trinkst du meine Seele in dich zurück?]. (Za IV, 10, KSA 4: 345)

In this section, Zarathustra is also said to be 'as from a strange intoxication' [wie aus einer fremden Trunkenheit], making it possible to link this chapter with 'The Intoxicated Song', as well as to the Dionysos motif in general. Jung's reference to 'the lowest' in 'Nox Tertia' seems to address Nietzsche again, and can be regarded as a proper response to his philosophy. In particular, it can be connected with Jung's annotation on 'The Intoxicated Song' cited above. As already written, Jung reads Nietzsche's chapter in relation to his unification with his 'underworld'. What is written before the quoted passage in *Liber Novus* is:

> The lowest in you is the source of mercy: We take this sickness upon ourselves, the inability to find peace, the baseness, and the contemptibility so that the God can be healed and radiantly ascend, purged of the decomposition of death and the mud of the underworld [Unterwelt]. The despicable prisoner will ascend to his salvation shining and wholly healed. (RB II, 16: 300)

Jung's confrontation with madness ends at the beginning of the next chapter, 'Nox Quarta', when Jung's 'I' wakes up and decides to return the book to the librarian. During the awakening, a few further references to *Zarathustra* can be mentioned. First of all, Jung's 'I' feels 'the roaring [Brausen] of the morning wind'. Then his soul cries out:

> The door should be lifted off its hinges to provide a free passage between here and there [zwischen hier und dort], between yes and no [zwischen Ja und Nein], between above and below [zwischen oben und unten], between

> left and right [zwischen rechts und links]. Airy passages should be built between all opposed things, light smooth streets should lead from one pole to the other. Scales should be set up, whose pointer sways gently. A flame should burn that cannot be blown out by the wind. A stream should flow to its deepest goal. The herds of wild animals should move to their feeding grounds along their old game paths. Life should proceed, from birth to death, from death to birth, unbroken like the path of the sun. Everything should proceed on this path. (RB II, 17, 'Nox Quarta': 302)

Although the two contexts cannot be compared in any way, these lines seem to evoke the very well-known aphorism 125 of *The Gay Science*, 'The Madman', precisely when the protagonist, while announcing the death of God, wonders: 'How were we able to drink up the sea? Who gave us the sponge to wipe away the entire horizon? [...] Are we not continually falling? And backwards, sidewards, forwards, in all directions? Is there still an up and a down left? [Und rückwärts, seitwärts, vorwärts, nach allen Seiten? Giebt es noch ein Oben und ein Unten?]' (FW 125, KSA 3: 480). However, the entire description, supported by what comes immediately after, presents other elements which can be read in relation to Nietzsche and, in particular, to *Zarathustra*. Jung's vision continues:

> Blind darkness besieges me—a great wall—a gray worm of twilight [Dämmerungswurm] crawls [kriecht] along it. It has a round face and laughs. The laughter is convulsive and actually relieving. I open my eyes: the fat cook is standing before me: "You're a sound sleeper, I must say. You've slept for more than an hour". (RB II, 17: 302)

The passage can be associated with *Zarathustra* chapter 'The Prophet', in which the protagonist, likewise Jung, has fallen asleep and had a nightmare, after having listened to a pessimistic prophet (most likely representing Arthur Schopenhauer) who spoke to his disciples of an approaching 'long twilight' [lange Dämmerung]. As Zarathustra wakes up, he tells his animals about his dream and asks them for help to disclose its meaning. First of all, he notes that his dream was about renouncing 'all life'. He had indeed 'become a night-watchman and grave-watchman yonder upon the lonely hill-fortress of death'. 'Up there, [he] guarded death's coffins: the musty vaults stood full of these symbols of death's victory. Life overcome regarded [him] from glass coffins'. With highly poetical tone, Zarathustra goes further in his account:

> Brightness of midnight was all around me, solitude crouched beside it; and, as a third, the rasping silence of death [Todenstille], the worst of my companions.
>
> I carried keys, the rustiest of all keys; and I could open with them the most creaking of all doors.
>
> When the wings of this corridor were open, the sound rang through the long corridors like an evil croaking [bitterbösen Gekrächze]; this bird cried out ill-temperedly, it did not want to be awakened. […]
>
> Tree blows were struck on the door like thunderbolts, the vault resounded and roared [heulten] three times again, then I went to the door.
>
> Alpa! I cried, who is bearing his ashes to the mountain? […]
>
> And I turned the key and tugged at the door and exerted myself. But it did not open by so much as a finger's breadth:
>
> Then a raging wind [ein brausender Wind] tore the door asunder: whistling, shrilling and piercing it threw to me a black coffin:
>
> and in the roaring [Brausen], the whistling and shrilling, the coffin burst asunder and vomited forth a thousand peals of laughter.
>
> And from a thousand masks of children, angels, owls, fools, and child-size butterflies it laughed [lachte] and sneered [höhnte] and roared [brauste] at me. (Za II, 19, 'The Prophet', KSA 4: 173–174, translation modified)

All of Nietzsche's references to the wind in this chapter and in *Zarathustra* will be later read by Jung as expressions of the Wotan archetype, understood as the destructive force underpinning not only Nietzsche's personal psychology but also both world wars, and twentieth-century totalitarianisms more generally (see Liebscher 2001; Bishop 1995a: 283–322). Similar tones and motifs are also to be found in the chapter 'The Funeral Song' (Za II, 11, KSA 4: 142–145). Both chapters present several markings and underlinings in Jung's copy, and alongside the section from 'The Prophet' quoted above, Jung traced a vertical sign and wrote 'Buffoon' [Possenreisser], referring to his own understanding of the *Prologue* as a prophecy on Nietzsche's forthcoming madness, for not being able to accept his 'lower functions'. This seems to indicate a link between this chapter and Jung's need for reconciling with 'the lowest' in himself. The reference to the 'silence of death' allows one to link this section to the previous ones. Ultimately, Jung's stylistic choice in his comment on the vision should not be overlooked: the phrase 'Thus speaks my soul' [Also spricht meine Seele] can somehow remind one of Nietzsche's title.

To draw some conclusion, one could say that, although Nietzsche's presence in *Liber Secundus* becomes explicit in chapters 'Divine Folly', 'Nox Secunda', 'Nox Tertia', a subtle, yet strong, Nietzschean motif permeates the whole section from its very first chapter to its ending. Indeed, among the first chapters of *Liber Secundus*, 'The Remains of Earlier Temples', 'First Day', 'Second Day', and 'The Incantations' presented already quite open allusions to Nietzsche; at the same time, the discourse on 'divine madness' which 'Nox Tertia' culminates with, will open up a new discourse on the role of Christianity, which will prevail in the conclusive block of chapters from *Liber Secundus*, namely: 'Nox Quarta', 'The Three Prophecies', 'The Gift Of Magic', 'The Way Of The Cross', 'The Magician'. In particular, Jung's questioning Nietzsche's 'death of God' on the one hand and traditional Christianity on the other will provide him with the right means to let his 'new god' be born again, and will consequently save him from the possibility of madness. Nietzsche's presence will then become predominant in *Scrutinies*, when layers 1 and 2 will literally merge together, leaving room for Jung's deliberate responses to Nietzsche and Zarathustra, understood as failing teachers.

3.3.2 *Teaching, Mocking, and Imitating: The Process of Self-Becoming*

Not only does Jung refer to Nietzsche in his urge to accept inferiority; by highlighting the similarity between the beginning of 'Nox Quarta' and 'The Prophet', another significant theme of *Zarathustra* is also introduced, i.e. *mockery*. As partially seen, it had been referenced in 'Divine Folly' and 'Nox Secunda'; now this topic seems to gain strength, becoming one of the key topics of the entire book. However, mockery is part of a wider discourse, referring to the idea of teaching as represented in *Liber Novus*. Such an idea can be thought of as a dialectical process, composed of three moments: imitation, self-mocking, self-becoming. As is quite often the case with *Liber Novus*, Nietzsche and the character of Zarathustra play an essential role in the whole process, going far beyond the issue of mockery, and embracing the moments of imitation and self-becoming too. Such three moments and their relation to Jung's idea of teaching on the one hand and to Jung's confrontation with Nietzsche on the other will be dealt with in the following paragraphs of this section.

As remarked, Jung's idea of teaching begins with the issue of *imitation*. As stated in the chapter 'The Anchorite', mankind itself seems incapable of not imitating: 'A new word is a new God for old men. Man remains the same, even if you create a new model of God for him. He remains an imitator' (RB II, 4: 270). As partially seen, one of the main topics of *Liber Novus* concerns imitation in relation to Christianity which, as a model, does not permit his followers to find their own way but force them to *copy* 'Christ'. The truest way to imitate 'Christ' would be to be like him, that is, to be oneself, seeking within oneself and not outside [Außer-uns]. According to the apocryphal gospels which Jung implicitly refers to, 'Christ' himself had to go to Hell; who goes to Hell, however, 'becomes Hell himself', so 'Christ' became the 'Antichrist' before being allowed to 'go to Heaven'. Among its many meanings and interpretative nuances, going to 'Hell' also means accepting the *natural* part of being human; in this sense, it does not differ from Nietzsche's idea. *The Anti-Christ* is probably the main example of how significant this concept was to Nietzsche:

> Contact between imaginary *entities* ("Gods", "spirits", "souls"); an imaginary *natural* science (anthropocentric; total absence of any concept of natural cause); an imaginary *psychology* (complete failure to understand oneself, interpretation of the pleasant or unpleasant general sensation—for instance, the states of *nervus sympathicus*—using the sign language of religious-moral idiosyncrasy,—"repentance", "the pangs of conscience", "temptation", "the presence of God"); an imaginary teleology ("the kingdom of God", "the Last Judgement", "eternal life").—This entirely *fictitious world* can be distinguished from the world of dreams (to the detriment of the former) in that dream reflects *reality* while Christianity falsifies, devalues, and negates reality. Once the concept of "nature" had been invented as a counter to the idea of "God", "natural" had to mean "reprehensible",—that whole fictitious world is rooted in a hatred of the natural (—of reality!—), it is the expression of a profound sense of unease concerning reality ... *But this explains everything*. Who are the only people motivated to *lie their way out of* reality? People who *suffer* from it. But to suffer from reality means that you are a piece of reality that has *gone wrong* ... the preponderance of feelings of displeasure over feelings of pleasure is the *cause* of that fictitious morality and religion: but a preponderance like this provides the *formula* for decadence. (AC 15, KSA 6: 181–182)

Furthermore, as will be further discussed in the next section, the separation between a 'true' and an 'apparent' world represents the core of *Twilights of the Idols*. Schopenhauer had already brought forward the same hypothesis in his essay 'On Religion': 'Through Christianity Europe acquired a tendency which had hitherto been foreign to her, by virtue of a knowledge of the fundamental truth that life cannot be an end in itself, but that the true purpose of our existence lies beyond it' (Schopenhauer 1851: § 178).

In *Liber Novus*, however, becoming one's own contrary seems a necessary step towards the reaching of the 'new God', namely, becoming 'Hell' oneself is the only way to be like 'Christ' and become godlike oneself. This implies that the first condition of becoming like 'Christ' should be becoming able to *self-mock*, that is, to recognise and accept one's own inferiority. Such an idea represents the second moment of the dialectical process of teaching in *Liber Novus*. The idea of self-mockery is first introduced by the feeling of shame of being mocked, as described in *Liber Secundus*, in the chapter 'Nox Quarta':

> If others mock [verspotten] me, it is nevertheless them doing this, and I can attribute guilt to them for this, and forget to mock myself. But he who cannot mock himself will be mocked by others. So accept your self-mockery [Selbstverspottung] so that everything divine and heroic falls from you and you become completely human. What is divine and heroic in you is a mockery [Spott] to the other in you. For the sake of the other in you, set off your admired role which you previously performed for your own self and become who you are [werde der, der du bist]. (RB II, 17: 303)

The last sentence definitely recalls Nietzsche's *Ecce Homo* motto. The same phrase 'Ecce Homo' derives from the Bible and refers to mockery. In fact, these are the words pronounced by Pilate during Jesus's trial. In that circumstance, Jesus wears a crown of thorns and a purple robe—mock-version of royal cloths—in order to be spotted by the crowd (Jn 19:5).[11] Moreover, the passage can also be read in relation to 'The Stillest Hour', where Zarathustra complains to his soul through these words:

> "They mocked [verspotteten] me when I found and walked my own way; and in truth my feet trembled then.
>
> "And they spoke thus to me: You have forgotten the way, now you will also forget how to walk!"

> Then again something said to me voicelessly: "Of what consequence is their mockery [Spott(e)]? You are one who has unlearned how to obey: now you shall command!" (Za II, 22, KSA 4: 188–189)

Reading Jung's marks and annotations in his copy, one can argue that, in a later period, he interpreted the chapter as a dialogue between Nietzsche and his Anima (only two paragraphs before the text just cited, he wrote down 'to his Anima' [an seine Anima]). In this sense, it is not to exclude a link between this text and Jung's vision, since this excerpt from 'Nox Quarta' represents another response to Nietzsche. Immediately below the cited section it is written, indeed:

> He who has the luck and misfortune of a particular talent falls prey to believing that he is this gift. Hence he is also often its fool [Narr]. A special gift is something outside of me. I am not the same as it. The nature of the gift has nothing to do with the nature of the man who carries it. It often even lives at the expense of the bearer's character. His character is marked by the disadvantage of his gift, indeed even through its opposite. Consequently he is never at the height of his gift but always beneath it. If he accepts his other he becomes capable of bearing his gift without disadvantage. But if he only wants to live in his gift and consequently rejects his other, he oversteps the mark, since the essence of his gift is extrahuman [außermenschlich] and a natural phenomenon, which he in reality is not. All the world sees his error, and he becomes the victim of its mockery [Spott(e)]. Then he says that others mock [verspotten] him, while it is only the disregard of his other that makes him ridiculous. (RB II, 17: 303)

These lines can be read in relation to Jung's later interpretation of Nietzsche's madness based on *Zarathustra*. In the *Prologue*, indeed, Zarathustra is mocked by the gravediggers at the town gate, while carrying the corpse of a ropedancer who had been killed by a buffoon, while trying to walk on a tightrope (Za I, *Prologue* 8, KSA 4: 24). Zarathustra sympathised with the ropedancer, as he recognised in his attitude that of the 'higher man': as the 'higher man' realises that man is to be overcome, in order for the *Übermensch* to arise, so the ropedancer wanted to cross the market square, walking on the tightrope (representing man indeed) above the crowd (symbolising the 'last man'), thus defying the uncertainty of his fate. Zarathustra respected the ropedancer, as he had 'made danger [his] calling', and for this reason, he decides to bury his corpse (ibid.: 6, KSA 4: 21–22). Right before the ropedancer's performance, Zarathustra had already been mocked by the market crowd while trying to teach them the *Übermensch* (ibid.: 5, KSA 4: 20–21; see also Za II, 3, 'Of the Compassionate', KSA 4: 113). One of Jung's most recurrent accusations to Nietzsche in his seminar on *Zarathustra* is that of identifying with the ropedancer and the *Übermensch*, trying to overleap the buffoon (hence the lowest in himself), rather than surpassing him. Due to his identification with the *Übermensch* (hence with the 'extrahuman'), Nietzsche would not be able to accept his human nature; therefore, he would constantly reject his instincts. As already argued, a more explicit reference to the ropedancer in relation to Nietzsche's failure occurs in 'The Way of the Cross', concerning the lion-desert symbolic constellation (see Sect. 3.2.1). To such a reference, however, the explicit accusation to Nietzsche's inadequacy to stand mockery is to be emphasised: 'He raged against the man of mockery [Man des Spottes] [...]. Ultimately the lowest in him got to him, his incapacity; and this crucified his spirit, so that, as he himself had predicted, his soul died before his body [seine Seele eher starb als sein Körper]' (RB II, 20: 310). As already said, the sentence 'his soul died before his body' [seine Seele eher starb als sein Körper] recalls the ropedancer episode indeed: the words 'your soul will be dead even before your body' [Deine Seele wird noch schneller todt sein als dein Leib] are pronounced by Zarathustra to give the dying ropedancer some comfort before he takes his last breath (Za I, *Prologue* 6, KSA 4: 22), and are underlined by Jung in his own copy of *Zarathustra*. Furthermore, Nietzsche writes in 'Of Redemption':

> Willing liberates: What does willing itself devise to free itself from its affliction and to mock [spotte] at its dungeon?
>
> Alas, every prisoner becomes a fool [Narr]! The imprisoned will, too, releases itself in a foolish way [Närrisch]. [...]
>
> Truly, a great foolishness dwells in our will; and that this foolishness [Narrheit] acquired spirit has become a curse to all human kind. (Za II, 20, KSA 4: 180)

The second sentence is accompanied by a vertical mark in Jung's copy. This can be considered a relevant element, if one thinks that this is the only part of the whole chapter presenting reading marks. Other text sections from *Zarathustra* where mockery is stressed are often underlined or marked by Jung in his personal copy, when not even annotated. The mockery theme in *Liber Novus* can be thus arguably regarded as another dialogue between Jung and Nietzsche. In particular, this time it seems to concern the philosopher's difficulty with self-mockery.[12]

A subtle aspect of mockery concerns not taking something seriously, which is important to the person who is being mocked. This may also reflect difficulty, when not impossibility, to understand the other's deep motivations. So, if on the one hand mockery and self-mockery are necessary in order to accept one's own inferiority, on the other hand mockery can also mean to grasp only the external aspects of someone else's acting, ignoring their reasons or meanings, and stopping at a very superficial level. In this sense, mockery leads one directly to the question of *imitation* and appears as one of its consequences: first, one experiences otherness through imitation, then, either one interiorises such otherness through self-mockery, or one stops at the level of the monkey. Only when one is able to mock oneself can self-becoming take place.

To remain stuck in the perspective of mockery means to look at oneself only from outside, and in relation to the others, and, if applied to the relationship between oneself and the others, mocking signifies not trying to identify with them, to understand them; rather, it means to simply *imitate* them:

> It was folly [Narrheit] and monkey business [Affenspiel], an atrocious Hell's masquerade of the holiest mysteries. How else could Christ have saved his Antichrist? Read the unknown books of the ancients, and you will learn much from them. Notice that Christ did not remain in Hell, but rose to the heights in the beyond. (RB I, 8, 'The Conception of the God': 243)

What emerges from this side of the problem is another key element, doubtless relevant to comprehend and complete the process of imitating in relation to mockery, i.e. the *monkey*. This figure is taken as an example in order to show the consequence of the risk indicated above:

> Imitation [Nachahmung] was a way of life when men still needed the heroic prototype. The monkey's manner [Des Affen Art und Weise] is a way of life for monkeys, and for man as long as he is like a monkey [äffisch]. Human apishness [Äffische] has lasted a terribly long time, but the time will come when a piece of that apishness will fall away from men.
>
> That will be a time of salvation and the dove, and the eternal fire, and redemption will descend. (ibid.: 245)

To abandon such a monkey standpoint seems quite hard a step to take, 'since we cannot desist from imitation', and it is easy to end up with confusing oneself with what one just sees, namely to identify with one's own experience (RB I, 10, 'Instruction': 251). Moreover, monkeys not only imitate and deprive gestures of their meaning but also ridicule, thus they highlight the lower and negative side of mockery.

References to the city, as well as of the *scorn* it may inspire, are well connected to the monkey symbol in *Zarathustra* chapter 'Of Passing By':

> He [Zarathustra] came unawares to the gate of the *great city* [die grosse Stadt]; here, however, a frothing fool [schäumender Narr] with hands outstretched sprang at him and blocked his path. But this was the fool the people called "Zarathustra's ape": for he had learned from him something of the composition and syntax of language and perhaps also liked to borrow from his store of wisdom. The fool, however, spoke thus to Zarathustra:
>
> "Oh Zarathustra, here is the great city: here you have nothing to seek and everything to lose.
>
> "Why do you want to wade through this muck? Take pity on your feet! Rather spit upon the gate and—turn back!
>
> "Here is the hell for hermits' thoughts: here great thoughts are boiled alive and cooked [gekocht] small.
>
> "Here all great emotions decay: here only little, dry emotions may rattle!
>
> "Do you not smell [riechst] already the slaughter-houses and cook-shops of the spirit?
>
> "Do you not see the souls hanging like dirty, limp rags? Does this city not reek of the fumes of slaughtered spirit? [Dampft nicht diese Stadt vom Dunst geschlachteten Geistes?] [...]
>
> "Here all blood flows foul and tepid and frothy through all veins: spit upon the great city that is the great rubbish pile where all the scum froths together!" (Za III, 7, KSA 4: 222–224)

The first part of the chapter presents several marks and some underlinings in Jung's copy, amongst which are 'a frothing fool' [ein schäumender Narr] and 'Zarathustra's ape' [den Affen Zarathustra's]. The same scorn theme towards the city is also present in the chapter 'Conversation with the Kings', and Jung's copy displays a vertical mark alongside that section too. Moreover, in 'On the Mount of Olives', Nietzsche wrote: 'Let me pity me and sigh with me over my chilblains: "He will yet *freeze to death* on the ice of knowledge!"—so they wail. In the meanwhile, I run with warm feet hither and thither upon my mount of olives: in the sunny corner of my mount of olives, do I sing and mock all pity. Thus sang Zarathustra' (Za III, 6, KSA 4: 221). Jung underlined 'He will yet *freeze to death* on the ice of knowledge! [am Eis der Erkenntniss *erfriert* er uns noch]', 'sing' [singe] and 'I [...] all pity' [ich alles Mitleids]. Alongside the text, referring to 'He will yet *freeze to death* on the ice of knowledge!', Jung wrote: 'in defiance of himself!' [Trotz gegen sich selber!]. Very similar phrases are used by Jung in 'Second Day', when he describes his 'I''s going through a town accompanied by Izdubar:

> Iz: "What a wondrous country! But look, isn't that a town [Stadt]? Don't you want to go there?"
>
> I: "No, God forbid. I don't want a crowd to gather, since the enlightened live there. Can't you smell them [Riechst du sie nicht]? They're actually dangerous, since they cook [Kochen] the strongest poisons from which even I must protect myself. The people there are totally paralyzed, wrapped in a brown poisonous vapor [Giftdampf] and can only move with artificial means." (RB II, 9: 282–283)

In comparison with the scene from *Zarathustra*, here the situation is reversed: Jung's 'I', rather than his accompanier, seems in fact to exhibit disgust towards the consequences of modern civilisation. In a certain way, he sounds like 'Izdubar's ape'. This does not contrast with the similarity between the two episodes: exactly as Zarathustra's ape, Jung's 'I' is here the product of Western civilisation, struggling to accept it. Both Izdubar and Zarathustra, in fact, represent the opposite attitude—coming from the East and not belonging to the European world. This section deals with the question of Zarathustra's skills as a teacher and his possibility to succeed in teaching his 'doctrine', indeed: his disciples do not seem yet able to comprehend such a profound wisdom, preferring to just imitate their teachers at a very superficial level. The same discourse will appear later in *Liber Secundus*, referring directly to the third moment of Jung's idea of teaching, namely, *self-becoming*.

The first point to be pointed out in relation to Jung's idea of self-becoming, as expressed in *Liber Novus*, is that in order for one to find their own way, one has to accept mockery and self-mockery, that is to say, one has to recognise and admit their own inferiority. Jung writes:

> What would mockery be, if it were not true mockery? What would doubt be, if it were not true doubt? What would opposition be, it if were not true opposition? He who wants to accept himself must also really accept his other. But in the yes not every no is true, and in the no every yes is a lie. But since I can be in the yes today and in the no tomorrow, yes and no are both true and untrue. Whereas yes and no cannot yield because they exist, our concepts of truth and error can. […] One cannot be enough for us since the

> other is in us. And if we were content with one, the other would suffer great need and afflict us with its hunger. But we misunderstand this hunger and still believe that we are hungry for the one and strive for it even more adamantly. (RB II, 17: 303)

Only once the possibility of being ridiculed has been accepted can one 'become who he is'. This leads directly to another important matter, concerning the role and the task a *teacher* must possess. In fact, if one is said to 'become who he is' by stopping to imitate and starting to live within himself, a valid teacher must teach his disciples how to take this step, that is to say, he or she must stop appearing to them as a model to *emulate*. But—and this is the essential point—because of that, the teacher first needs to gain such independence himself or herself. In order to gain and preserve such independence, however, the tension given by self-mockery has to be kept, so that a certain sense of otherness can remain within.

Again, whenever teaching appears in *Liber Novus*, several similarities with *Zarathustra*, in particular in the chapter 'Of the Bestowing Virtue'—where this topic is mainly thematised—can be brought out. Even more than this, whenever Jung refers to teaching in *Liber Novus*, he seems to constantly address both Nietzsche and Zarathustra, questioning their role as teachers. In 'The Gift of Magic' (23 January 1914), Jung is given a black 'rod' [Stab], 'formed like a serpent' (RB II, 19: 307). Zarathustra is also given a 'staff' [Stab], 'upon the golden haft of which a serpent was coiled about a sun' (Za I, 22, KSA 4: 97; 'a serpent was coiled about a sun' is underlined in Jung's copy). Furthermore, the main figure responsible for teaching in *Liber Novus* is Philemon, who appears in the chapter 'The Magician' (27 January 1914) and in *Scrutinies*, and shares important features with Zarathustra.

Some very general characteristics belonging to both Zarathustra and Philemon which cannot be disregarded are: their solitude; their 'slowness of life'; their not being understood by men; their possession of a nonconventional wisdom, far from traditional values and ideas. Moreover, more specific allusions to Nietzsche can be found in the same sections just cited. First of all, Philemon is compared to a 'serpent that coils around itself' and lies in the sun; his wisdom is indeed 'serpentlike'. Then he is said to be 'hospitable': 'you took the dirty wanderers unsuspectingly into your hut. Your house then became a golden temple, and did I really leave your table unsatisfied? What did you give me? Did you invite me for a meal?'. Zarathustra lives in a cave with two animals: an eagle and a serpent.

Moreover, as already written, Zarathustra's cave becomes the place where all of the 'Higher Men' of the fourth book—generally symbolised through the figure of the *wanderer* in Nietzsche's works—are invited and offered a meal, the 'Last Supper'. Referring to the same Bible-*Zarathustra* scene, Philemon will prepare a 'Last Supper' a bit later. Philemon is then said to be 'no light that shines in the darkness, no savior who establishes an eternal truth and thus extinguishes the nocturnal light of human understanding' (RB II, 21, 'The Magician': 314–317). It is undeniable that the reference here is to the Bible and John's Gospel (I:5), but the image of the contrast light-darkness is also a recurrent theme in *Zarathustra*. Besides, a similar image also appears in the aphorism 125 of *The Gay Science*, where the last words pronounced by the madman sound like: 'Lightning and thunder need time, deeds need time after they have been done before they can be seen and heard. This deed is still more distant from them than the most distant stars—*and yet we have done it ourselves*' (FW 125, KSA 3: 482). Moreover, in the same scene from *Liber Novus*, an allusion to playing flute occurs. As stressed by Nietzsche in *The Birth of Tragedy*, the flute is Dionysos's favourite instrument.

Finally, some peculiarities attributed to a new conception of virtue in *Scrutinies* can be linked to the similar idea introduced by Nietzsche in the same *Zarathustra* chapter mentioned above. Here Jung speaks to himself with these words:

> I want you to speak about your shame, and that instead of speaking great words, you utter a discordant clamor before those whose respect you wanted to exact. You deserve mockery; not respect.
>
> I will burn out of you the contents of which you were proud, so that you will become empty like a poured-out vessel [ausgeschüttetes Gefäß]. You should be proud of nothing more than your emptiness and wretchedness. You should be a vessel of life, so kill your idols [schlachte deine Abgötter].
>
> Freedom does not belong to you, but form; not power, but suffering and conceiving.
>
> You should make a virtue out of your self-contempt [Du sollst aus der Geringschätzung deiner selbst eine Tugend machen], which I will spread out before men like a carpet. They should wall over it with dirty [schmutzigen] feet and you should see to it that you are dirtier than all the feet that step on you. (RB *Scrutinies*, § 1: 334; 19 April 1914)

Motifs such as the 'empty vessel', or the transformation of vice—in this case one's self-contempt—into virtue have already been discussed. What has still to be added is the emphasis on killing 'your idols', doubtless one of the most popular leitmotifs of Nietzsche's. Moreover, only a few lines below, Jung mentions the 'taming' [Zähmung] and the necessity to 'whip' [peitschen]. Both words recall Nietzsche's idea of morality, particularly expressed not only in *Zarathustra* but also in *Genealogy of Morals*.[13] Other phrases with Zarathustrian echoes present in the same chapter are: 'your compassion is sick' and 'I know that I doubt, because of my love for men' (ibid.: 335). At the very beginning of *Scrutinies*, another allusion seems to recall Nietzsche, namely the words: 'Perhaps the whip will help?' (ibid., § 1: 333). The whip-motif is quite recurrent in *Zarathustra*, as well as in traditional imagery of Nietzsche.[14] Among these references in the sentence from *Zarathustra* 'But there are indeed those to whom virtue is a writhing under the whip', the phrase 'writhing under the whip' [Kampf unter einer Peitsche] is underlined by Jung in his own copy (Za II, 5, 'Of the Virtuous', KSA 4: 121), whilst alongside the passage 'To the rhythm of my whip shalt thou dance and cry! I forgot not my whip?—Not I!', Jung wrote: 'survive' [weiterleben] (Za III, 15, 'The Second Dance Song', KSA 4: 284). The first one of these references seems to directly recall the meaning given by Jung in *Liber Novus*.

When Philemon reappears to Jung, in Autumn 1915, he discusses his idea of teaching with words that recall again 'Of the Bestowing Virtue'. First, the same gold metaphor used by Nietzsche to describe Zarathustra's virtue and wisdom is here invoked and reversed, to bring out the mechanism of dependence implied in such a construct. Philemon explains: 'Gold is no master out of its own will and yet it rules the whole, despised and greedily demanded, an inexorable ruler: it lies and waits'. He describes it as 'self-sufficient, a king that needs no proof of its power [...] it neither gives nor squanders itself [es gibt sich nicht, es verschwendet sich nicht]. [...] Everyone denies that he depends on it, and yet he secretly stretches out his hand longingly toward it. Must gold prove its necessity? It is proven through the longing of men'. Gold brilliance, in fact, 'confuses the senses', and exactly through that keeps men and women under control. As the value of gold is determined by his seekers exclusively, and would be of no importance per se, so the value of a teacher is established by his disciples. Then he adds:

> Not only to teach, but also to disavow [verleugnen], or why then did I teach? If I do not teach, I do not have to disavow [verleugnen]. But if I have taught, I must disavow [verleugnen] thereafter. For if I teach, I must give

others what they should have taken. What he acquires is good, but the gift that was not acquired is bad. To waste oneself means: to want to suppress many. Deceitfulness surrounds the giver because his own enterprise is deceitful. He is forced to revoke his gift and to deny [verleugnen] his virtue. (RB Scrutinies, § 6: 348)

And some paragraphs below:

How could I teach what I believe? Who would give me the right to such belief? It is what I know how to say; not because I believe it, but because I know it. If I knew better, I would teach better. But it would be easy for me to believe more. Yet should I teach a belief to those who have discarded belief? And, I ask you, is it good to believe something even more, if one does not know better? (RB Scrutinies, § 6: 348)

In a similar way Zarathustra expresses his scepticism towards teaching:

I now go away alone, my disciples! You too now go away and be alone! So I will have it.

Truly, I advise you: go away from me and guard yourselves against Zarathustra! And better still: be ashamed of him! Perhaps he has deceived you.

The man of knowledge must be able not only to love his enemies but also to hate his friends.

One repays a teacher badly if one always remains only a pupil. And why, then, should you not pluck at my laurels?

You respect [verehrt] me; but what if one day your respect [Verehrung] should tumble? Take care that a statue does not strike you dead!

You say you believe in Zarathustra? But of what importance is Zarathustra? You are my believers: but of what importance are all believers?

You had not yet sought yourselves: then you found me. Thus do all believers; therefore all belief [Glauben] is of so little account.

Now I bid you lose me and find yourselves; and only when you have all denied [verleugnet] me will I return to you. (Za I, 22, KSA 4: 101)

The passage comprehending the lines 'The man of knowledge must not only love his enemies, he must also be able to hate his friends. One repays a teacher badly if one always remains only a pupil' is accompanied by a vertical mark in Jung's text, while the sentence 'you had not yet sought yourselves when you found me' is underlined. Jung made use of the sentence 'One repays a teacher badly if one always remains only a pupil' also in his letter to Freud, dating 3 March 1912, with which he vocalised his estrangement from him for the first time (Freud and Jung 1974: 544; letter 303j). At the beginning of the chapter, Zarathustra had compared his virtue to gold and its value, by telling his disciples:

> Tell me, how did gold come to have its highest value? Because it is uncommon and useless and shining and mellow in lustre; it always bestows itself. Only as an image of the highest virtue did gold come to have the highest value. Gold-like gleams the glance of the giver. Gold-lustre makes peace between moon and sun. The highest virtue is uncommon and useless, it is shining and mellow in lustre: the highest virtue is the bestowing virtue. Truly, I divine you well, my disciples, you aspire to the bestowing virtue, as I do. (Za I, 22, KSA 4: 97)[15]

Whereas Zarathustra puts the main stress on gold wholeness, meant as the characteristic which allows it to 'bestow itself', Philemon seems to respond by highlighting the meaninglessness of its value, if nobody were there for it to be given. As a last remark, one of the very last dialogues between Philemon, Jung, and the dead in *Liber Novus* (February 1916) has to be mentioned. So Philemon addresses the dead: 'But how do you reach the eternal light? You mock my stupidity, which you too possess: you mock yourselves. Knowledge frees one from danger. But mockery is the other side of your belief is black less than white? You rejected faith and retained mockery: Are you thus saved from faith? No, you bound yourselves to mockery and hence again to faith. And therefore you are miserable'. However, the dead affirm that they 'praise [their] reason', and 'mock superstition'. In this way, they think to be immune from Philemon's 'old folly'. To which Philemon responds:

> What can do you any good? I free you from what still holds you to the shadow of life. Take this wisdom [Wissen] with you, add this folly [Torheit] to your cleverness [Klugheit], this unreason to your reason, and you will find yourselves. If you were men, you would then begin your life and your life's way between reason and unreason and live onward to the eternal light, whose shadow you lived in advance. But since you are dead, this knowledge frees you from life and strips you of your greed for men and it also frees your self from the shrouds that the light and the shadow lay on you, compassion with men will overcome you and from the stream you will reach solid ground, you will step forth from the eternal whirl onto the unmoving stone of rest, the circle that breaks flowing duration, and the flame will die down. (RB *Scrutinies*, § 11: 353)

Then, Philemon admits to have 'given the murderer a knife', and, among other things, to have 'given the madman [Wahnsinnigen] more intoxicating [Rauschtrank] drink'. So, he concludes: 'I have made the cold colder, the heat hotter, falseness even falser, goodness even better, weakness even weaker. This knowledge is the axe of the sacrificer'. However, the dead reply: 'Your wisdom is foolishness and a curse. You want to turn the wheel back? It will tear you apart, blinded one!' (ibid.). Phrases concerning madness, as well as the need of adding 'folly to [...] cleverness' in order to find oneself, remind one of the *Zarathustra* chapter, 'The Intoxicated Song', and therefore deal with the specific task of a teacher. In Nietzsche's chapter, Zarathustra expresses again his reluctance to be considered a model to imitate and stresses the importance of integrating folly in one's own *wisdom*, in order to become a real 'wise man'. He cries out:

> What do you think, you Higher Men? Am I a prophet? A dreamer? An intoxicated [Trunkener]? An interpreter of dreams? A midnight bell [Mitternachts-Glocke]?
>
> A drop of dew? An odour or scent of eternity? Do you not hear it? Do you not smell it? My world has just become perfect, midnight is also noonday, pain is also joy, a curse is also a blessing, the night is also a sun,—be gone, or you will learn: a wise man is also a fool [ein Weiser ist auch ein Narr]. (Za IV, 19, KSA 4: 402; translation modified)

By chasing his disciples away, Zarathustra refuses again the traditional role expected from a teacher and, in this sense, he seems to anticipate Philemon's role in *Scrutinies.* Nietzsche writes in 'Of the Three Metamorphoses': 'Is it not this: to debase yourself in order to injure your pride? To let your folly shine out in order to mock [spotten] your wisdom?' (Za I, 1, KSA 4: 29), and 'The Dance Song' is said to be also a 'mocking-song' [Spottlied] (Za II, 10, KSA 4: 140). Moreover, not only does the 'teacher' Zarathustra stress the importance of the recurring playing and mocking but he also plays the role of a mocker himself on a few occasions.

For instance, Nietzsche writes in 'The Higher Man':

> Timid, ashamed, awkward, like a tiger whose leap has failed: this is how I have often seen you slink aside, you Higher Men. A *throw* you made has failed. But what of that you dice-throwers! You have not learned to play [spielen] and mock [spotten] as a man ought to play and mock! Are we not always seated at a great table for play and mockery [Sitzen wir nicht immer

an einem grossen Spott- und Spieltische]? And if great things you attempted have turned out failures, does that mean you yourselves are—failures? And if you yourselves have turned out failure, does that mean—man is a failure? If man has turned out a failure, however: very well! come on!' (Za IV, 13, KSA 4, 363–364)

Despite several marks and annotations occurring in the whole chapter, however, these lines do not seem to interest Jung at all. Again, Zarathustra cannot reach his contemporaries, therefore he says: 'The men of the present [...] are strange to me and a mockery [Spott]' (Za II, 14, 'Of the Land of Culture', KSA 4: 155). Further references to mockery can be found in other sections from *Zarathustra*. Most significantly, in 'Of the Three Evil Things', Zarathustra is mocked by a personification of his wisdom (Za III, 10, KSA 4: 235); near the phrase 'divine nutcrackers', Jung annotates: 'here is the missed God' [hier ist der vermisste Gott]. In 'The Second Dance Song', instead, a personification of life mocks Zarathustra (Za III, 15, KSA 4: 283); in 'The Honey Offering', mocking is said to be part of Zarathustra's wickedness (Za IV, 1, KSA 4: 298). In the final part of the book, the two kings describe the wrong impression that Zarathustra's enemies have of him, as one who 'gazed the grimace of a devil, and with mocking laughter [hohnlachend]' (Za IV, 3, 'Conversation with the Kings' KSA 4: 307). It can be interesting to notice that, during this dialogue, Zarathustra almost cannot help but to mock the king's eagerness: 'As the kings thus eagerly talked and babbled of the happiness of their fathers, Zarathustra was overcome by no small desire to mock [spotten] their eagerness: for they were apparently very peaceable kings that he saw before him, with aged, refined faces' (KSA 4: 308).

Returning to the initial question raised regarding the relation between mockery and becoming 'who one is' in *Liber Novus* with particular focus on Nietzsche, a few significant points deserve to be emphasised. First of all, mockery is the presupposition of what could be defined as a healthy self-development. It can be regarded from two different perspectives: as the capacity of self-ironising, or as the apish attitude of ridiculing the other by stopping at a superficial level. Only the first of these meanings promotes psychological growth, but it is also strongly linked to the latter, from which it derives: self-irony means indeed to act as a monkey towards oneself. Therefore, the monkey-like behaviour appears as the first step to take, hardly overcome by most people. The ground of a monkey-like attitude lies in an undeveloped form of imitation; such undeveloped form of imitation, however, can be even extended to an entire collective action or religion, such as Christianity, which seems to have forgotten its premises of originality and independence—achievable only through deep introspection and self-confrontation. 'Christ', therefore, cannot be considered by Jung as a good example for a teacher, having become an empty model to emulate, instead of teaching how to achieve self-knowledge and independence, that is, how to become 'who one is'. Philemon, on the contrary, is presented as a valid symbol to express a new and different kind of teacher, who teaches how to find and develop one's own originality.

What emerges most loudly from the *Liber Novus* excerpts just analysed, however, is Jung's questioning the role of Zarathustra as a teacher. Indeed, incapable to bear himself being mocked, Zarathustra would not be able to recognise the inferior in himself despite his teaching. This is likely the reason why Zarathustra appears to be simply *imitated* by his disciples, without being understood. Furthermore, through the plausible allusion to the ropedancer episode, it is possible to extend such a consideration to Nietzsche himself, and his personal rejection of inferiority. As already said in relation to the process of transformation, the ropedancer's death is one of the most recurrent examples used by Jung, in order to show Nietzsche's obstinacy to deny the unconscious. Jung's question seems now to address Nietzsche's role as a teacher.

3.3.3 Death and Rebirth of God

If one follows the self-becoming path just shown, the result will be a 'new God'. Jung writes: 'The new God laughs at imitation and discipleship. He needs no imitators and no pupils. He forces men through himself. The God is his own follower in man. He imitates himself' (RB I, 8, 'The Conception of the God': 245). Whereas Nietzsche spoke of 'death of God' as a primary condition for being independent, Jung seems to express the same possibility through a divine symbol again; for divinity appears to him as a *necessity* in human psychology. Nevertheless, while facing this aspect, he once more seems to evoke Nietzsche and his symbols. Due to the Western rational attitude, godliness is bound to disappear: rather than being accepted in the irrational possibility of its independence from reason, the divine is perceived only as an idea or a concept. Therefore, God is said to be 'sick', or even believed to be dead:

> Something always happens, but we do not happen, since our God is sick. We have seen him dead with the venomous gaze of the Basilisk [giftigem Basiliskenbick] on his face, and we have understood that he is dead. We must think of his healing. And yet again I feel it quite clearly that my life would have broken in half had I failed to heal my God. Hence I abided with him in the long cold night. (RB II, 8, 'First Day': 281)

'Basilisk eggs' [Basilisken-Eier] appear also at the very end of Nietzsche's *Anti-Christ*: 'Third proposition.—The execrable location where Christianity brooded over its basilisk eggs should be razed to the ground and, being the depraved spot on earth, it should be the horror of all posterity. Poisonous serpents should be bred on top of it' (AC 'Epilogue', 1, 'Law against Christianity', KSA 6: 254; translation modified). What must also be remarked is the link to the 'poisonous serpents' [giftige Schlangen], directly recalling Jung's phrase, thus justifying the possibility of a real allusion to Nietzsche in this *Liber Novus* chapter. With similar tones, in the dithyramb 'Fame and Eternity' [Ruhm und Ewigkeit], Nietzsche writes:

> How long have you already been sitting
> On your misfortune for?
> Watch out! You brood me yet
> Another egg
> A basilisk-egg
> Out of your long misery. (DD, 8, KSA 6: 402)

Returning to *Liber Novus*, the only way for God to be healed is to be reborn again in the Western civilised world. The birth of a new 'God' is symbolised by Izdubar's episode. As already seen, the giant Izdubar represents the East, along with its non-scientific thinking. As Jung's 'I' makes him conscious about his own land and culture, these *poisoning* truths make him ill and fragile, since he is as innocent and naive as 'a child, a primordial grown child that required human Logos' (ibid.). So, Jung's 'I' decides to reduce his companion's weight in order to carry him to the 'Western land'. Izdubar, in fact, is perceived as a fantasy and his size can change depending on the will of Jung's 'I'. Once 'the God' has become 'lighter than a feather', the protagonist is able to carry him through his own land. There Jung's 'I' intends to spend the night in the house of someone he knows, but the door seems to be too small for the giant Izdubar, so he uses his fantasy again in order to 'squeeze' him 'into the size of an egg' and put him in his pocket. At this point, 'the God' can be considered safe and ready to come back to life in a new shape. While commenting on this episode, Jung presumably refers to Nietzsche. The first thing he notices is: 'How often has it been assumed that the Gods have been brought to their end in this way. This was obviously a serious mistake, since this was precisely what saved the God. He did not pass away, but became a living fantasy, whose workings I could feel on my own body'. Then he argues: 'One used to believe that one could murder a God'. And again:

> This tangible and apparent world is one reality, but fantasy is the other reality: So long as we leave the God outside us apparent and tangible, he is unbearable and hopeless. But if we turn the God into fantasy, he is in us and is easy to bear. The God outside us increases the weight of everything heavy, while the God within us lightens everything heavy. (RB II, 9, 'Second Day': 282–283)

When the 'new God' is born again, in the chapter 'The Opening of the Egg', he will be compared to 'the sun, the eternal light', evoking again *Zarathustra* tones (RB II, 11: 286).[16] The assumption of a sort of natural self-destruction in the gods, as well as the difference between a 'tangible and apparent world' and a different 'reality', can be read as referred to Nietzsche's *Twilight of the Idols*, as discussed. Similarly, the idea of self-suppression of morality is also brilliantly exposed in one of Nietzsche's most famous unpublished texts, written in Lenzerheide in 1887, and bearing the title of 'European Nihilism'. In the *Twilight of the Idols* chapter 'How the "True" World finally Became a Fable' (subtitle 'The history of an error'), Nietzsche exposes a short and metaphorical revisitation of the history of metaphysics. From the Platonic distinction between a 'true' and an 'apparent' world, according to which the 'true world' could be reached only through knowledge, metaphysics would be transposed to a religious layer throughout the development of Christianity, by promising the truth through devotion. Then it would finally reach the point of the Kantian noumenic *unattainability* of such a truth, which should therefore remain *unknown*. From there, Positivism would then develop, eliminating Plato's distinction, and permitting nihilism to evolve. Now it is about time for Zarathustra to announce his doctrine: 'The true world is gone: which world is left? The illusory one, perhaps? ... But no! we got rid of the illusory world along with the true one! (Noon; moment of shortest shadow; end of longest error; high point of humanity; INCIPIT ZARATHUSTRA)' (GD

IV, 1, KSA 6: 80–81). Still in Nietzsche's *Twilight*, the following chapter is entitled 'Morality as Anti-nature' [Moral als Widernatur] and describes the contradictory aspect of morals towards nature, that is to say, 'all passions go through a phase where they are just a disaster [...] and a later, much later phase [...] where they "spiritualise" themselves'. In this second phase, the instincts are suppressed (Nietzsche speaks indeed of 'castration' [Castratismus]) and become 'enemies' of oneself. However, this means to fight against life itself. 'Every naturalism in morality [...] is governed by an instinct of life', but 'anti-natural morality [...] condemns these instincts, sometimes in secret, sometimes in loud and impudent tones' and, as Nietzsche concludes, 'by saying "God sees into the heart", it says no to both the lowest and the highest desires of life, and treats God as the enemy of life'. Therefore, morality appears as the 'negation of [Schopenhauer's] will to life', as an *instinct of the decadence* and, consequently, as a form, again, of *self-destroying* life. Furthermore, this kind of morality tends to change individuals' inner attitude, according to a merely *exterior* ideal, originated by 'an idiosyncrasy of degenerates' which simply condemns life (GD V, 1–6, KSA 6: 82–87).

In 1887, in Lenzerheide (Switzerland), Nietzsche reflected on nihilism systematically for the first time. Once more, what emerges from these very personal annotations, is the self-contradictory aspect of Christian morality, containing in itself the germ of self-destruction and leading to the final crisis of values (NF 5[71], June 1887, KSA 12: 211–217). In reality, Nietzsche's reflection on nihilism began earlier, as well as his utilisation of the word. Interestingly, in 1879, after the publication of *Human, All too Human*, the Wagnerian Édouard Schuré accused Nietzsche of *nihilisme écoeurant* (see Campioni 2006). The somewhat long fragment written in Lenzerheide was unfortunately split into several sections by Elisabeth Förster-Nietzsche, together with Peter Gast. At the time of *Liber Novus*, therefore, its contents were still available, but scattered within other texts of Nietzsche's and were therefore hardly accessible for consultation.

The sentence 'One used to believe that one could murder a God', instead, recalls the 'last men' and 'the ugliest man' from *Zarathustra*. Many times it is written by Nietzsche that we are all responsible for the death of God, that is to say, we, as human beings, did kill him. The last men correspond to those who do realise their guilt but do not suffer from it and carry on with their own lives as if nothing had happened. 'The ugliest man' represents the counterpart of this attitude, that is, that kind of man who is more than aware about his own guilt, but is far too weak to bear the situation and overcome his nature. In Jung's *Zarathustra* copy, the chapter 'The Ugliest Man' [Der hässlichste Mann] presents several underlinings, marks, and three meaningful annotations. The first of these appears at the beginning of the chapter, where Zarathustra manifests happiness for the characters he has just encountered (the two kings, the leech, the sorcerer, and the retired Pope) and bears the inscription: 'Last Supper motif' [Abendmahls Motiv], which, as already shown, is also an important image in *Liber Novus.* Only a few lines below, near the sentences 'For it was a valley which all beasts avoided, even the beasts of prey; except that kind of ugly, thick, green serpent, when it grew old, came here to die. Therefore the shepherds called this valley "Serpent's Death" ' (where 'Serpent's Death' [Schlangen-Tod] is underlined), Jung annotates: 'Death of life' [Lebenstod]. Finally, the most significant inscription appears precisely alongside the underlined sentence '*you are the murderer of God*! [...] You could not *endure* him who saw *you*'. This might be easily linked to the murdering of God exposed in *Liber Novus.* Jung comments on the text with these words: 'You murderer, Zarathustra! he could not endure ugliness' [Du Mörder, Zarathustra! er ertrug den Hässlichen nicht] (Za IV, 7, 'The Ugliest Man', KSA 4: 327–332).

Putting all of these details together, the words expressed by Jung in his encounter with Izdubar seem to allude to Nietzsche's wrongly believing that God is irreversibly dead and that it could not be different—God being nothing but the product of the unjustified distinction between a 'true' and an 'illusory' world. Rejecting this difference, there would no longer be room for a fantasy-like God. According to Jung, instead, it is such not-belonging to the 'real' world that makes God's power stronger and more effective in our 'tangible' reality. Nietzsche's error would therefore consist in refusing fantasy as such, instead of realising its potentiality and efficacy in reality in our everyday life.

Ultimately, the sentence 'Bring your God down to the haze pregnant with poison, but not like those blinded ones who try to illuminate the darkness with lanterns which it does not comprehend' (RB II, 9: 283) recalls again *The Gay Science*, 125; precisely when 'the madman' is portrayed as bringing a lantern in the daylight, reminding one of the cynic Diogenes and the attitude of the men of knowledge that he represents. Holding a source of light during the day, in fact, means not to arrest before appearance, but to try and investigate further and further, exclusively relying on a rational attitude. If linked to *Liber Novus*, this can be read as a criticism to Nietzsche's presumably still too rational attitude towards religion. If Jung acknowledges Nietzsche's philosophy for showing a certain attempt to overcome rationality unilateralism on the one hand, he denies Nietzsche's actual capability to put his attempt into practice at a personal and psychological level on the other. Jung's reading of Nietzsche's 'death of God' represents one of the most emblematic corollaries of such an understanding of Nietzsche's philosophy and life, which will emerge quite clearly during the 1930s seminar on *Zarathustra*.

Returning to *Liber Novus*, not only has Izdubar become of the same size of an egg, he has even been transformed into an egg indeed, or, to better express it, his divine nature has been enclosed in it. In order that the egg may open, Jung chants a series of incantations until the egg opens up and the new 'God' comes to life. Although in this part of the text there seems to be no apparent evidence of Nietzsche's inspiration, the way Jung comments on *Zarathustra* chapter 'Before Sunrise' in his own copy makes it evident to postulate a connection between these two passages: precisely underneath the title of the chapter, Jung wrote 'incantation of the egg' [Incantation des Eies]. Moreover, the first part of this *Zarathustra* chapter presents a couple of marks, likely indicating beginning and end of the reference to *Liber Novus* according to Jung. Right at the beginning of the text, are a few motifs recalling *Liber Novus* indeed:

> O Sky above me, o pure sky! You abyss of light! Gazing into you, I tremble with divine desire. To cast myself into your height—that is *my* depth! To hide myself in your purity—that is *my* innocence! The god is veiled by his beauty: thus you hide your stars. You do not speak: thus you proclaim to me your wisdom. You have risen for me today, mute over the raging sea; your love and your modesty speak a revelation to my raging soul. That you have come to me, beautiful, veiled in your beauty; that you have spoken to me mutely, manifest in your *wisdom*: Oh how should I not divine all that is modest in your soul! You came to me *before* the sun, to me the most solitary man. (Za III, 4, KSA 4: 207–208, the word 'wisdom' [Weisheit] is underlined by Jung)

Phrases such as 'divine desire' [göttlichen Begierden] and 'The god is veiled by his beauty' [Den Gott verhüllt seine Schönheit] surely let one guess a similarity with the Izdubar episode. Moreover, towards the end of the section marked by Jung, occur other motifs, reminding one of Jung's journey, such as the description of lonely wanderings and 'treacherous paths' [Irr-Pfaden], while seeking god:

> We have been friends from the beginning: we have grief and terror and world in common; we have even the sun in common. We do not speak to one another, because we know too much: we are silent together, we smile our knowledge to one another. Are you not the light of my fire? Do you not have the sister-soul of my insight? Together we learned everything; together we learned to mount above ourselves and to smile uncloudedly—to smile uncloudedly down from bright eyes and from miles away when under us compulsion and purpose and guilt stream like rain. And when I wandered alone, *what* did my soul hunger after by night and on treacherous paths? And when I climbed mountains, *whom* did I always seek, if not you, upon mountains? And all my wandering and mountain-climbing: it was merely a necessity and an expedient of clumsiness: my whole will desires only to *fly*, to *fly* into *you*! (ibid.)

In particular, presenting the *sun* as the common element to both Zarathustra and this craved god, the already mentioned *Eastern wisdom* seems to come up again. As already discussed, *Liber Novus* chapters 'First Day', 'Second Day', and 'The Incantations' represent the core of Jung's confrontation with European culture, as well as the will to integrate it with a different and wider perspective, symbolised by the East. The sun plays a meaningful role in this process, and the fact that Jung reads 'Before Sunrise' in connection with his own need for a god validates such hypothesis even more. In 'The Incantations' he writes:

> Christmas has come. The God is in the egg. I have prepared a rug for my God, an expensive red rug from the land
> of morning. He shall be surrounded by the shimmer of magnificence of his Eastern land. I am the mother, the simple maiden, who gave birth and did not know how. I am the careful father, who protected the maiden. I am the shepherd, who received the message as he guarded his herd at
> night on the dark fields.
> I am the holy animal that stood astonished and cannot grasp the becoming of the God…
> I am the wise man who came from the East, suspecting the miracle from afar.
> And I am the egg that surrounds and nurtures the seed of the God in me.
> The solemn hours lengthen.
> And my humanity is wretched and suffers torment. Since I am a giver of birth. Whence do you delight me, Oh God! He is the eternal emptiness and the eternal fullness. Nothing resembles him and he resembles everything.

> Eternal darkness and eternal brightness. Eternal below and eternal above.
> Double nature in one. [...]
> Oh light of the middle way,
> enclosed in the egg,
> embryonic,
> full or ardor, oppressed.
> Fully expectant,
> dreamlike, awaiting lost memories.
> As heavy as stone, hardened.
> Molten, transparent.
> Streaming bright, coiled on itself. (RB II, 10: 284)

The same idea of 'the egg of the Gods' comes back later in *Liber Novus*, in 'The Magician' (RB II, 21, §§ 164–189: 320–327). What is important to dwell upon here, are the references to East and Eastern wisdom (especially 'I am the wise man who came from the East'), offering a deeper connection between this chapter and Nietzsche's. Furthermore, motifs such as 'the eternal emptiness and the eternal fullness', as well as the 'eternal darkness and eternal brightness', 'eternal below and eternal above' not only anticipate Abraxas's features but also present some elements which strongly occur in Nietzsche's 'The Night Song' and characterise Zarathustra's wisdom. Moreover, it can be observed that these expressions sound quite close to Taoism, letting a strong Eastern echo emerge in both texts. Even though there seem to be no direct evidence to prove Nietzsche's knowledge of old Chinese scriptures—differently from Jung, who was well accustomed with Chinese culture and philosophy—there are several elements in *Zarathustra* and its imagery that remind one of Lao-tsu and Chuang-tsu, as has been shown in some studies. For instance, *Zarathustra*'s purpose of abandoning an anthropocentric perspective can be regarded as a Taoist perspective; again, Nietzsche's apparent emphasis on 'self-cultivation', alongside with references to animals and symbols drawn from nature can lead one to connect *Zarathustra* with Taoism (Parkes 1989). Moreover, other studies have tried to read Nietzsche's nihilism as a European expression of Taoism (Sloterdijk 1989: 161–210). In addition to this, another common feature can be traced in the importance given to the relation between weakness and strength, in which to be really strong means to look softer, whereas what appears strong and rigid hides the true weakness within. This represents one of the key elements of Nietzsche's philosophy, as well as one of the most important statements of Lao-tsu's teaching.

In the aforementioned passage from 'The Magician', moreover, phrases such as 'Star of the East', 'fire of old night', or 'We filled your cup with red wine. We set out fragrant fruit on golden dishes' resonate with Zarathustrian motifs and evoke certain indisputable religious tones (RB II, 10: 284–285). In particular, the following excerpt ought to be recalled: 'I have overthrown all the Gods, broken the laws, eaten the impure. I have thrown down my sword and dressed in women's clothing. I shattered my firm castle and played like a child in the sand. I saw warriors form into line of battle and I destroyed my suit of armor with a hammer' (ibid.: 285). The image of the child playing in the sand can be linked to *Zarathustra* and, at an even deeper level, evokes at the same time the metaphor used by Heraclitus's fragment 52, as quoted by Hippolytus in his *Refutatio Omnium Haeresium* (§ 9.4) to describe the fugacity of existence ('Time is a child playing draughts; the kingship is a child's', See Kirk 1954). Nietzsche writes, in fact: 'They were playing on the sea-shore [am Meere]—then came a wave and swept their playthings into the deep: now thy cry. But the same wave shall bring them new playthings and pour out new coloured sea-shells before them! Thus they will be consoled; and you too, my friends, shall, like them, have your consolation—and new coloured sea-shells!' (Za II, 5, 'Of the Virtuous', KSA 4: 123). Still referred to the quoted section from *Liber Novus*, the hammer element has ultimately to be highlighted: Nietzsche's *Twilight of the Idols* has *How to philosophise with a Hammer* as its subtitle and is defined by Nietzsche as a 'declaration of war', as will be further developed in the conclusion. After these incantations, Jung comments on what is taking place with these words:

> You force the gates of Hell: the sound of cackling masks [Maskengekicher] and the music of fools [Narrenmusik] approaches you. You storm Heaven: stage scenery totters and the prompter in the box falls into a swoon. You notice: you are not true, it is not true above, it is not true below, left and right are deceptions. Wherever you grasp is air, air, air. (RB II, 10: 285)

Zarathustra's dream described in the chapter 'The Prophet', where similar images are present, has been already recalled. Also, in 'The Funeral Song' a 'gruesome, gloomy melody' [schaurige dumpfe Weise] occurs. Ultimately, the connection between the new god in the egg and the sun will return again towards the end of *Liber Secundus*. After that Jung's 'I' accepted and recognised this newborn as his own child; he speaks to him:

> I: "Where is your country?"
>
> He: "In the light, in the egg, in the sun, in what is innermost and compressed, in the eternal longing embers. So rises the sun in your heart and streams out into the cold world."
>
> I: "How you transfigure yourself!"
>
> He: "I want to vanish from your sight. You ought to live in darkest solitude, men-not Gods-should illumine your darkness." (RB II, 21, 'The Magician': 329)

If *Liber Novus* really represents Jung's confrontation with his old 'idols', and if Nietzsche is one of those, then his idea of Abraxas can represent an attempt to react to Nietzsche's 'death of God'. Still while discussing with himself, Jung seems to doubt about his situation and paraphrases Nietzsche: 'You call on God for help? The dear old God has died, and it is good that way; otherwise he would have had *pity* on your repentant sinfulness and spared me the execution by granting mercy' (RB *Scrutinies*, §: 333, italic added). In reality, Jung's God is alive, as argued by Philemon in the second sermon:

> God is not dead. He is as alive as ever. God is creation, for he is something definite, and therefore differentiated from the Pleroma. God is a quality of the Pleroma, and everything I have said about creation also applies to him. (RB *Scrutinies*, § 7: 348)

Although here the main reference is to the Gnostic representation of Abraxas, Jung's endeavour to develop a concept of godliness that counterbalances the nihilist void he could easily go through, can be really read as a possible response to Nietzsche. As already remarked, 'pity' is also Zarathustra's 'last sin'. Still to remind one of Nietzsche's imagery, Abraxas is even compared to Pan a few lines below the text just quoted (RB *Scrutinies*, § 8: 350).

Notes

1. The other three quotations from the Bible are: 'Isaiah said: Who hath believed our report? and to whom is the arm of the Lord revealed? For he shall grow up before him as a tender plant, and as a root out of a dry ground: he hath no form nor comeliness; and when we shall see him, there is no beauty that we should desire him. He is despised and rejected of men; a man of sorrows, and acquainted with grief: and we hid as it were our faces from him; he was despised, and we esteemed him not. Surely he hath borne our griefs, and carried our sorrows: yet we did esteem him stricken,

smitten of God, and afflicted' (Isaiah 53: 1–4); 'For unto us a child is born, unto us a son is given: and the government shall be upon his shoulder: and his name shall be called Wonderful, Counsellor, The mighty God, The everlasting Father, The Prince of Peace (Isaiah 9:6)'; 'And the Word was made flesh, and dwelt among us (and we be held his glory; the glory as of the only begotten of the Father), full of grace and truth (John 1:14)'.

2. Interestingly, Paul Bourget makes use of this novel, and precisely of the character of St Anthony, in order to explain Flaubert's psychology in terms of 'decadence'. The stress on an intellectual *image* of 'reality', 'feelings', and 'sensations', before 'reality', 'feelings', and 'sensations' on their own, mirrors the central role of thinking. The temptation would represent indeed a desire to become one with 'matter', which would perfectly contrast such intellectualism, showing the 'disproportion', typical of the decadence (Bourget 1883: 111–173).
3. Eigentlich um nun die gewonnene Einsicht in die menschliche Natur wirklich zu leben und nicht bloss zu denken. Daraus würde ein Kampf mit den Löwen entstehen und aus seiner Überwindung würde der puer aeternus, eben das Kind entstehen. Das fällt aber schon in die Krankheit.
4. The 'swamp water' [Sumpfwasser] was already mentioned in Jung's comment on his fantasy from the chapter 'One of the Lowly' (29 December 1913) (RB II, 3: 266).
5. Some lines above, Jung had presumably already referred to Nietzsche by writing: 'the disgust of whoever wants to enter into his own life can hardly be measured. Aversion will sicken him. He makes him self vomit'.
6. On the role of the ass in *Zarathustra*, IV, with particular regard to its religious meaning and tradition, see Salaquarda (1973).
7. Another reference to Wagner in *Liber Novus* is given by the unusual representation of *Parsifal* after the asylum episode in 'Nox Quarta', *Liber Secundus* (RB II, 17: 302–303). Besides, the sacrifice of Siegfried in 'Murder of the Hero', *Liber Primus*, might be also linked to Wagner and his *Ring* (RB I, 7: 241–242).
8. In the chapter 'Death', Jung also experiences unindifferentiation and values overturn. He will later understand these in regard to the approaching of the First World War and the North-European situation in general. It is also interesting to notice, to this end, that after accepting 'death' as a condition of life, the 'red sun' rises again (RB II, 6: 273–275).
9. Philo of Alexandria (also called Philo Judaeus) brought Jewish elements into Greek philosophy. In particular, Jung referred to him in a letter to James Kirsch: 'The gnosis from which John the Evangelist emanated, is definitely Jewish, but its essence is Hellenistic, in the style of Philo Judaeus, the founder of the teachings of the Logos' (Jung Archives, cited in Shamdasani 2009, RB II, 4: 268). Regarding the character of Ammonius, Jung wrote that he came from the third century (letter from 31 December

1913; Jung's Family Archives). As pointed out by Sonu Shamdasani, 'there are three historical figures named Ammonius in Alexandria from this period: Ammonius, a Christian philosopher in the third century, once thought to have been responsible for the medieval divisions of the gospels; Ammonius Cetus, who was born a Christian but turned to Greek philosophy and whose work presents a transition from Platonism to Neoplatonism; a Neoplatonic Ammonius in the fifth century, who tried to reconcile Aristotle and the Bible. At Alexandria, there was accommodation between Neoplatonism and Christianity, and some of the pupils of the latter Ammonius converted to Christianity' (ibid.: 267).

10. According to Ammonius, 'a succession of words does not have only one meaning. But men strive to assign only a single meaning to the sequence of words, in order to have an unambiguous language. This striving is worldly and constricted, and belongs to the deepest layers of the divine creative plan. On the higher levels of insight into divine thoughts, you recognize that the sequence of words has more than one valid meaning. Only to the all-knowing is it given to know all the meanings of the sequence of words. Increasingly we try to grasp a few more meanings' (ibid.: 268). It is also interesting to notice that Philo himself is defined by Ammonius as 'slave of his own words' (ibid.).
11. The mockery episode is also narrated in Mt 27:29. On Nietzsche's 'genealogical' approach to Christianity, see Salaquarda (1996). The phrase 'become who you are' has been very likely borrowed by Nietzsche from Pindar's second *Pythian Ode* (Hamilton 2004: 57). Pindar was known to Jung as well.
12. In this regard, it can be observed that the extreme form of self-mockery is represented by the attitude of the Cynics. Interestingly, Nietzsche takes a similar position in *Beyond Good and Evil*, § 26, by stating that 'Cynicism is the only form in which base souls approach honesty [Cynismus ist die einzige Form, in welcher gemeine Seelen an Das streifen, was Redlichkeit ist]' (JGB I, 26, KSA 5: 44; my own translation).
13. Here, Nietzsche describes 'bad conscience' [Schlechtes Gewissen] in terms of a moral conduct which judges as wrong—and therefore represses—every human attempt to follow natural instincts (GM II, 16–25, KSA 5: 331–332). According to this definition, 'slave morality' would be born together with the necessity of suppressing the instincts from the outer world and turning them towards interiority. In this sense, men are seen as in need of being *tamed*: 'that will to self-torment, that repressed cruelty of animal man pushed inward and forced back into himself, imprisoned in the "state" to make him tame [zum Zweck der Zähmung], who invented bad conscience in order to lacerate himself, after the more natural discharge of this will to inflict pain had been blocked—this man of bad conscience seized upon religious assumptions to drive his self-torment to its most

horrifying hardship and ferocity' (ibid.: 22; with the same meaning, *Zähmung* appears also in GM III, 13, KSA 5: 365). The reference to this text occurs again twice in the same section from *Liber Novus*. Once, still referring to himself, Jung uses the word 'slaves' [Sklaven] (RB *Scrutinies*, 1: 334). Just a few pages further on, Christian morality is said to be 'for burden' (ibid.: 337), recalling again not only the same distinction between slaves' and masters' moral, but also *Zarathustra*—with particular regard to 'Of The Three Metamorphoses' and the camel.

14. One can think, for instance, of the well-known picture of Nietzsche, Paul Ree, and Lou von Salomé, taken in Lucerne in 1882, in which the three of them are on a carriage and Lou is holding a whip, pretending to hit her friends.
15. References to a kind of virtue that enlightens similarly to stars is to be found in the chapter 'Of the Virtuous', too, precisely in relation to the sentence 'your virtue is your dearest friend' (KSA 4: 121).
16. Such understanding of the divine might be also read in opposition to Karl Barth's theology. Although never openly exhibited, Jung and Barth showed their mutual disagreements in a few occasions (Jehle-Wildberger 2014: Introduction).

References

Bishop, Paul. 1993. The Jung/Förster-Nietzsche Correspondence. *German Life and Letters* 46: 319–330.

———. 1995a. *The Dionysian Self: C. G. Jung's Reception of Friedrich Nietzsche*. Berlin and New York: De Gruyter.

———. 1995b. Jung's Annotation of Nietzsche's Works: An Analysis. *Nietzsche-Studien* 24: 271–314.

———. 1999. Estrangement from the Deed and the Memory Thereof: Freud and Jung on the Pale Criminal in Nietzsche's *Zarathustra*. *Orbis Litterarum* 54: 424–438.

Bourget, Paul. 1883. *Essays de psychologie contemporaine*. Paris: Plon-Nourrit.

Campioni, Giuliano. 2006. Il 'sentimento del deserto'. Dalle pianure slave al vecchio occidente. In *Il nichilismo europeo. Frammento di Lenzerheide*, ed. Friedrich Wilhelm Nietzsche, 47–60. Edited by Giuliano Campioni. Milan: Adelphi.

Creuzer, George Friedrich. 1822. *Symbolik und Mythologie der alten Völker*. Leipzig and Darmstadt: Leske.

Domenici, Gaia. 2015. Il 'ruggito del leone morale'. C. G. Jung si confronta con *Zarathustra*. In *Prospettive. Omaggio a Giuliano Campioni*, ed. Paolo D'Iorio, Maria Cristina Fornari, Luca Lupo, and Chiara Piazzesi, 197–202. Pisa: ETS.

———. 2018. 'Crush the Head of the Serpent and it will bite you in the heel'. A Historical Reconstruction of C. G. Jung's Understanding of the Poisonous Serpents in *Zarathustra* through *Liber Novus*. *Phanês: Journal for Jung History* 1: 1–27.

Flaubert, Gustave. 1849. *La Tentation de Saint Antoine*. Paris: Charpentier Et Cie, 1874.
Freud, Sigmund, and Carl Gustav Jung. 1974. *Briefwechsel*. Edited by William McGuire and Wolfgang Sauerländer. Frankfurt am Main: Fischer.
Hamilton, John. 2004. Ecce Philologus: Nietzsche and Pindar's Second Pythian Ode. In *Nietzsche and the Antiquity. His Reaction and Response to the Classical Tradition*, ed. Paul Bishop, 54–69. Rochester, NY: Camden House.
Jehle-Wildberger, Marianne, ed. 2014. *C. G. Jung Und Adolf Keller: Über Theologie Und Psychologie: Briefe Und Gesprache*. Zurich: Theologischer Verlag.
Jung, Carl Gustav. 1902. *On the Psychology and Pathology of So-called Occult Phenomena*. Collected Works of C. G. Jung. Vol. 1, §§ 1–150.
———. 1905. *Cryptomnesia*. Cof C. G. Jung. Vol. 1, §§ 166–186.
———. 1909/1949. *The Significance of the Father in the Destiny of the Individual*. Collected Works of C. G. Jung. Vol. 4, §§ 693–744.
———. 1912a. *Wandlungen und Symbole der Libido. Beiträge zur Entwicklung des Denkens*. 2nd ed. Leipzig and Vienna: Franz Deuticke, 1925.
———. 1912b. *Psychology of the Unconscious. A study of the Transformations and Symbolisms of the Libido. A contribution to the History of the Evolution of Thought*. New York: Moffat, Yard and Company, 1917.
———. 1916/1958. *The Transcendent Function*. Collected Works of C. G. Jung. Vol. 8, §§ 131–193.
———. 1917. *On the Psychology of the Unconscious*. 7, §§ 1–201.
———. 1930/1950. *Psychology and Literature*. Collected Works of C. G. Jung. Vol. 15, §§ 133–162.
———. 1934. *Archetypes of The Collective Unconscious*. Collected Works of C. G. Jung. Vol. 9, 1, §§ 1–86.
———. 1936. *Wotan*. Collected Works of C. G. Jung. Vol. 10, §§ 371–399.
———. 1945. *After the Catastrophe*. Collected Works of C. G. Jung. Vol. 10, §§ 400–443.
———. 1952. *Symbols of Transformation*. Collected Works of C. G. Jung. Vol. 5.
———. 1989. *Nietzsche's Zarathustra: Notes of the Seminar Given in 1934–9*. 2nd ed. Edited by James L. Jarrett in Two Parts. London: Routledge, 1994.
———. 2009. *The Red Book: Liber Novus*. Edited and Introduced by Sonu Shamdasani, Translated by Mark Kyburz, John Peck, and Sonu Shamdasani. New York and London: W. W. Norton & Company.
Jung, Carl Gustav, and Aniela Jaffé. 1962. *Memories, Dreams, Reflections by Carl Gustav Jung*. Recorded and Edited by Aniela Jaffé. New York: Vintage Books, 1989.
Kirk, G. S. (ed.). 1954. *Heraclitus. The Cosmic Fragments. A Critical Study with Introduction, Text and Translation by G. S. Kirk*. Cambridge and New York: Cambridge University Press.
Liebscher, Martin. 2001. 'Wotan' und 'Puer Aeternus'. Die Zeithistorische Verstrickung von C. G. Jungs Zarathustrainterpretation. *Nietzsche Studien* 30: 329–350.

Nietzsche, Friedrich Wilhelm. 1878. *Human, All Too Human I*. Translated by Alexander Harvey. Chicago: Charles H. Kerr & Company, 1908.

———. 1879. *Human, All Too Human II*. Translated by Paul V. Cohn. London: George Allen and Unwin, 1911/1924.

———. 1883–1885. *Thus Spoke Zarathustra*. 2nd ed. Translated by R. J. Hollingdale. New York: Penguin Classics, 1969.

———. 1887a. *The Gay Science*. Translated by Josefine Nauckhoff. Edited by Bernard Williams. Poems Translated by Adrian Del Caro. Cambridge and New York: Cambridge University Press, 2001–2008.

———. 1887b. *Genealogy of Morals. A Polemical Tract*. Translated by Ian Johnston. Arlington, VA: Richer Resources Publications, 2009.

———. 1888–1889. *Dithyrambs of Dionysus*, www.thenietzschechannel.com.

———. 1899–1911. *Kleinoktav-Gesamtausgabe*. Leipzig: Naumann und Kröner.

———. 1930 [1883–1885]. *Thus Spake Zarathustra*. Translated by Thomas Common. New York: The Modern Library.

———. 1967–. *Kritische Gesamtausgabe der Werke Nietzsches*. Edited by Giorgio Colli and Mazzino Montinari. Berlin and New York: De Gruyter.

———. 1980–. *Kritische Studienausgabe*. Edited by Giorgio Colli and Mazzino Montinari. Berlin and New York: De Gruyter.

———. 2009–. *Digital Critical Edition*. Edited by P. D'Iorio.

Parkes, Graham. 1989. Human/Nature in Nietzsche and Taoism. In *Nature in Asian Traditions of Thought. Essays in Environmental Philosophy*, ed. J. Baird Callicot and Roger T. Ames, 79–97. Albany: SUNY Press.

Salaquarda, Jörg. 1973. Zarathustra und der Esel: eine Untersuchung der Rolle des Esels im Vierten Teil von Nietzsches 'Also sprach Zarathustra'. *Theologia Viatorum* 11: 181–213.

———. 1996. Nietzsche and the Judaeo-Christian Tradition. In *The Cambridge Companion to Nietzsche*, ed. Bernard Magnus and Kathleen Higgins, 90–118. Cambridge and New York: Cambridge University Press.

Schopenhauer, Arthur. 1851. *Parerga and Paralipomena: Short Philosophical Essays*. 2 vols. Translated by E. F. J. Payne. Oxford: Caledonian Press, 1974.

Shamdasani, Sonu. 2009. Introduction and Footnotes. In *The Red Book: Liber Novus*, ed. C.G. Jung. Edited and Introduced by Sonu Shamdasani. Translated by Mark Kyburz, John Peck, and Sonu Shamdasani. New York and London: W. W. Norton & Company.

Sloterdijk, Peter. 1989. *Eurotaoismus. Zur Kritik der politischen Kinetik*. Frankfurt am Main: Suhrkamp Verlag.

Spitteler, Carl. 1906. *Imago*. Jena: Eugen Diederichs, 1922.

Vischer, Friedrich Theodor. 1878. *Auch Einer. Eine Reisebekanntschaft*. Leipzig: Heffe & Becker Verlag.

CHAPTER 4

Liber Novus in Nietzsche: Jung's Seminar on *Zarathustra*

The solitary went into the desert to find himself. But he did not want to find himself but rather the manifold meaning of holy scripture. You can suck the immensity of the small and the great into yourself and you will become emptier and emptier, since immense fullness and immense emptiness are one and the same. (RB II, 5, 'Dies II': 273)

4.1 Jung's Interpretation of *Zarathustra*

4.1.1 Introductory Remarks

As noted, Jung was asked to dedicate one of his *Psychologischer Club Zürich* seminars to *Zarathustra*. This took place in Zurich, on Wednesday mornings, from 2 May 1934 to 15 February 1939. Until spring 1936, three terms per year were held (spring, autumn, winter), each of them lasting two months (eight to ten sessions). In autumn and winter 1936, no session took place; in 1937, the seminar happened only during the spring term, then again in spring and autumn 1938, and finally in winter 1939. This was the last term, suddenly interrupted after the fifth session, and never continued, probably due to the beginning of the Second World War a few months later. For this reason, the last four chapters of the third part and the entire fourth book of *Zarathustra* were left aside. The seminar notes remained unpublished until 1989, when they were posthumously

G. Domenici, *Jung's Nietzsche*,
https://doi.org/10.1007/978-3-030-17670-9_4

edited by J. Jarrett in two volumes entitled *Nietzsche's Zarathustra. Notes of the Seminar Given in 1934–1939.* Jung never gave permission for his notes to be distributed until 1957. Between then and their publication, three short excerpts appeared: 'Answer by Dr. Jung to a Question Concerning the Archaic element in the Self. Zurich Seminar June 3, 1936'. In *Bulletin of the Analytical Psychology Club*, 30:5 [May]: 14–19; 'Comments on a Passage from Nietzsche's Zarathustra [1936]'. In *Spring* 1972: 149–161; 'Zurich: Analytical Psychology Club of New York. Excerpted from the seminar notes, Pt. 7, Lecture 2 [13 May 1936]: 18–29' (*Seminar Notes*, CW 19), as well as the already mentioned article by Peggy Nill. Interestingly, however, Peggy Nill's permission was restricted to consult but not quote from the unedited material, although the text would come out one year later (Bishop 1995a: 266–270; Nill 1988: 258, footnote 31). A complete list of the participants in the seminar appears briefly in the introduction to the seminar (Jarrett 1989, SNZ I: ix–xxi) and has also been reconstructed historically by Bishop (1994). The most relevant consequence of all this is that, as for *Liber Novus*, the material available was neither directly edited by Jung, nor meant to be published by him. Moreover, differently from *Liber Novus*, the 1544 pages which compose the text were not directly written by him, but collected from the notes written down by various participants in the seminar. However, the overall interpretation does not come across as different from Jung's understanding of *Zarathustra* at the time, appearing in his voluntarily published texts.

The apparent misreading emerging from this seminar has already been discussed in the introduction, along with the existing literature on the subject. The most relevant aspect of Jung's interpretation concerns his regarding *Zarathustra* as an example of Nietzsche's failed individuation. Such a failed individuation would be caused by both Nietzsche's being incapable of accepting the unconscious as something independent from his consciousness, and his being 'inflated' with the Old Wise Man archetype. As already discussed, not only might this interpretation sound a bit *ambitious* for a valid and complete comprehension of such a complex work as *Zarathustra*, but, at some specific points, it also appears completely outside the context of Nietzsche's philosophy, as some scholars have already observed (Nill 1988; Parkes 1999; Liebscher 2001, 2002, 2003, 2012). However, these peculiarities in Jung's reading can be justified, when compared with *Liber Novus*. Some elements of his *Zarathustra* seminar can be correctly re-contextualised within the framework of Jung's thinking development by keeping in mind some of the episodes narrated in *Liber Novus*. In particular, as pointed out at the end of last chapter, the last sections of *Liber Secundus* and *Scrutinies* can be read as Jung's response to Zarathustra through his dialogues with Philemon; several are the elements, indeed, which remind one of *Zarathustra*, both stylistically and in terms of contents. What can effectively endorse such a hypothesis, however, is the fact that those visions happened to Jung a few months before, during, and two years after having engaged with *Zarathustra* for the second time (November 1914). In 'The Magician' and in *Scrutinies*, all of the main accusations that Jung makes against Nietzsche in the 1930s are already present; this is going to be the starting point of this chapter. Beginning with Jung's apparent *misreading* in his seminar, parallels in the last chapters of *Liber Secundus* and in *Scrutinies* will be found first; then in other passages from *Liber Primus* and *Liber Secundus*, where similar elements occur in layer 2. Remarkably, another significant element in the development of Jung's interpretation of *Zarathustra* is given by alchemy, which contributed to enrich the evolving of many motifs present in *Liber Novus* and anticipating the seminar.

In the following sections, two different aspects characterising Jung's seminar interpretation will be investigated: *Zarathustra* as a representation of Nietzsche's failed individuation process and *Zarathustra* animals. Regarding the first point, Jung's opinion on Zarathustra as a representation of the Old Wise Man will be firstly considered, showing the problematic elements of Jung's thesis and confronting his interpretation of Zarathustra with his characterisation of Philemon. Then the most relevant points of Nietzsche's 'inflation' will be investigated by comparing them with Jung's 'intoxication'; a comparison between Nietzsche's *Übermensch* and Jung's *Übersinn* will be crucial in this respect. Lastly, Jung's opinion on Nietzsche's solitude will be brought out and, again, a comparison with fantasies and comments from *Liber Novus* will be furnished, where Jung expresses himself in similar manner. In this first part, Jung's understanding of concepts such as 'will to power', 'death of God', and 'eternal return' will also emerge. In the last part of this chapter, the focus will be on Jung's peculiar interpretation of *Zarathustra* animals, in relation to the same symbols occurring in *Liber Novus*. First, serpents will be considered again, this time in connection with other animals, namely birds, spiders, and scarabs. Second, the relation between frogs, toads, and swamp in Jung's reading of *Zarathustra* will be compared with Jung's corresponding understanding in *Liber Novus*. Lastly, Jung's opinion about Nietzsche's failed acknowledgement of the Anima in *Zarathustra* emerging through the doves symbol will be confronted with his idea of a feminine soul, represented in *Liber Novus* by the same symbol.

4.2 *Zarathustra* as Nietzsche's Failed Individuation

4.2.1 *The 'Old Wise Man': Zarathustra and Philemon*

In Jung's personal *Zarathustra* German copy, the phrase 'old man' is underlined in both sections 2 and 8 of *Prologue*, that is, referring to both the saint in the forest and the hermit in the woods. During the 1934–1939 seminar, these two characters will be analysed as manifestations of the 'old wise man' archetype indeed. More precisely, they both seem to represent, to Jung, the earlier Christian attitude, and are therefore defined as 'anchorite[s]' (SNZ I: 33–47, 9–16 May 1934 and 173–175, 17 October 1934, respectively). The strong presence of Zarathustrian echoes in Jung's account of his encounter with Ammonious in *Liber Novus* has been already discussed. What is still to be recalled, is that while referring to the first 'old man' from *Zarathustra*, *Prologue* in the seminar, Jung mentions 'Philo Judaeus, a Jew, also called Philo of Alexandria', in order to stress the impact of the 'Logos philosophy'—as well as of its connection with John's Gospel—on early Christianity (ibid.: 41). This immediately reminds one of the 'The Anchorite' episode in *Liber Novus* (RB II, 4: 268). The Old Wise Man [Alter Weiser] (sometimes translated as 'Wise Old Man') represents a manifestation of the wider archetype of the Spirit. In *The Phenomenology of the Spirit in Fairytales* (1948), Jung explains that, by 'spirit', he means 'the principle that stands in opposition to matter', that is, 'an immaterial substance or form of existence which on the highest and most universal level is called "God"' (CW 9, 1: § 385). According to his view, 'the psychic manifestations of the spirit indicate at once that they are of an archetypal nature—in other words, the phenomenon we call spirit depends on the existence of an autonomous primordial image which is universally present in the preconscious makeup of human psyche' (ibid.: § 396). This means it can manifest in dreams, as well as in fairytales or in myths. In all of these categories, in fact, 'the psyche tells its own story', and through an uninterrupted game of formation and transformation, the 'interplay of the archetypes is revealed in its natural settings'. The first personification of this archetype introduced by Jung is 'the old man' indeed. When the 'hero' finds himself in a 'hopeless and desperate situation from which only profound reflection or a lucky idea—in other words, a spiritual function or an endopsychic automatism of some kind—can extricate him', the 'old man' appears to help him, with the same frequency 'in fairytales as in dreams'. This figure usually forces the 'hero' 'to face the issue', thus saving him 'the trouble of making up his mind'. 'Indeed the old man is himself this purposeful reflection and concentration of moral and physical forces that comes about spontaneously in the psychic space outside consciousness when conscious thought is not yet—or is no longer—possible'; such a strength of 'psychic forces' brings behind elements that 'always look like magic'. The 'old man' does not reveal anything new to the 'hero'; nevertheless, by obliging him to reflect, he solves a situation of tension. In the traditional imagery, the 'old man' shows himself as a 'very critical old man', a magician, a dwarf. He 'represents knowledge, reflection, insight, wisdom, cleverness, and intuition on the one hand, and on the other, moral qualities such as goodwill and readiness to help, which make his "spiritual" character sufficiently plain'. In some primitive stories, this archetype appears as the sun; in a legend popular among North American Indians, the 'old man' is 'a witch-doctor who owns the fire'. The 'old man' being an archetype, he presents a downside as well, which occurs when the 'hero' has to face characters such as wicked magicians, elves, and so on. (ibid.: §§ 400–418). It might be of interest to notice that Jung puts the Pentecostal miracle, as well as 'the language of the Old Testament' on the same level of 'primitive fairytales' in which the spirit was associated with the fire (§ 409). Other representations of the 'spirit' can take place through theriomorphic figures, such as 'helpful animals', capable of speaking, acting like humans, and gifted with superior 'sagacity' and 'knowledge' (ibid.: § 421). In this particular case, Jung analyses the specific manifestation of the Spirit archetype through its personification as an 'old man'. As will be better argued below, the 'wise old man' referred to in Jung's seminar on *Zarathustra* does not differ at all from this later characterisation of the 'old man'.

According to Jung's *Zarathustra* interpretation, the 'spirit' would be the only unconscious phenomenon accessible to Nietzsche. His intuition and thinking functions, indeed, would prevent him from accepting any possible contact with feeling or sensation, without rejecting and projecting. His only way towards a possible individuation has thus to get through his preference for rationality, daylight, masculine, and spiritual aspects, before integrating their opposites. In the seminar, the 'Old Wise Man' par excellence is said to be Zarathustra, with whom Nietzsche appears to Jung as identified and, therefore, inflated. In the session held on 12 December 1934, Tadeus Reichstein gave a brief lecture on 'the archetype of the Old Wise Man'. The topic is carried out by focusing on two aspects, namely 'the function of the old man in human society' and 'the Gods or superhuman beings in whom this function is expressed, according to myth and tradition'. Regarding the first point, Reichstein highlights characteristics from the 'extraverted side' of the Old Wise Man archetype, as well as from his 'introverted side'. These do not really differ from Jung's later definition of the Old Man mentioned above. In fact, regarding his extraverted side, the Old Wise Man is characterised by 'experiences accumulated over a long period of time', which give him a certain steadiness towards situations of change. Socially, he tends to play the role of guardian, teacher, or 'regulators generally'. From the point of view of introversion, the Old Wise Man possesses 'the secret knowledge', and is in contact with 'the secret side of the world, the invisible'. Therefore, he is usually a sorcerer, a medicine man, a priest, and so on. Due to this close link with the other side of the world, he is also viewed as the 'embodiment of the supernatural or the deputy of a God or Demon'. Usually, the introverted and the extraverted sides of this archetype are both to be found in a single individual, who is given 'the necessary mana (like an electric charge), by a special ordination and is thus set apart from ordinary people'. On the second point brought out by Reichstein, namely 'The old wise man in Religion and Myth', a historical excursus is exposed, which starts from primitives, and goes all the way through Egypt, Iran, Poimandres, and alchemy. Reichstein points out that among the primitives, the main role played by the Old Wise Man was related to his 'mana'; therefore his strongest attribution was his magical power, usually with immediate effect. Moreover, this archetype was normally represented 'in personal form', material but invisible. In ancient Egypt, Thoth, the main expression of the Old Wise Man at that time, was considered a 'doctor among the Gods'; he was in charge of keeping equilibrium between the opposites, as well as of judging. Later on, this figure seemed to be identified with Hermes Trismegistos, closely entwined with the Iranian development of the same archetype. In fact, according to Reichstein, in Persia the Old Wise Man was incarnated by 'God Ormuzd (Primal Man, Anthropos)', who 'at least from the fragments of the syncretistic era is identified with the "psyche"', meant as 'essence', or 'self'. From there to Christianity, he represented the chance that the 'World of Light' defeated the darkness. Ormuzd needs to 'return home', that is 'the soul or the self of man' has to reach back the 'World of Light'. Ormuzd is sometimes represented as a 'divine messenger' who leads the souls; therefore this myth is often applied in the form of 'Cult of the Dead' and linked to the experience of resurrection. Analogies are also found in Indian and Chinese Myths, regarded by Reichstein as possible sources. About Poimandres, Reichstein notices that the major attribution of the 'Old Wise Man' was to be 'shepherd of men'. Again in this Gnostic sect, which is said to have had 'a great influence on Early Christianity', the stress is on the separation between two worlds and their consequent necessity to be reunited. The 'process of transformation consists in having to repeat the work of creation of the world', where a correspondence between 'the micro- and the macro-cosmos' must be achieved. Again, a 'primal man' is postulated by Poimandres's conception, and this time this is very much related with the 'Logos', that 'consists of light' and 'is the son of god. Know what sees in thee and hears in thee is the Lord's Word'. According to a myth on world creation, Reichstein reports that 'Male-female primal god created the demiurgos and he created the seven planets, the visible world and fate. Out of the lower elements rose the Logos and united with the demiurgos his brother, so the lower elements are abandoned by the Logos and are purely material. Out of them came the dumb animals'. Therefore, 'nature and primal man were longing for each other in love and primal man took his home in the unintelligent form, in the body'. For this reason men are said to have a 'double nature': mortal in their body; immortal in their essence, and, also in this case, their purpose is to let their immortal essence reconnect to its own world. In order to investigate the evolving of the Old Wise Man archetype in alchemy, Reichstein cites from two books from the seventeenth century. An 'old man' actually appears in a vision narrated by Franz Kieser in the first of the two books, *Cabala Chymica* (Mühlhausen, 1606), where a pupil sees this figure 'with a long, snow-white beard, in a black robe, with a compass and square'. He 'draws the lines and calls a magic number spell with a horrible voice. On the top of the quadrangle appears a dove. This he calls the spirit of conjunction and vivification'. Then a star symbol appears, representing the 'philosopher's stone which illuminates everything', and the 'old man' prays to God that 'for once evil is put down and the truth revealed', thus putting an end to the darkness. The 'eternal rotation' of the world stops, or a new world, immune to it, is created. In the other story, instead, the Old Wise Man appears as a 'divine messenger' (Johannes Valentinus Andreä 1602/1616). As a remark at the end of Reichstein's exposition, Jung describes this archetype as 'the medicine man simply, who is called when something is wrong', arises in a period of great difficulty and helps solve the situation (SNZ I: 300–313).

Martin Liebscher has exhaustively discussed the elements brought out by Reichstein in relation to the character of Zarathustra. First, he notices that Zarathustra has slowly accumulated wisdom; in this sense he carries knowledge behind, as in the primitives' representation of the Old Wise Man as a 'medicine man'. Differently from this figure, however, Zarathustra reckons that his disciples are not ready for his wisdom yet, despite his strong will to share his knowledge with them. Second, Zarathustra rejects the possibility of being considered a 'medicine man' [Artz] in the traditional sense. He does not offer cure or healing, but he is more like a 'prophet', a visionary man. The main difference with the Egyptian Thoth, as well as with Hermes Trismegistos—Liebscher points out—is that 'Zarathustra cannot keep his knowledge on future happenings for himself', but constantly feels the need of sharing it as a gift. Differently from Iranian mythology, then, it is observed that Zarathustra is no leader; since his recurrent failures with the crowd from the marketplace reveal his inability to be taken seriously and to be followed. Furthermore, Zarathustra speaks against writing and expresses his teaching through speeches exclusively. In comparison with Poimandres, Zarathustra explicitly claims that he does not intend to be a shepherd to men and the frequent biblical parodies make clear his position against such a concept. Lastly, in relation to alchemy, Liebscher explains that the strength of Zarathustra's teaching lies in his eternally repeating failure, which prevents him from being considered a 'teacher' who suddenly appears and proposes the solution for a complex situation, as recurrently narrated in alchemical texts. Nevertheless, Zarathustra is a teacher and his 'doctrine' on the eternal return can be read—as Jung does—in terms of solution against the emptiness of nihilism (Liebscher 2002, 2012: 68–83). In addition to this, and considering Jung's definition of the 'old man' published in 1948, it can be stated that Zarathustra does not possess 'moral qualities', meant in a positive or negative sense—his goal being to overcome morals itself.

The amount of problems with the interpretation of Zarathustra as the Old Wise Man is high enough to wonder whether Jung's idea could not be better contextualised by confronting it with figures from *Liber Novus*, that will later contribute to delineate this archetype features, in particular Philemon. First of all, it must be noted, according to what reported in *Memories, Dreams, Reflexions*, Philemon is described as 'a pagan and brought with him an Egypto-Hellenistic atmosphere with a Gnostic coloration'. He appeared for the first time in a dream about a kingfisher which Jung could not interpret, so he decided to paint its main character. To Jung, Philemon 'represented a force which was not' himself; in his 'fantasies [Jung] held conversations with him, and he said things which [Jung] had not consciously thought'. He 'represented superior insight', a 'guru' (MDR: 182–184). According to this description, Philemon would be also developed out of the character of Elijah. Furthermore, Jung's narration adds another interesting element:

> Later, Philemon became relativized by the emergence of yet another figure, whom I called Ka. In ancient Egypt the "king's ka" was his earthly form, the embodied soul. In my fantasy the ka-soul came from below, out of the earth as if out of a deep shaft. I did a painting of him, showing him in his earth-bound form, as a herm with base of stone and upper part of bronze. High up in the painting appears a kingfisher's wing, and between it and the head of Ka floats a round, glowing nebula of stars. Ka's expression has something demonic about it one might also say, Mephistophelian. In one hand he holds something like a colored pagoda, or a reliquary, and in the other a stylus with which he is working on the reliquary. He is saying, "I am he who buries the gods in gold and gems". Philemon had a lame foot, but was a winged spirit, whereas Ka represented a kind of earth demon or metal demon. Philemon was the spiritual aspect, or "meaning". Ka, on the other hand, was a spirit of nature like the Anthroparion of Greek alchemy with which at the time I was still unfamiliar. Ka was he who made everything real, but who also obscured the halcyon spirit, Meaning, or replaced it by beauty, the "eternal reflection". In time I was able to integrate both figures through the study of alchemy. (ibid.)

Still in *Memories, Dreams Reflexions*, it is written:

> At Bollingen I am in the midst of my true life, I am most deeply myself. Here I am, as it were, the "age-old son of the mother." That is how alchemy puts it, very wisely, for the "*old man*," the "ancient," whom I had already experienced as a child, is personality No. 2, who has always been and always will be. He exists outside time and is the son of the maternal un-conscious.

In my fantasies he took the form of Philemon, and he comes to life again at Bollingen. (ibid.: 225, italic added)[1]

The dialogue between Jung's 'I' and Philemon in the later part of *Liber Secundus* evokes several elements recalling Zarathustra and his role as a teacher. As already noted, Philemon and Zarathustra are depicted with similar features and, in Jung's description of his final meeting with Philemon, are elements which remind one of Nietzsche's text. Besides, a few characteristics belonging to Philemon will be attributed to Zarathustra in the 1930s. At the beginning of his seminar, Jung interprets Zarathustra as a 'Saoshyant', namely 'a mediator between god and man', 'a reaper, a saviour', that appears 'every thousand years—[...] about half of a month of the great platonic year', and 'teaches people a new revelation, a new truth, or renews old truths'. This is a 'Zoroastrian teaching', indeed, and, according to Jung, it would have evolved through Christianity, turning into the *enantiodromia* of an alternation of positive and 'negative Saoshyant[s]'. He then finds coherency with historical facts: the coming of Christ (after Zoroaster), and that of the Antichrist, that is to say of the widespread angst about the end of the world (happening around the year 1000); after that, finally, the Church took his power back again, until the final schism of Protestantism. Despite the historical inaccuracy of such happenings if compared with their expected dates, Jung seems to firmly believe in the possibility that Nietzsche's need for destroying old values could be read in the sense that 'he feels himself [...] as a positive Saoshyant, in spite of the fact that he accepts the title of "immoralist" and "Antichrist"'. Due to the archetypical essence of Zarathustra, 'a feeling of remote times, as if time were at a complete standstill' would characterise Nietzsche's meeting with him, and complete his sense of having a timeless task to take on (SNZ I: 12–13, 2 May 1934. As Jung shows exhaustively, the same idea of a saviour is present in India and Japan too). With these words, Jung retrospectively comments on his encounter with Philemon, at the end of *Liber Secundus*:

When the month of the Twins had ended, the men said to their shadows: "You are I", since they had previously had their spirit around them as a second person. Thus the two became one, and through this collision the formidable broke out, precisely that spring of consciousness that one calls culture and which lasted until the time of Christ. But the fish indicated the moment when what was united split, according to the eternal law of contrasts, into

> an underworld and upperworld. If the power of growth begins to cease, then the united falls into its opposites. Christ sent what is beneath to Hell, since it strives toward the good. That had to be. But the separated cannot remain separated forever. It will be united again and the month of the fish will soon be over. We suspect and understand that growth needs both, and hence we keep good and evil close together. Because we know that too far into the good means the same as too far into evil, we keep them both together. (RB II, 21, 'The Magician': 314)

Still in his first seminar sessions, Jung utilises this phrase to describe Nietzsche's experience as an archetypal one: 'Zarathustra [...] became manifest as a second personality in himself'. Because of the lack of convincing psychological theories on a non-materialistic nature of the unconscious at his time, Nietzsche's only choice to accept that event, was identifying with the Old Wise Man archetype, that is, Zarathustra. By experiencing the unconscious and its independence, Nietzsche would go through 'a peculiar sense of destiny', or better 'the Dionysian experience *par excellence*' (SNZ I: 10). Back to *Liber Novus*, Jung's 'I' addresses Philemon this way:

> You are legendary and unreachable. You were and will be, returning periodically: Your wisdom is invisible, your truth is unknowable, entirely untrue in any given age, and yet true in all eternity; but you pour out living water, from which the flowers of your garden bloom, a starry water, a dew of the night. (RB II, 21: 316)

Similarities between this *Liber Novus* chapter and *Zarathustra* chapter 'Of the Bestowing Virtue' have been previously investigated, particularly referring to Zarathustra and Philemon as teachers. If these two characters share some features, there are also differences to be noticed. When analysing these in the light of Jung's later *Zarathustra* interpretation, it is remarkable that the same way of regarding Zarathustra's wisdom can be already found in his dialogue with Philemon. In fact, Philemon cries out: 'Giving is as childish as power. He who gives presumes himself powerful. The virtue of giving is the sky-blue mantle of the tyrant', therefore he is said to be 'wise', for he does not give. He wants his 'garden to bloom, and for everything to grow from itself'. Philemon is said to be 'no shepherd who runs after stray sheep, since [he] believe[s] in the dignity of man, who is not necessarily a sheep. But if he happens to be a sheep, [Philemon] would leave him the rights and dignity of sheep' (ibid.). Giving is one of the leitmotifs in *Zarathustra*, as well as the core of Zarathustra's 'virtue', which is also his ‘wisdom’ and, as has been previously pointed out, is meant as an unconventional one. In a few seminar comments, Jung criticises Nietzsche’s attitude in terms of power and ‘feeling of inferiority’. On 4 May 1938, by analysing the chapter ‘Of Self-Overcoming’ (‘Self-Surpassing’ in Jung’s translation), Jung argues that Nietzsche ‘produced the psychological power theory first, anticipating, thus, Adlerian psychology, the so-called individual psychology, though it is not individual at all, but is very collective, as one sees from the way Nietzsche states the case’. He then declares: ‘People with a power attitude are always inclined to *accuse*, either to accuse in themselves a gesture of power, or anything suggesting such an attitude in anybody else. You see, that so-called power attitude is always expressed on the other side by feelings of inferiority; otherwise power makes no sense’ (SNZ II: 1211). Nietzsche represents to Jung such a case, as made clear by the description of his personality:

> Now when Nietzsche sees the power aspect of things [...] he is quite right inasmuch as there is a misuse of power. But if he sees it everywhere, at the core of everything, it has crept in as the secret of life even, if he sees it as the will to be and to create, then he makes a great mistake. Then he is blindfolded by his own complex, for he is the man who, on the one side, has feelings of inferiority, and on the other, a tremendous power complex. What was the man Nietzsche in reality? A neurotic, a poor devil who suffered from migraine and a bad digestion, and had such bad eyes that he could read very little and was forced to give up his academic career. And he couldn’t marry because an early syphilitic infection blighted his whole Eros side. Of course, all that contributed to the most beautiful inferiority complex you can imagine; such a fellow is made for an inferiority complex, and will therefore build up an immense power attitude on the other side. [...] If you know your one passion is power and assume that other people have such a passion too, you are not far from the mark. But there are people who *have* power, who have good eyes and no migraine and can swing things, and to accuse people of “power” is perfectly ridiculous, for they create something, they are positive. Then the devil gets them naturally by another corner and that is what the power psychologist does not see.
>
> Now of course, Nietzsche is very much on the side on the inferiority, where the only passion, the only ambition, is: how can I get to the top? (ibid.: 1213–1214)

On 19 October 1938, while commenting on *Zarathustra* chapter ‘The Bedwarfing Virtue’, Jung associates Nietzsche’s ‘feelings of inferiority’ to a ‘psychology [...] born out of [...] resentment’ against the others. He warns his participants: ‘Nietzsche is the author of the *Will-to-Power*, don’t forget' (ibid.: 1353–1354). If, in the above case, Nietzsche's 'psychology of power' was associated with Adler's, now his 'resentment' against society is linked to Freud: 'Nietzsche, not being a doctor, did the social part of the critique as it were; and Freud, being a doctor, saw behind the screen and showed the intricacies of the individual' (ibid.: 1354). Previously, Jung had stated: 'If you go on through the text ['The Thousand and one Goals'] or if you read his *Genealogy of Morals*, it is perfectly plain that he derives morality entirely from the instinct of power, no matter whether the instinct is love or not' (SNZ I: 672, 6 November 1935). Although Adler openly refers to Nietzsche while introducing his concept of 'will to power' [Wille zur Macht] for the very first time, in 1912, his understanding of the phrase appears far from Nietzsche's original conception. Similarly to Jung, Adler understands Nietzsche's personality in terms of inferiority feeling, and the concept of 'power' [Macht] is considered a form of 'compensation' [Kompensation] or 'overcompensation' [Überkompensation] for such an inferiority feeling (Adler 1912: 19).[2] About 20 years later, still dealing with the question of 'overcompensation' but in relation to society, he will take Nietzsche's *Übermensch* as an example for an unnatural attempt to compensate for his inferiority feeling: such an 'elitist' superhuman being would represent the opposite of human natural strivings, normally orientated towards 'community feelings' (Adler 1933–1937: 22). Elsewhere Adler relates 'personal superiority' to neurosis and sadism (Adler 1933: 84). Returning to Jung, the same way of understanding Nietzsche's idea of 'will to power' was already present at the time of *Liber Novus*. In *On the Psychology of the Unconscious* (1917–1943), after having depicted Nietzsche as someone who 'with a rare passion [...] sacrificed himself, his whole life, to the idea of the Superman—to the idea of the man who through obedience to instincts transcends himself', Jung calls Nietzsche's personality a 'pathological' one, and writes: 'It is of this last instinct, the will to power, that Nietzsche obviously speaks. Whatever else is instinctual only follows, for him, in the train of the will to power' (CW 7: §§ 36–38). The aim of Jung's criticism is Adler's individual psychology. Already in the *Preface to the First Edition (1917)*, written in 1916, referring to the changes that had been made since the first publication of the essay in 1912, Jung made clear that 'Adler's psychology was taken into account', whereas 'a number of passages on Freud were shortened' (ibid.: 3–4).

Associating Nietzsche with the concept of 'will to power' was a common attitude in those years. Although Nietzsche gave up the publication of a work called 'The Will to Power' (started in 1885), and preferred to publish smaller volumes separately in 1888 (*The Case of Wagner*, *The Twilight of the Idols* [*Die Götzen Dämmerung*], *Ecce Homo* [*Ecce Homo*], *The Anti-Christ* [*Der Antichrist*], *Dithyrambs of Dionysus* [*Dionysos-Dithyramben*], *Nietzsche Contra Wagner* [*Nietzsche contra Wagner*]; this last two came out in 1889), his sister decided to involve his collaborator Heinrich Köselitz (Peter Gast) and carry on her late brother's project. The main reason why Nietzsche gave up his idea, was the inadequacy of a single, ambitious volume in order to contrast and 'transvalue' the notion of systematisation present in any metaphysical conception; rather, he would attack his philosophical 'archenemies' from various different angles, or, to put it as Nietzsche, 'perspectives'. Nietzsche's understandings of 'power' and 'will to power', in fact, are to be read in terms of interpretation: 'What urges you on, and arouses your ardor, you wisest of men, do you call it "will to truth"? Will to conceivability of all being: That is what I call your will. [...] That is your entire will, you wisest men; it is a will to power, and that is so even when you talk of good and evil and of the assessment of values' (Za II, 'Of Self-Overcoming', KSA 4: 146). Will to power means nothing outside life itself, that is, no individualism or social implications are meant in Nietzsche's conception, for such concepts are created by life in its evaluation process and are given only as a result: 'Where I found a living creature, there I found will to power; and even in the will of the servant I found the will to be master. [...] The living creatures value many things higher than life itself; yet out of this evaluation itself speaks—the will to power' (ibid., KSA 4: 147–149). In *Beyond Good and Evil* (1886), the same meaning is expressed through the famous sentence, at the end of the aphorism 22, with which Nietzsche anticipates a response to possible criticisms to his notion of will to power: 'Supposing that this also is only an interpretation—and you will be eager enough to raise that objection?—well, so much the better' [Gesetzt, dass auch dies nur Interpretation ist—und ihr werdet eifrig genug sein, dies einzuwenden?—nun, um so besser] (JGB I, 22, KSA 5: 37). As long as everything is subject to interpretation, in fact, the same concept of interpretation stops making sense, when thought in terms of 'truth'.

Nevertheless, due to her intense commitment to nationalism, as well as to antisemitism, Elisabeth Förster-Nietzsche struggled to insert her brother's name in the same tradition of systematic German philosophers'. Not only did she edit *The Will to Power* in a completely arbitrary order—that is, by conforming to only one of the plans drawn by her brother—but in 1894 (when the philosopher was still alive, even if insane) she had already decided to publish all of Nietzsche's works in a unique collection of 19 volumes (plus an index added later on, in 1926). Until 1913, Elisabeth, Peter Gast, and the editor Naumann from Leipzig edited the so-called *Großoktavausgabe*; the project then switched to the editor Kröner. Several editions of *The Will to Power* were printed until 1930, when the contract with Kröner expired, as well as Elisabeth's property rights to her brother's material, as 30 years had passed since his death and she had not been able to prolong the legal expiry. At that time, the posthumous material kept in the so-called Nietzsche-Archiv in Weimar—of course created by Elisabeth herself—was available for consultation and citation. The first questions on *Nachlaß* arose, even though nobody seemed to really question the reliability of *The Will to Power*. For instance, in 1931, Alfred Bäumler claimed that *The Will to Power* edited in 1906 was the only reliable source of investigation on Nietzsche (Bäumler 1931b: 7–15). However, in the same year, he himself edited a collection of excerpts from *Nachlaß* with the same Kröner Verlag (*Die Unschuld des Werdens*). Similarly, Martin Heidegger made use of Elisabeth's relation to her brother and, above all of Gast's (disputable) 'friendship' with him, as well as of his ability to decipher Nietzsche's handwriting, in order to explain the reliability of their work (Heidegger 1961, I: 328–329). In order to show how strong a metaphysical reading of Nietzsche's philosophy was, Karl Jasper's interpretation might be shortly recalled too. Although he openly recognised the impossibility of systematising Nietzsche's thinking, he made use of such an impossibility to draw a system out of it. Precisely in the apparent unintelligibility of his aphorisms, Nietzsche's 'philosophy of life' would express itself to the best (Jasper 1981). At the end of the 1950s, the idea of a critical edition came eventually about, thanks to two Italian scholars, Giorgio Colli and Mazzino Montinari, although scholars such as Karl Schlechta had previously questioned Elisabeth Förster-Nietzsche's criteria, especially in relation to her significant forgeries. As already written, Jung had a short correspondence with Elisabeth while writing his dissertation and the same edition *Kleinoktavausgabe* of Nietzsche's *Gesammelte Werke* possessed by him followed her original project, the *Großoktavausgabe*; it was only a smaller version.[3] No wonder the general opinion on Nietzsche at that time was strongly influenced by *The Will to Power* misconception, and Jung's opinion on the matter seems to be no exception.

Philemon's attributions of wisdom might sound as criticisms to Zarathustra's virtue, meant as an expression of Nietzsche's 'feeling of inferiority'. In Jung's own copy, both chapters 'Of Self-Overcoming' and

'The Bedwarfing Virtue' display several underlinings. In particular, in 'Of Self-Overcoming', along the text 'You first want to *make* all being conceivable: for, with a healthy mistrust, you doubt whether it is in fact conceivable', Jung wrote 'introv'. The 'i' not being capitalised suggests that Jung intended to refer to Nietzsche as an introverted type; this annotation is thus likely to belong to a different period than *Liber Novus*. At that time, Jung's reading was not indeed oriented towards a psychological analysis of Nietzsche's personality, as it would be in a later period. It is difficult to say whether it was written in preparation for the *Zarathustra* seminar though, as that paragraph is omitted by Jung in his analysis. Right at the beginning of 'The Bedwarfing Virtue' in Jung's exemplar of Nietzsche's *Zarathustra*, instead, another inscription reads: 'man reduction' [Verkleinerung des Menschen]—which is the main theme of the chapter, in fact. Underneath the phrase there is a cross-reference, in red, to p. 303, namely to the chapter 'The Shadow'. Here the reference is very probably directed to his seminar, where he faces the issue in terms of 'inflation'. Although Jung did not have time to comment on the last part of *Zarathustra* in his seminar, he often mentioned sections from it, in order to make clear his interpretation of previous chapters. In most cases, with such examples Jung intends to address Nietzsche's rejection of inferiority, expressed by Jung as the Shadow, indeed.

In Autumn 1915, Philemon reappears to Jung. The closeness of such an apparition to 'Of the Bestowing Virtue' has been already highlighted; what is still to be pointed out, is that all of Philemon speeches, here, are directed towards Jung's 'I'. This seems somehow to anticipate Jung's concept of inflation, as will be better argued in the next section. Lastly, to show how closely entwined Philemon and Zarathustra might be thought of, it can be recalled that on the night of 21 February 1916, Philemon appears again 'wearing a long coat and a turban', thus evoking the historical features of Zoroaster (RB *Scrutinies*, § 13: 355). In the *Black Books*, the character is described by Jung as a 'Turk' who intends to speak 'of polygamy, houris, and paradise'.

4.2.2 *Intoxication, Inflation, the* Übermensch *and the* Übersinn

It has already been said that *Scrutinies* can be considered as a dialogue between Jung and Zarathustra, supported by Philemon. All of the most significant similarities between this section and *Zarathustra* have been already pointed out. However, a few relevant remarks can be made, concerning Nietzsche's presumed 'inflation'. Jung argues, in his seminar on *Zarathustra*:

> Yes, he is identical with the archetype. Of course he makes a difference between himself and Zarathustra [...] but he cannot help feeling gripped by that figure and he even *is* Zarathustra at times, and that is an inflation. [...] Nietzsche cannot help being partly identical with Zarathustra, because that was the time of the culmination of materialistic science and philosophy and nobody had a hint of psychology, nobody had thought of the possibility of making a difference between oneself and something psychical. (SNZ I: 27).

For this reason, the language is also said to be 'terribly pregnant'; since it compensates 'human being feelings of inferiority which are not admitted' by an inflated individual. In the same circumstance, Zarathustra is depicted in terms of 'mana' personality, too (ibid.: 27–29). In the second part of *The Relations Between the Ego and the Unconscious* (1928–1935/1938), Jung describes the 'mana personality' as 'on one side a being of superior wisdom, on the other a being of superior will'. He adds:

> Meister Eckhardt, Goethe in his *Faust*, Nietzsche in his *Zarathustra* have again brought this problem somewhat closer to us. Goethe and Nietzsche try to solve it by the idea of mastery, the former through the figure of the magician and ruthless man of will who makes a pact with the devil, the latter through the masterman and supreme sage who knows neither God nor devil. With Nietzsche man stands alone, as he himself did, neurotic, financially dependent, godless and worldless. This is no ideal for a real man who has a family to support and taxes to pay. Nothing can argue the reality of the world out of existence, there is no miraculous way round it. Similarly, nothing can argue the effects of the unconscious out of existence. Or can the neurotic philosopher prove to us that he has no neurosis? He cannot prove it even to himself. (CW 7: §§ 396–397)

The essay, slowly developed by Jung, was first published in French in 1916, under the title 'La structure de l'inconscient', then in English, under the title 'The Conception of the Unconscious' (1917/1920). The references to *Zarathustra* and *Faust* concerning the role of the magician were already present in these first editions, but the comment on Nietzsche's personality misses. The 'mana personality' appears when an 'autonomous complex' is not recognised as such, therefore it keeps one's I under its spell. This is particularly the case with the Anima/Animus, whose fascination is initially too strong to figure out the difference between oneself and the archetypal power. When the Anima 'can no longer exercise the power of possession, since it is depotentiated', her function is assimilated and integrated in one's own personality. At this point, 'no longer is the soul to be called "Mistress", but a psychological function of an intuitive nature' (ibid.: § 374). Similarly, 'In differentiating the ego from the archetype of the mana-personality one is now forced [...] to make conscious those contents which are specific of the mana-personality. Historically, the mana-personality is always in possession of the secret name, or of the esoteric knowledge, or has the prerogative of a special way of acting—*quod licet Jovi, non licet bovi*—in a word, it has individual distinction' (ibid.: § 393. Jung remarkably describes the role of this archetype in terms of 'initiation', too: § 384). At the very end of *Zarathustra*, II, Nietzsche calls his 'stillest hour' his 'terrible mistress [furchtbare() Herrin]' (Za II, 22, 'The Stillest Hour', KSA 4: 187). In his seminar, Jung interprets the passage as a dialogue between Nietzsche and his Anima, and comments on the sentence 'Thou knowest it, Zarathustra' by affirming: 'This allusion to a secret knowledge in him is most uncanny'. Indeed, according to Jung, Nietzsche's Anima is trying to make him aware of his own psychological situation, and to let him react—'The Anima speaks absolutely to the point, as if she were a first-rate psychotherapist'—but Nietzsche's inflation is far too deep, so is his Anima rejection (SNZ II: 1244–1246, 11 May 1938). Remarkably, in *Symbols of Transoformation*, Jung writes: 'The vengeful Hera would then appear as the stern "Mistress Soul", who imposes the most difficult labours on her hero and threatens him with destruction unless he plucks up courage for the supreme deed and actually becomes what he always potentially was' (CW 5: § 459). Although Jung's exemplar of Nietzsche's *Zarathustra* does not show marginalia relating to 'The Stillest Hour', the chapter presents markings and underlinings throughout.

Nietzsche, according to Jung, is therefore under the spell of Zarathustra; what this means, is that this is the only unconscious part he is able to recognise and accept. In terms of his philosophy, Jung associates such a psychological attitude with the assumption of the 'death of God'. In one of the first seminar sessions, Jung raises the question: 'What happens when he declares that God is dead?' (SNZ I: 50, 16 May 1934). What happens, in fact, is that one becomes God oneself: 'So when Nietzsche declares that God is dead, instantly he begins to transform. [...] He immediately gets into the process of that archetype of rebirth, because those vital powers in us which we call "God" are powers of self-renewal, powers of eternal change'. As a consequence, one comes to possess the most powerful creative skills, as well as the responsibility for all good and evil in the world. Indeed, even Goethe might have experienced a similar situation in *Faust* (ibid.: 54). By contrast, 'If a person is conscious of it [that "God had worked in the worth hitherto"], his responsibility can heighten to such an extent that he will have a hellish inflation of consciousness'. However, he continues, 'also if he does not realize it, if he does not know what he has done by saying that God is dead, he can have an inflation of his whole personality. Then his unconscious will get inflated; he will be hampered by the continuous presence of God in the unconscious, which is of course the most terrible thing. Things happen to him, and he thinks he is responsible' (ibid.: 51). In another session, Jung points out the difference between an identification caused by inflation, and the conscious undertaking of a Christian attitude:

> If a man says he is Jesus Christ you tell him he is a fool and belongs in a clinic. But if a man says he throws his whole load on Christ to take care of, it is considered marvellous; he preaches it and confesses it and nobody has any doubt its being right. [...] *To identify with a suffering God is no small business.* Something is going to happen to you. You cannot have all the advantages of an inflation and no disadvantages. That the god has all the human disadvantages, and you all the advantages of a god, is not possible, and it will cost very dearly in the end. (ibid.: 758, 11 December 1935, italics added)

A few sessions later, it is the same contradiction implicit in the inflation to be brought out: 'As soon as you identify with God you needs must transcend him because God is a stream; and you are not the air or the rushing waters, but are just a definite form called human, so you can only personify God in yourself' (SNZ II: 860, 26 February 1936). On another occasion, as a consequence derived from this contradiction, Zarathustra's being '*numinosum*' is highlighted by Jung:

> when a definite image has been reduced to apparent nothingness, it is just as if the *pneuma*, what we call "spirit", were also reduced to its primeval form which is just air. You see, when you have the experience of the deity, the *numinosum*, and you have an image of it, you can say this is experience of the spirit, but when you reduce it and deny its existence, you are simply filled with air. (ibid.: 1039, 5 May 1937)

At the very beginning of *Scrutinies*, Jung talks to his 'I' and accuses him to be 'craving for power'. He adds: 'You call on God for help? The dear old God has died' (RB, *Scrutinies*, § 1: 333). Still in *Scrutinies*, on 18 September 1915, when reflecting on Philemon's discussion on virtue, Jung affirms:

> We must presumably often go to ourselves to re-establish the connection with the self since it is torn apart all too often, not only by our vices but also by our virtues. For vices as well as virtues always want to live outside. But through constant outer life we forget the self and through this we also become secretly selfish in our best endeavors. What we neglect in ourselves blends itself secretly into our actions toward others. (ibid.., § 3: 337–338)

The assonance with *Zarathustra* implied by the relation vices-virtues, as well as by the necessity of finding balance within oneself, has been previously discussed. However, the following section of Jung's comment deserves attention, as he reflects on his conversation with Philemon with these words:

> But I must say that the God makes us sick. I experience the God in sickness. A living God afflicts our reason like a sickness. He fills the soul with intoxication. He fills us with reeling chaos. How many will the God break?
>
> The God appears to us in a certain state of the soul. Therefore we reach the God through the self. Not the self is God, although we reach the God through the self. The God is behind the self, above the self, the self itself, when he appears. But he appears as our sickness, from which we must heal ourselves. We must heal ourselves from the God, since he is also our heaviest wound. (ibid.: 338)

This passage appears significantly close to a few lines from two chapters from *Zarathustra*. The first one is 'Of the Despiser of the Body', particularly concerning the section: 'The Self also seeks with the eyes of sense, it listens too with the ears of the spirit. The Self is always listening and seeking: it compares, subdues, conquers, destroys. It rules and is also the I's ruler. Behind your thoughts and feelings, my brother, stands a mighty commander, an unknown sage—he is called Self' (Za I, 4, KSA 4: 39–40). The second chapter is 'Of Love of One's Neighbour', more precisely when Zarathustra says: 'You crowd together with your neighbours and have beautiful words for it. But I tell you: Your love of your neighbour is your bad love of yourself. You flee away from yourselves and would like to make a virtue of it: but I see through your "selflessness"' (Za I, 16, KSA 4: 77). Both passages display underlinings and markings in Jung's personal copy. Jung's understanding of self-redemption and love for oneself seems to have a similar meaning in *Zarathustra*. However, a few lines above the excerpt from *Liber Novus* just cited, Jung makes clear that 'we benefit in particular from removing every sense of beauty from the thought of redemption'. With such an assumption, he clearly distances himself from any aesthetic justification and moves towards a moral dimension. According to him, in the union with the self, God is experienced, whatever the nature of such experience.

On the one hand, it is required not to confuse 'the God' with 'the self', on the other hand, God is put in connection with sickness and wounds. Another aspect is also anticipated, which will be predominant in the seminar on *Zarathustra*, namely the relation between the 'death of God' and what Jung will later call 'inflation'. Since in *Liber Novus* the 'self' can be regarded as a sort of symbol of the 'God', killing the 'God' implies to suppress the independence of the 'self', and to constrain it within the I. 'It is certainly possible and even quite easy for our reason to deny the God and to speak only of sickness. Thus we accept the sick part and can also heal it. But it will be a healing with loss. We lose a part of life. We go on living, but as ones lamed by the God'. In fact: 'I must free my self from the God, since the God I experienced is more than love; he is also hate, he is more than beauty, he is also the abomination, he is more than wisdom, he is also meaninglessness, he is more than power, he is also powerlessness, he is more than omnipresence, he is also my creature ' (ibid.: 339). This seems to be the case with Nietzsche, who frequently speaks of sickness—particularly in relation to the decadence—and struggles to deal with a godless world (WA 5, KSA 6: 21; AC 52, KSA 6: 232; NF 14[13], KSA 13: 223–224 [Spring 1888]; NF 15[110], KSA 13: 470 [Spring 1888]). In particular, in *The Anti-Christ*, the link between Christianity (especially Catholicism), decadence, and sickness (meant in terms of mental disorder, even) is expressed quite strongly:

> The fact that, under certain circumstances, faith can make blessed, that this blessedness originated by a fix idea makes the idea itself *true*, that faith does not move mountains, but rather *sets mountains down* where there are not any: a quick walk through a *lunatic asylum* makes all this sufficiently clear. *Not* to a priest, of course: for he will instinctively deny that sickness is sickness and lunatic asylums is lunatic asylums. To Christianity, sickness is *neces-*

> *sary*, more or less like to the Greek spirit a superabundance of health was necessary—*making* people ill is the actual ulterior purpose of the whole system of salvation of the Church. And the Church itself—doesn't it have the Catholic lunatic asylum as its ultimate ideal?—The whole earth as a madhouse?—The sort of religious man that the church *wants* is a typical *décadent*; the moment at which a religious crisis takes control over people is always marked by epidemics of nervous disorder; the "inner world" of the religious man looks so much like the "inner world" of over-excited and exhausted ones, that it is easy to confuse them; the "highest" conditions, which Christianity held up before mankind as the supreme value, are epileptoid in form. (AC 51, KSA 6, 230–232, translation modified)

In Jung's own *Anti-Christ* volume (*Kleinoktav-Gesamtausgabe*, available at Jung's personal library in Küsnacht), the following phrases are underlined: 'lunatic asylum' [Irrenhaus], 'To Christianity, sickness is *necessary*' [Das Christenthum hat die Krankheit nöthig], 'the Catholic lunatic asylum as its ultimate ideal?—The whole earth as a madhouse?' [das katholische Irrenhaus als letzetes Ideal?—Die Erde überhaupt als Irrenhaus?]. Even more significant, however, is another section from the same chapter, which captivated Jung's attention even more, as demonstrated by his markings and annotations along the text:

> Nobody is free to become Christian: one is not "converted" to Christianity—one must first be sick enough for it. … We others, who have the courage for health, as well as for contempt,—we may well despise a religion that taught how to misunderstand the body! that does not intend to rid itself of the superstition about the soul! that makes a "merit" out of insufficient nourishment! that fights health as a sort of enemy, devil, temptation! that persuades itself that it is possible to carry around a "perfect soul" in a *cadaver* of a body, and that, to this end, it was necessary to devise for itself a new concept of "perfection", a pale, sickly, idiotically fanatic essence, so-called "holiness"—a holiness that is itself merely a series of symptoms of an impoverished, enervated and incurably spoilt body. (ibid., translation modified, italic added)

Near the word 'cadaver' [Cadaver], which Jung underlined, Jung wrote: 'Your soul died before your body. Zarathustra' [Deine Seele starb vor Deinem Körper. Zarathustra]. Such a reference demonstrates not only how strong Jung's conviction is about *Zarathustra* representing

Nietzsche's psychological breakdown, but also how impactful *Zarathustra* is on his own overall reception of Nietzsche.

Returning to *Liber Novus*, the following night, through Philemon's voice, Jung makes use of the phrase 'grave of the God', in order to express the necessity to 'live in the God', and not let 'the God [...] live[] in you'. Later on, when reflecting on his experience with Philemon, Jung also realises that he was 'intoxicated' [in einem Rausche] by him, who gave him 'language that was foreign to [him] and of a different sensitivity', and who now looks different to him. In fact, 'probably the most part of what' Jung has 'written in the earlier part of this book was given to' him by Philemon (RB *Scrutinies*, § 3: 339). Jung has come to realise the difference between himself and Philemon, and is now trying to differentiate from him. In this sense, 'intoxicated' could be arguably substituted by 'inflated', and Jung's *Liber Novus* would in a certain way achieve the same meaning to him, as that of Nietzsche's *Zarathustra* in the seminar. As argued in the previous section, Philemon too represents the expression of a divine power whose characteristics are defined in terms of 'spirit'.

One of the major topics of *Liber Novus* is surely the realisation of the 'supreme meaning' [Übersinn], namely the 'birth of a new God'. What this means in the context of *Zarathustra*, is that no God can effectively die, without being replaced by a new symbol. If this process is not consciously admitted, then it must happen unconsciously. Jung reads Nietzsche as if he had not reached any 'self' intuition consciously, nonetheless he appears able to project such an idea on an unconscious level, namely onto the *Übermensch*. Therefore he would confuse 'self' and 'I', and would tend to confine the wholeness represented by the former to the narrowness of the latter. Furthermore, because of his inflation, Nietzsche himself would even identify with the *Übermensch*. The problem with this opinion is that Nietzsche is actually aware of the possibility of the 'I' being transcended by autonomous phenomena, and the whole first part of *Beyond Good and Evil*—as already explained in the introduction—represents a significant piece of evidence. It can be stated that Jung interprets the *Übermensch* as Nietzsche's 'new God'; in fact, from *Zarathustra*, *Prologue* to its last chapters, Jung understands the *Übermensch* as a symbol for the 'self'. In his second seminar session, on 9 May 1934, Jung responds to a question from Linda Fierz on the 'urge for individuation' in *Zarathustra* by saying: 'the self is in it' (SNZ I: 32).[4] While discussing Nietzsche's conception of the 'self', Jung affirms:

> *Gemüt* and *Geist* would be contents or qualities of consciousness. Therefore, there was the possibility—which I saw even then in *Zarathustra*—of the mistake which Nietzsche actually makes; namely, he identifies the ego with the self and therefore with the Superman, as we have seen. That would be an incarnation of the self. But the self is much too big; you cannot possibly identify with it without incurring the risk of a fatal inflation. (ibid.: 391, 20 February 1935)

Nietzsche's perception of the 'self' appears to Jung as a distort one, due to his inflation. On 20 November 1935, Jung discusses 'Of the Neighbour-Love' in this sense:

> Obviously, he recommends love for the furthest in order to protect oneself against that easy dodging of oneself that one has offered to other people in the immediate vicinity. [...] The quest is the quest of the self—that is the precious thing which is difficult to attain; that is the hero's fight and you are alone, and even have no weapons. [...] From a psychological point of view it would be the shadow, because that would be the precondition for the union with the self; without the realization of the shadow there is no such union. But on account of the identity of Nietzsche with the archetype of Zarathustra, he is not aware of his shadow [...]. In a later part of *Zarathustra* the shadow incarnates the ugliest man and he rejects him because of his inflation. Anybody who is inflated by an archetype naturally cannot accept the shadow because it would deflate him; yet that deflation is absolutely necessary for individuation. In ['Of The Neighbour-Love'], you see that he is inclined to identify that man with the Superman: he is the foretaste of the Superman. As the Superman is most definitely not a shadow, he is dreaming of a Superman who is friend of the self, yet without a shadow. But if he should try to identify or reunite with the self, he would come across the shadow and it would interfere. When the shadow does interfere later, he does not recognise it. There is the tragedy. (SNZ I: 702–703)

During the same session, in relation to the chapter 'The Way of the Creating One', Jung comments: 'On account of identification with the creative self, he feels himself a creator, and you will see how he experiences the fact of being a creator' (ibid.: 703). Similarly, Jung's idea of a 'supreme meaning' is introduced, in a retrospective comment, at the very beginning of *Liber Primus*:

> But the supreme meaning is the path, the way and the bridge to what is to come. That is the God yet to come. It is not the coming God himself but his

> image which appears in the supreme meaning. God is an image, and those who worship him must worship him in the images of the supreme meaning.
>
> The supreme meaning is not a meaning and not an absurdity, it is image and force in one, magnificence and force together.
>
> The supreme meaning is the beginning and the end. It is the bridge of going across and fulfillment.
>
> The other Gods died of their temporality, yet the supreme meaning never dies, it turns into meaning and then into absurdity, and out of the fire and blood of their collision the supreme meaning rises up rejuvenated anew.
>
> The image of God has a shadow. The supreme meaning is real and casts a shadow. For what can be actual and corporeal and have no shadow?
>
> The shadow is nonsense. It lacks force and has no continued existence through itself. But nonsense is the inseparable and undying brother of the supreme meaning.
>
> Like plants, so men also grow, some in the light, others in the shadows. There are many who need the shadows and not the light.
>
> The image of God throws a shadow that is just as great as itself.
>
> The supreme meaning is great and small, it is as wide as the space of the starry Heaven and as narrow as the cell of the living body. (RB I, 1: 229–230)

A couple of strong Nietzschean echoes in this passage need to be brought out, beginning with the bridge metaphor. In this respect, what is important to be highlighted, is the context of this metaphor in *Zarathustra*. It appears in the *Prologue*, and is used in order to depict the relationship between man and *Übermensch* indeed: man is compared to a bridge towards the *Übermensch* (Za I, *Prologue* 4, KSA 4: 16–18; see also Za I, 3, KSA 4: 42). It can be stated that both Nietzsche's *Übermensch* and Jung's *Übersinn* are associated with a bridge, as Gerhard Schmitt has also pointed out (2011). As Schmitt remarks, what in *Zarathustra* represents a linear structure from animal-like beings to the *Übermensch*, corresponds in *Liber Novus* to a 'climax of the conscience' [Klimax des Bewusstseins], which cannot go back to a 'polar relationship' with the 'unconscious', once the initial unconscious perspective has been abandoned (Schmitt 2011: 126). Moreover, it can be observed, in either case, the bridge metaphorically stands for a transitional element towards a new achievement: to Jung, it is just an image for the forthcoming God—and not the God himself; to Nietzsche, it represents the necessity of men being overcome by the *Übermensch*. However, in such a close similarity, a crucial difference must be brought out as well. Nietzsche's *Übermensch* is not the bridge, but one of its ends; Jung's *Übersinn* is the bridge itself, as this represents a symbol for an otherwise incomprehensible

God. Since the time of *Liber Novus*, Jung has conceived the process of transformation as a path orientated towards the realisation of the divine. In this sense, he tends to regard any transformation process in terms of transcendence, thus he interprets the *Übermensch* as a symbol of the self, a sort of *Übersinn*. The very fact that, to Nietzsche, the *Übermensch* is the goal itself might explain Jung's understanding of it as a symptom of inflation indeed: not admitting any transcendence, Nietzsche's *Übermensch* can by no means be compared to Jung's *Übersinn* from Nietzsche's perspective; from Jung's perspective, however, transcendence cannot be denied, and any attempt to deny it would result in inflation.

A last remark concerns another metaphor, that is, the shadow. Phrases such as 'The image of God has a shadow. The supreme meaning is real and casts a shadow. For what can be actual and corporeal and have no shadow?' and 'The image of God throws a shadow that is just as great as itself' (RB I, 1: 229–230) recall a significant motif from *Zarathustra*. Indeed, Nietzsche uses the same image in relation to the *Übermensch* in a similar context at the very end of chapter 'On the Blissful Islands': 'I will complete it: for a shadow came to me—the most silent, the lightest of all things came to me! The beauty of the *Übermensch* came to me as a shadow. Ah, my brothers! What are the gods to me now' (Za II, 2, KSA 4: 112, translation modified). Paul Bishop has exhaustively dwelt upon the tradition lying behind the symbolic constellation shadow-beauty-divine not only in relation to these two chapters from *Zarathustra* and *Liber Novus*, but also to the significance of such a symbolic constellation to Jung's depth psychology, understood as a form of 'self-sculpting', oriented towards what Bishop defines—at the end of his book—'a new kind of *vitalistic aesthetics*' (Bishop 2017: 209). What can be added to his discourse is that the relation shadow-divine in Nietzsche has an even deeper meaning relating to the 'death of God', thus bringing back in the discourse on Nietzsche's inflation, as understood by Jung. In two aphorisms from *The Gay Science*, Nietzsche compares several contemporary attitudes—such as the unconditioned faith in science of Positivism—to religions without God. He defines them in terms of 'shadows of God' [Schatten Gottes], meaning that although 'God is dead', his image is still strong and effective in individuals (FW 108–109, KSA 3: 467–469. See Campioni 2009: 121–148). As in the case of the bridge, the same metaphor is used by Nietzsche and Jung in the same way, but again, what for Nietzsche intends to express the end of metaphysics, is used by Jung precisely in the opposite direction. And, by virtue of this, Jung cannot help but to interpret Nietzsche's anti-metaphysical attitude as a symptom of inflation.

4.2.3 *Isolated Suns, The Island of the Dead, and the 'Wheel of Creation'*

Another aspect of Nietzsche's negation of the unconscious, according to Jung's interpretation, is connected to the motif of *solitude*. From a merely psychological point of view, Nietzsche is certainly isolated in his inflation; however, the phenomenon of solitude has also a wider meaning, which appears as a consequence of the 'death of God' and represents its unavoidable *collectivisation*. While commenting on 'Of the New Idol', where Nietzsche expresses himself against the idealisation of the 'state', Jung explains the process:

> You see, what has happened there, is that the idea of the Superman, or the differentiated individual, having not reached the surface of consciousness, remains in the dark, and therefore it is everywhere; it is in everybody, and everybody becomes so individualized and also so inflated in consciousness that they needs must make a state in order to be able to live. For, when everyone has an inflation they are no longer able to understand one another, and the human and social organizations will disintegrate. (SNZ I: 602, 16 October 1935)

Then he adds:

> You see, the unconscious, activated archetype is like a rising sun, a source of energy or warmth which warms up the ego personality from within, and then the ego personality begins to radiate as if it were God-knows what. But it radiates its own colours, expresses the archetype in its own personal way, and therefore it appears as if the ego were all-important. Whereas the ego is of no importance at all in reality, but is simply urged from within, pushed forward and made to perform as if it *were* important. (ibid.: 611)

Denying the possibility of an independent element from the 'ego' corresponds to a closure in each individual, which brings them to consider themselves as gods. In this sense, the 'contagion' is the other aspect implicitly suggested by the issue of solitude. In fact, 'the cause according to Nietzsche is the all-pervading archetypal idea of the Superman, the greatness of man—and his idealism or ambition is to attain greatness'. But to the extent that the same idea is present in anyone—and only on an unconscious level—the extreme consequence this problem leads to, is a widespread solitude, which makes everyone incapable of communicating, and prevents them from interaction, in order to preserve the feeling of godliness. Else, the inflation would come to an end:

> Now, if Nietzsche is conscious of this idea and identical with it, it is quite to be expected that he will become suspect, for when people meet the apparent carrier of the source of their inflation, they naturally will immediately try to suppress that individual who sticks out, just because he threatens that inflation. *For they are no longer the only sun in heaven*—there is another sun, and that should not be. (ibid.: 612–613, italics added)

This idea is very much present in Jung's interpretation of chapters 'The Night-Song' and 'The Grave-Song'. As already pointed out, Jung reads beginning and ending of the former in German, because of the musicality given by the unconscious—namely 'the peculiar emotion of a man who experiences the spirit, the superhuman light and its cosmic coldness' (SNZ II: 1144, 9 June 1937). The middle section is read in English, however, as the sentence '"And oft have I dreamt that stealing must be more blessed than receiving" [...] is the point where, to [Jung's] feeling, the whole rhythm and poetry of the passage before comes to an end. This is also the point where [Nietzsche] touches upon his own ego, and there we can begin our critical examination of his text'. Jung comments on the text by saying:

> he felt as if he were pouring out a full vessel. *Zarathustra* flowed out of him till he became aware finally of the inner emptiness caused by it. First, he was pouring it out with the feeling that he should fill the whole world, and then no echo came back, apparently nothing has happened. He had poured out his very blood and nothing came back, and naturally he developed a tremendous hunger, a desire to be filled up again. (ibid.: 1145–1146)

Jung describes this as 'an example of the humility of the spirit: inasmuch as the spirit is shining and hot like the sun, it is positive, but inasmuch as it is cold, it is negative, and inasmuch a man is filled with the warmth of the spirit he will give, and inasmuch he is filled with the coldness of the spirit, he will take, but not in a human way. It will be less than human' (ibid.). At the moment of commenting on the lines 'Many suns circle in desert space: to all that is dark do they speak with their light—but to me they are silent. / Oh, this is the hostility of light to the shining one: unpityngly doth it pursue its course. / Unfair to the shining one in its innermost heart, cold to the suns:—thus travelleth every sun', Jung argues:

'Here he identifies with the sun, the hottest thing we know of; he is identical with Yang'. As a response to 'Their [the suns'] inexorable will do they follow: that is their coldness', Jung affirms: 'Here we see the fact that the sun or the suns, the fixed stars, etc., are following a mechanical principle which is utterly inhuman; therefore they are cold, despite all heat. And that is the image or the allegory of the hunger of the spirit' (ibid: 1148.).

In *Liber Novus*, similar images are evoked in the chapter 'Hell', where Jung expresses himself in relation to his need for giving birth to his 'God', while reflecting on his fantasy in retrospect:

> Because I wanted to give birth to my God, I also wanted evil. He who wants to create an eternal fullness will also create eternal emptiness. You cannot undertake one without the other. But if you want to escape evil, you will create no God, everything that you do is tepid and gray. I wanted my God for the sake of grace and disgrace.
>
> [...]
>
> Nothing is more valuable to the evil one than his eye, since only through his eye can emptiness seize gleaming fullness. Because the emptiness lacks fullness, it craves fullness and its shining power. And it drinks it in by means of its eye, which is able to grasp the beauty and unsullied radiance of fullness. The emptiness is poor, and if it lacked its eye it would be hopeless. It sees the most beautiful and wants to devour it in order to spoil it. (RB II, 12: 288)

On 23 June 1937, Jung deals with the chapter 'The Grave-Song', and states:

> Yes, it is the utter stillness and solitude of the grave. A man is completely cut off on such an island. For who goes there? Only the dead that never return. So it is also an eternal prison, and he himself is a sort of ghost landing there. The psychological condition that he now becomes aware of is his absolute loneliness. Before, he was Zarathustra surrounded by imaginary disciples, talking to crowds in the marketplaces of town. Ha had a mission, he represented something. His heart was full to overflowing with all that he wanted to bestow on people; he bestowed his gift upon nations. And now he is on the island of the dead. The inflation has gone, as even the worse inflation comes to an end at times. [...] He suddenly realizes his real isolation and falls into himself, into his human existence. (SNZ II: 1183)

In December 1915, Jung comes across 'the dead' for the first time. These are the only figures that can intercede with God on behalf of men. In fact, 'He has neither goodwill nor ill will', whilst 'the dead hear your prayers since they are still of human nature and not free of good will and ill will' (RB *Scrutinies*, § 4: 342). A few weeks later, on 10 December 1916, Philemon reappears and warns Jung's 'I' against them. Or, better, against keeping a divine element in his soul:

> Remove, Oh man, the divine, too, from your soul, as far as you can manage. What a devilish farce she carries on with you, as long as she still arrogates divine power over you! She's an unruly child and a bloodthirsty daimon at the same time, a tormentor of humans without equal, precisely because she has divinity. Why? Where from? Because you venerate her. The dead too want the same thing. Why don't they stay quiet? Because they have not crossed over to the other side. Why do they want sacrifice? So they can live. But why do they still want to live with men? Because they want to rule. They have not come to an end with their craving for power, since they died still lusting for power. A child, an old man, an evil woman, a spirit of the dead, and a devil are beings who need to be humored. Fear the soul, despise her, love her, just like the Gods. May they be far from us! But above all never lose them! Because when lost they are as malicious as the serpent, as bloodthirsty as the tiger that pounces on the unsuspecting from behind. A man who goes astray becomes an animal, a lost soul becomes a devil. (ibid., § 5: 342–343)

Dealing with the dead demands to understand their 'craving for power', and to act accordingly, namely by humouring them, and by never forgetting their presence, too. Again, Jung's stress on 'craving for power' [Machtgier] and 'lusting for power' [Machtlust] recalls his idea of Nietzsche's failure to individuate, which can be expressed as his incapacity to create a new 'God'. Furthermore, a few lines above, a reference to a 'Last Supper' appears, as well as to the emptiness-fullness paradox in relation to God (ibid.). This represents the core of Philemon's 'first sermon to the dead', which is better summarised by the formula 'Nothingness is the same as the fullness. In infinity full is as good as empty. Nothingness is empty and full' (ibid., § 6: 346). In the third sermon the same idea appears again, when Philemon has to describe Abraxas, 'the God who is difficult to grasp': 'He is the fullness that seeks union with emptiness' (ibid., § 8: 350). As already mentioned, a few lines above, Abraxas is compared to Pan: 'He is the great and the small Pan alike' (ibid.). In the whole episode, a few allusions to the vessel motif appear too. In a similar sense, while speaking of 'the dead', Philemon explains that they 'rejected the God of love, of the good and the beautiful; they had to reject him and so they rejected unity and community in love, in the good and the beautiful. And thus they killed one another and dissolved the community of men' (ibid., § 7: 349). The dead's attitude does not come across as different from Jung's interpretation of Nietzsche's 'death of God' and its consequent leading to solitude. Indeed, similarly to 'The Night-Song', in the fourth sermon to the dead, it is also said that 'Each star is a God, and each space that a star fills is a devil. But the empty fullness of the whole is the Pleroma' (ibid., § 9: 351). The concept of God as Pleroma reminds one of Gnosticism, but the idea expressed by the dead seems to anticipate the core of Jung's criticisms of Nietzsche in the seminar. On 5 February 1916, it is said:

> For the Gods are many, while men are few. The Gods are mighty and endure their manifoldness. Like the stars they abide in solitude, separated by vast distances. [...]
>
> The multiplicity of the Gods corresponds to the multiplicity of men.
>
> Numberless Gods await the human state. Numberless Gods have been men. Man shares in the nature of the Gods. He comes from the Gods and goes unto the God.
>
> Thus, just as it is no use to reflect upon the Pleroma, it is not worthwhile to worship the multiplicity of the Gods. Least of all does it serve to worship the first God, the effective fullness, and the *summum bonum*. By our prayer we can add nothing to it, and take nothing from it; because effective emptiness gulps down everything. The bright Gods form the heavenly world. It is manifold and extends and increases infinitely: The Sun God is the supreme lord of the world. (ibid.)

Not too far from the passage above, namely in the sixth sermon to the dead, a few further Nietzschean allusions appear:

> I was probably very confused when ΦΙΛΗΜΩΝ approached me the following night, since I called to him saying, "What did you do, Oh ΦΙΛΗΜΩΝ? What fires have you kindled? What have you broken asunder? Does the wheel of creations stand still?"
>
> But he answered and said, "Everything is running its usual course. Nothing has happened, and yet a sweet and indescribable mystery has taken place: I stepped out of the whirling circle."
>
> "What's that?" I exclaimed, "Your words move my lips, your voice sounds from my ears, my eyes see you from within me. Truly, you are a magician! You stepped out of the whirling circle? What confusion! Are you

> I, am I you? Did I not feel as if the wheel of creation was standing still? And yet you say that you have stepped out of the whirling circle? I am truly bound to the wheel-I feel the rushing swaying of it-and yet the wheel of creation also stands still for me. What did you do, father, teach me!"
>
> Then ΦΙΛΗΜΩΝ said, "I stepped onto what is solid and took it with me and saved it from the wave surge, from the cycle of births, and from the revolving wheel of endless happening. It has been stilled. The dead have received the folly of the teaching, they have been blinded by truth and see by mistake". (ibid., § 11: 353)

The link between the 'wheel of creation' and the 'cycle of births' makes possible to put the text in connection with something close to Nietzsche's eternal return. Indeed with similar expressions, Jung interprets Nietzsche's wheel symbol in his seminar. In particular, on 28 November 1934, while analysing 'Of the three Metamorphoses', he comments on the image of the 'self-rolling wheel' by saying: 'The center of the impetus of the wheel being in itself, it is self-creative. And Nietzsche means that the attitude of the child is self-creative'. Then he adds: 'the child must be self-creative, in order to put something into the place of the dragon that has been overcome; it must create a new subjective, individual value' (SNZ I: 270). On 20 November 1935, during a session dedicated to 'The Way of the Creating One', Jung argues: 'The rolling wheel is very clearly the symbol of the self and the stars rolling about the self would be the Milky Way, the center of the heavens. So Nietzsche would ask here, "Are thou the self? If you are, then you can risk it." He assumes that one can only risk that way if one is the wheel—only the self could risk that way of being alone' (ibid.: 708). The strongest link with the passage from *Scrutinies* appears on 22 January 1936, in regard to *Zarathustra* chapter 'Voluntary Dead', when the symbol of the 'golden ball' appears for the first time. First, Jung compares it to Nietzsche's 'dancing star', and adds: 'It is a symbol of the self'. Then Jung connects the 'pelote game' with 'depreciatory rumors about the ritual murder which was supposed to take place in Gnostic circles, as well as among the Christians and the Jews; it was said in antiquity that they played the game of pelote with a child they threw to one another until he was dead. The child represents the god'. So, he comments: 'It was a sacrifice of the god and a human sacrifice in order to renew the life of the god'. However, as Jung remarks, 'the ball is a symbol of the sun; it is the golden ball, an entirely round thing which expresses the state of perfection, of the highest value, of gold'. In this, it anticipates the main motif of 'Of the

Bestowing Virtue', which follows 'Voluntary Dead' indeed. In regard to the 'golden ball' symbol as it appears in 'Of the Bestowing Virtue', Jung considers the sun with the snake coiled around it on Zarathustra's stick, and compares it to 'the golden germ, the *Hiranyagarbha* as it is the *Upanishads*', which 'is another symbol of the self'. Like the sun, he observes, 'it is also called the golden child, the precious, perfect substance that is made by man or born out of man; and it is of course the alchemistic gold and the all-roundness of the Platonic being and the *sphairos*, the most blissful god of Empedocles'. So Jung concludes his meditation on the 'self' as expressed through the 'golden ball' symbol:

> It is the idea that the self is not identical with one particular individual. No individual can boast of having *the* self: there is only the self that can boast of having many individuals. You see, the self is an extraneous unit in one's existence. It is a center of personality, a center of gravity that does not coincide with the ego; it is as if it were something outside. Also, it is not this *individual*, but a connection with individuals. So one could say the self was the one thing, yet it is the many. It has a paradoxical existence which cannot define and limit by any particular definition. It is a metaphysical concept. But we must create such a concept in order to express the peculiar psychological fact that one can feel as the subject and one can also feel as the object [...]. Therefore, my definition of the self is a non-personal center, the center of the psychical non-ego—of all that in the psyche which is not ego. And presumably it is to be found everywhere in all people. [...] Now, Zarathustra says here that his goal is connected to that ball. [...] And he has thrown the ball among his brethren or disciples, which means that he is bringing up or instigating the self and setting in motion. (SNZ II: 781–783)

In Jung's cosmology, 'the Sun God is the highest good, the devil the opposite' (RB *Scrutinies*, § 9: 351). Furthermore, in the seminar, the same topic is also linked by Jung to Buddhistic literature and the symbol of the wheel indeed: 'As Zarathustra has thrown a ball, so Buddha brings a wheel among men and sets it in motion' (SNZ II: 783). In the *Scrutinies* section mentioned above, it is also written: 'compassion with men will overcome you and from the stream you will reach solid ground, you will step forth from the eternal whirl onto the unmoving stone of rest, the circle that breaks flowing duration, and the flame will die down' (RB Scrutinies, § 11: 353). The reference to compassion, besides Zarathustra's 'last sin' and Schopenhauer, reminds one of the Buddhistic tradition. When dealing with the eternal return more specifically, Jung interprets Nietzsche's intuition very closely to the Indian conception. For instance, on 24 October

1934, while reading *Zarathustra, Prologue*, he defines the eternal return as 'a peculiar way of talking of rebirth' (SNZ I: 191). On 20 February 1935, about 'The Despisers of the Body', Jung exclaims: 'Nietzsche is far more concerned with the actual time than with the general aspect of the world that lives and dies—after birth, death and then birth again. That is characteristic of *Upanishad* philosophy and later on you find it in Nietzsche too, in his idea of the eternal return of things' (ibid.: 399). Shortly after, he adds: 'That Nietzsche identifies the self with the body is of course illogical, for you then come necessarily to the conclusion that if the body died, therefore the self wants to die' (ibid.: 405). Again, while reading 'On the Blissful Islands' on 20 May 1936, Jung explains:

> In the collective unconscious you discover the identity of different times for instance, that things have been practically always the same, they never change so why should you do anything about it? Why invent? Or why should you translate them into the language of this time? You can disappear into them without ever saying a word about them. But the fact is of course that externally, to your surroundings, to your world, you are lost. (SNZ II: 933)

Jung's understanding of Nietzsche's eternal return is always about an attempt to escape reality—and its responsibilities—on behalf of an idea of divine eternity, which recalls the 'self'. This emerges quite clearly during Jung's interpretation of the symbol of the 'ring' in *Zarathustra* section 'Of the Virtuous', on 5 May 1937:

> I cannot quite understand it [Nietzsche's idea of the eternal return] but that does not matter. It belongs with this symbolism of the ring, the ring of the rings, the ring of Eternal Recurrence. Now, this ring is the idea of totality and it is the idea of individuation naturally, an individuation symbol. It means absolute completeness of the self, and you will see that this is confirmed in the text.
>
> In my edition of the English text there is a mistake. In the sentence, "It is your dearest Self, your virtue", *self* should not be written with a capital S—that is wrong. Nietzsche does not mean here *the* Self, he means "it is even your dearest". [...] You see, the fact which he tries to express here, that virtue is the thing you love the most, means that the intensity of your love is the virtue, and there he takes the word *virtue* in its antique sense. [...]
>
> [...] Thirst is the dynamic element and that is the value, or the virtue. With the ring comes in the idea of duration, of immortality, the eternal return. This is substantiated by the fact that the actual psychological experi-

ence of totality, which is a religious experience, always expressed or formulated as the presence of God, has the quality of immortality, the quality of eternal duration. (ibid.: 1043–1045)

Again, on 18 May 1938, Jung comments on 'The Vision and the Riddle' by pointing out the same concept: 'It is the idea of *die ewige Wiederkunft*, the eternal return, his idea of immortality. Why should one be afraid of the death since everything eternally returns? So onslaught of the dwarf brings out in him the idea of the eternity of life' (ibid.: 1263). On 25 May 1938, still on the same chapter, Jung discusses the eternal return in terms of a 'primitive fear of the overwhelming power of the unconscious'. According to him, Zarathustra believes to dominate the dwarf, but he is actually possessed by the dwarf, as this sits on his back as someone who is riding a horse. Therefore, 'he is afraid of the spirit of gravity, afraid of the thing that possesses him. Now, in such a moment one could expect a reaction from the side of the instincts' (ibid.: 1271–1273). Again:

> if he takes this moment that has been emphasized by the dwarf and himself in mutual collaboration, as a unique moment, with no return, no repetition, then he would be forced to realize it completely. [...] But if you see flatness only, you cease to exist—there is only an immense continuity of flatness, and that is of course not worthwhile. Why should we continue such a string of nonentities, mere repetitions? (ibid.: 1288, 8 June 1938)

In the section 'The Convalescent', Zarathustra becomes annoyed when his animals make a 'hurdy-gurdy song' [Leier-Lied] out of the profundity of his 'abysmal thought'. In fact, they sing:

> Everything rolls, everything returns; the wheel of existence rolls for ever. [...] Everything breaks, everything is joined anew; the same house of existence builds itself for ever. Everything departs, everything meets again; the ring of existence is true to itself for ever. Existence begins in every instant; the ball There rolls around every Here. The middle is everywhere. The path of eternity is crooked. (Za III, 13, KSA 4: 273)

This represents an extreme exemplification of the complexity of the problem, and does not differ from the dwarf's discourse. They both correspond to a temptation from the 'spirit of gravity', which makes everything heavy or tragic in order not to allow one to face the question and really overcome it. This aspect describes only the first impression of Nietzsche's 'abysmal thought', that is to say, the frightful intuition that time is nonsense, and that any purpose is vane. Instead, thinking the eternal return in a deeper way leads to a further stage, where temporality gains a new and more intense meaning, as the moment loses its link to determinism and becomes valuable for the sake of itself. Moreover, if it is true that any decision made has already been made countless times, it is also true that whatever is chosen is meant to be chosen forever. This should be enough to speak against any attempt to think the question in terms of superficiality; rather, it introduces Nietzsche's emphasis on responsibility. In this sense, Jung's understanding of the eternal return resembles more what Zarathustra's animals think, rather than Nietzsche's attempt to overcome temporality. Nonetheless, it represents a consistent element in Jung's understanding of the issue. By pointing out the superficial aspect connected to repetition, that is to say the nonsense of the moment, Jung highlights Nietzsche's justification for escaping his confrontation with the unconscious and stopping his inflation with Zarathustra. On the other end, by stressing the eternity element implicit in the eternal return, he also links Nietzsche's 'abysmal thought' to the same need for projecting the 'self' which would appear in Nietzsche's idealisation of the *Übermensch*. This is another manifestation of the immortal 'God' whom Nietzsche has tried to kill. In this sense indeed, while commenting on 'Of the Bedwarfing Virtue', Jung associates a particular meaning of the eternal return with Christianity, the Cabala and Gnosticism. In this case, it is the aspect concerning 'restoration' which is stressed, namely 'the return of everything that has been lost' (SNZ II: 1341–1342, 19 October 1938). Both these aspects were already present in *Scrutinies*. At the end of Philemon's 'Sermons to the Dead ', Elijah and Salome appear again. Jung's 'I' states that 'The multiplicity of individual things is the one multiple God from whose body many Gods arise, but the uniqueness of the one thing is the other God, whose body is a man but whose spirit is as large as the world', to which Elijah responds:

> That is new, my son. Is the new good? What was, is good; and what was, will be. Is that not the truth? Has there ever been anything new? And was what you call new, ever good? Everything remains the same if you give it a new name. There is nothing new, there can be nothing new; how could I then look ahead? I look at the past and therein I see the future, as in a mirror. And I see that nothing new happens, everything is but mere recurrence of what has been since time immemorial. What is your being? An appearance, a darting light; tomorrow it is no longer true. It is gone; it is as if it never was. (RB *Scrutinies*, § 14: 358)

Just to emphasise the recurrence of elements common to Nietzsche's imagery in the same vision, one can also observe that the 'Gods' are depicted by Jung's 'soul' as suffering and in need of being redeemed (ibid).

4.3 Animals

4.3.1 *Serpent, Bird, and Black Scarab*

Much has been already said about the serpent motif in *Liber Novus*, in relation to Nietzsche's utilisation of the same image. What is still to be investigated is the proximity of Jung's interpretation of *Zarathustra* serpent symbology to the meaning given to it in *Liber Novus*. Throughout Nietzsche's text, Zarathustra is accompanied by two animals that live in the cave with him: an eagle and a serpent. These two animals are introduced by Nietzsche at the very beginning of *Zarathustra*. Jung interprets them in terms of 'instincts', the serpent representing the chthonic world—what is more connected to the earth and the body—and the eagle symbolising the spirit, in all of its aspects. In this sense, he mentions Ganymede, 'the messenger of Zeus', who 'is lifted up by the eagle to Olympian heights', and adds: 'it is the genius and enthusiasm of youth that seize him and carry him up to the heights of the gods. So one could say it was a spiritual, uplifting power'. According to Jung's interpretation, Nietzsche would feel close to his instincts—both in their chthonic and spiritual meaning—when he makes the decision of going under, that is to say, to abandon the realm of 'consciousness' and meet the unconscious would represent his conscious choice (SNZ I: 18–19). In *Zarathustra*, the eagle and the serpent appear to be good friends, and, at the end of the *Prologue*, are said by Zarathustra to represent pride and wisdom, respectively: 'The proudest animal [Das stolzeste Thier] under the sun and the wisest animal [das klügste Thier] under the sun'. On that occasion, the eagle 'was sweeping through the air in wide circles, and from it was hanging a serpent, not like a prey but like a friend: for it was coiled [geringelt] around the eagle's neck' (Za I, *Prologue* 10, KSA 4: 27). In Jung's personal copy, 'eagle', 'hanging a serpent', 'coiled [...] neck' are underlined, and a significant inscription—most likely written down in preparation for the seminar—reads: '[He] would need pride and wisdom. They both broke away in animal-likeness' [(Er) bedürfte des Stolzes und der Klugheit. Beide sind ins Thierische abgespalten]. On 7 November 1934, towards the end of his *Prologue* analysis, Jung explains:

> The snake would be a symbol of the earth, for things chthonic. More psychologically, the eagle is like thought, a messenger of the highest god; thought is also understood to be a winged being and a product of the brain, which is on top of man, on top of the world. It is Mount Meru where the city of light lies, the light of consciousness. While the snake, on the other side, chiefly consists of a vertebral column, and is therefore a personification of the lower motor centers of the body, of the spinal cord and the corresponding centers of the brain. As a personification of the physiological instincts, it is also associated with sexuality, or with the low instinctive cunning of the primitive or animal mind of man.
>
> Zarathustra sees those animals together, representing pairs of opposites, because spirit is always supposed to be the irreconcilable opponent of the chthonic, eternally fighting against the earth according to the dogmatic idea and the idea of old philosophies in general. [...] You are probably impressed with the fact that the serpent has coiled itself round the neck of the eagle. (SNZ I: 227–228)

In reply to his question as to what the 'usual presentation of this symbolism' would be, Martha Sigg—one of the participants in Jung's seminar—suggests that 'the eagle has the snake in its claws'. Here is Jung's comment on such a reply:

> Yes, showing that the spirit has overcome matter, or that the eagle, personifying the light, has overcome the power of darkness or the devil. For instance, you remember having seen the so-called lecterns in churches, sort of reading-desks on which the Bible is supported by an eagle. The eagle is the symbol of St. John the Evangelist, whose philosophy is the idea of the Logos, the word, the light that comes from God and shines into the darkness of man. Antique fantasy ascribed the eagle to John because the eagle was the messenger of Zeus, the god of the sky, the personification of the light. Therefore, the symbolism on the lecterns, where the word of God as given to us in the Bible comes down to the earth supported on the wings of the eagle. Now, the eagle is in a way predominating here, he carries the snake but not in its claws; the snake is coiled round his neck. (ibid.)

Shortly after, it is stated: 'You think it is rather dangerous for the eagle to have such a necktie? It is. I would not like it. [...] Well, if he [the snake] clings to the neck of the eagle, he won't fall down, but it is not a pleasant situation. I don't think the serpent likes such an airplane stuff' (ibid.: 230). And, again:

> Of course, the most impressive thing in this picture is that the snake is lifted up out of her usual abode into a medium in which it depends entirely upon the good will of the eagle. It is a hellishly uncomfortable situation. After a while the eagle will certainly become very hungry and eat the snake. He [Nietzsche] is just lifted out of the ground, and as a material man, as a man of the earth, he is in the power of that enormous bird. The eagle is the archetype, you see: the wise old man is the wise old bird. (ibid.)

In fact, he explains a couple of pages after:

> To a man like Nietzsche, for instance, a dream will appear which contains this image of the eagle and the snake. If such a case should happen in reality, I would explain it in this way: the light of heaven, the eagle, the divine word has caught you; naturally, how could you resist? So you gave yourself to it. But you must know that it is exceedingly dangerous; we don't know how it will turn out in the future. I should say it was a precarious situation for that serpent—probably less for the eagle, because the serpent is chiefly under the illusion of friendship. You see if the eagle were under that illusion, he would have been persuaded by the serpent to stay on the ground and to hop about while she crept up and sat on his back. He would have to hop along carrying the snake—or some other grotesque arrangement could be thought of. But it is clearly the serpent that follows. It is Nietzsche who follows the insinuation or the intimation of the archetype and is carried into the air. (ibid.: 232)

In the same session, the couple is also interpreted in terms of 'universal principles', such as Yin and Yang. On 21 November 1934, Jung dwells upon the couple eagle-serpent again, and compares it with the same image present in the Gilgamesh epic; although this is said to be 'a different kind of symbolism, yet the meaning is particularly clear'. Gilgamesh is for one-third human and for two-thirds divine, 'he is a sort of superhuman being with a tremendous spirit of power'. After that the women complained to the Gods because Gilgamesh treats everyone as slaves while building his town (Uruk), '[the gods] create a peculiar counterfigure to Gilgamesh, a man of equal size and strength, also a sort of superhuman nature, called Enkidu'. This is 'half animal', 'an inferior man, a sort of ape-man, a shadow but of equal strength. He simply personifies the inferior psyche of man', while Gilgamesh 'represents the will, consciousness, the spiritual attitude'. 'Enkidu being overcome by Gilgamesh would mean, then, the lower mind or psyche overcome by consciousness and will, and thus it is a representation of a problem which in those century was, of course, of the highest importance to man' (ibid.: 246–247). In this respect, it might be recalled that Jung borrowed the name Izdubar from one of the first transcriptions of the name 'Gilgamesh', indeed. In Jung's own copy of Nietzsche's *Genealogy of Morals* (available at Jung's personal library in Küsnacht), the words 'Pair of opposites' [Gegensatz Paare] and 'Gilgemesch' are annotated alongside the paragraph 13 from the third essay. The first phrase is referred to the question: 'this man who denies [the priest]—he belongs precisely with all the great conserving and affirming forces of life ... To what can we ascribe this pathology?'. The second refers to Nietzsche's description of the 'great experimenter with himself': 'still unconquered, always a man of the future, who no longer gets any rest from the force of his own powers, so that his future relentlessly burrows like a thorn into the flesh of his entire present' (GM III, 13, KSA 5: 366–367). Both sections are also marked by a vertical line. Gilgamesh is also recurrently mentioned throughout *Wandlungen und Symbole der Libido*.

While focussing on the chapter 'Of the Pale Criminal' and reading it in terms of an inflation, Jung affirms:

> Nietzsche means here that he is committing his crime on order to reach death; the lust for murder, the greed for the blood, is simply the preparation for death. [...] He is seeking to end his existence because—as the text afterwards says—he is nothing but a mass of diseases, a coil of wild serpents which can only wind up in its own destruction. So the Pale Criminal is in that respect the symbol for the man who must end his existence because he is no good—in order to make room for the Superman. [...] You see, if the criminal knows in committing his crime that he really means his own undoing, that he commits the crime in order to kill himself, then one can only agree [...]. One judges a crime differently when the murderer immediately afterwards kills himself too: one has the feeling that he has judged himself and sentenced himself to death. If the murderer is also put out of life it is satisfactory. (SNZ I: 465, 8 May 1935)

On 11 December 1935, in his analysis of 'Of the Adder's Bite', Jung points out that 'the anima is represented as woman above and serpent below, as the serpent in paradise is often represented with a woman's head; the snake element is always connected with the anima problem'. Then he adds: 'It is a coldblooded animal with a non-human psychology; one can establish a sort of *rapport* with almost any warmblooded animal but with snake there is no parallel feeling'. In fact, due to its representing our sympathetic system, to fear it means having troubles with the acceptance of one's own body:

> And that is the secret of the anima, human on the one side and that most paradoxical and incomprehensible thing on the other. On the one side she is an inferior woman with all the bad qualities of a merely biological woman, an intriguing and plotting devil who always tries to entangle a man and make a perfect fool of him; yet she winds up with the snake's tail, with that peculiar insight and awareness. She is a psychopompos, and leads you into the understanding of the collective unconscious just by the way of the fool. So wherever you touch upon that anima business you will have a paradoxical picture. (ibid.: 748–751. Jung introduces the symbol of the serpent as a 'reaction to the unconscious, to what Zarathustra said in the chapter before', 'Of Old and Young Women', ibid.: 252)

Following this interpretation, Jung proposes to read the 'bite' as linked to Nietzsche's inflation: 'It is a dangerous catastrophe when a man falls into a trap laid by the anima. To be caught by the heel is the usual fate of a man. Crush the head of the serpent and it will bite you in the heel. This is a regular occurrence and it can finish a man's career, his hopes, or even his life'. The throat is said to represent the logos, and by getting it bitten, Zarathustra would lose his speech skills, thus permitting Nietzsche to interrupt the inflation. 'The same motif comes again later', Jung adds, in 'On the Vision and the Riddle', 'so we must assume that the throat region is the active organ'. In fact, 'Zarathustra is very obviously the *logos*, and you cannot reach the *logos* with the feet because it has none; you can only reach it by the throat where the words come from' (ibid.: 755–756). Remarkably, in *The Significance of the Father in the Destiny of the Individual* (1909–1949), Jung interprets the dreams of a boy, where a black serpent bites his face and explains: 'The serpent's attack on the boy's face, the part that "sees," represents the danger to consciousness (blinding)' (CW 4: § 737, translation modified).

According to what has been just pointed out, three different aspects of Jung's dealing with the serpent in *Zarathustra* are to be considered: its relationship with the bird symbol; its link with murder and sacrifice; its close relation with the Anima.[5] In particular, what majorly arises in the first case, is the resolutive aspect of the couple serpent-bird, regarded as a symbol for the unification of opposites, in the sense of both contrasting principles and psychological functions. In the second case, it is the ancient link between serpents and evil to be particularly highlighted. Ultimately, regarding the serpent as an Anima representation, its chthonic side is mainly stressed, along with its 'poisonous' effect. These three perspectives are recurrent in *Liber Novus* as well, even though in some cases they are expressed differently—as for the Anima, that had not been yet conceptualised as an archetype. Similarly to *Zarathustra*, as has been already pointed out, there are several different serpents in *Liber Novus*, each of them having a specific meaning. Regarding the first point, the most representative scene appears at the very beginning of 'The Way of the Cross' (27 January 1914). Jung describes a fantasy:

> I saw the black serpent, as it wound itself upward around the wood of the cross. It crept into the body of the crucified and emerged again transformed from his mouth. It had become white. It wound itself around the head of the dead one like a diadem, and a light gleamed above his head, and the sun rose shining in the east. I stood and watched and was confused and a great weight burdened my soul. But the white bird that sat on my shoulder spoke to me: "Let it rain, let the wind blow, let the waters flow and the fire burn. Let each thing have its development, let becoming have its day". (RB II: 309–310)

As already highlighted, this chapter presents several important references to Nietzsche and *Zarathustra*, regarding both layers of visions and style. Assuming that, the serpent emerging from the mouth might be linked to 'Of the Vision and the Riddle', even. Differently from Nietzsche's description, however, in this case it is the serpent itself which has undergone a transformation and has become white. Moreover, a 'white bird' is sitting on a shoulder of Jung's 'I', representing the counterbalancing element to the serpent. Indeed, it is said to symbolise a different kind of wisdom which in a sense reassures Jung's 'I' and encourages him with confidence to let 'becoming have its day'. A few years later, the 'soul' appears to Jung's 'I' again and explains:

> If I am not conjoined through the uniting of the Below and the Above, I break down into three parts: the *serpent,* and in that or some other animal form I roam, living nature daimonically, arousing fear and longing. The *human soul,* living forever within you. The *celestial soul,* as such dwelling with the Gods, far from you and unknown to you, appearing in the form of a bird. Each of these three parts then is independent. (RB *Scrutinies,* 'Appendix C': 370; *Black Books 5,* 16 January 1916)

It can be interesting to note that in a letter dated 2 February 1913, Dr. Loÿ took the couple 'serpent and bird' as an example for the hypnotic effects of the analyst on the patient, in contrast to Freud's theory of sexual Libido (CW 4: § 591; translation modified).

In the chapter following 'The Way of the Cross', namely 'The Magician', the same image of the bird as a counterbalance, necessary to contrast the influence of serpentlike nature and keep a human median position, is shown again. So Jung interprets his fantasy:

> You find all this between men but not between men and serpents, even if they are serpent souls. But wherever there is love, the serpentlike abides also. Christ himself compared himself to a serpent, and his hellish brother, the Antichrist, is the old dragon himself. What is beyond the human that appears in love has the nature of the serpent and the bird, and the serpent often enchants the bird, and more rarely the bird bears off the serpent. Man stands in-between. What seems like a bird to you is a serpent to the other, and what seems like a serpent to you is a bird to the other. Therefore you will meet the other only in human form. If you want to become, then a battle between bird and serpent breaks out. And if you only want to be, you will be a man to yourself and to others. He who is becoming belongs in the desert or in a prison, for he is beyond the human. If men want to become, they behave like animals. No one saves us from the evil of becoming, unless we choose to go through Hell. (RB II, 21: 318)[6]

On the one hand, Jung stresses the dynamism of both symbols: 'what seems like a bird to you is a serpent to the other, and what seems like a serpent to you is a bird to the other'. On the other hand, the same relationship present in *Zarathustra* is depicted, and the same perplexity about the plausibility of such situation is expressed: 'the serpent often enchants the bird, and more rarely the bird bears off the serpent'. Furthermore, the 'becoming' motif occurs again, and, also this time, it cannot neglect a battle between opposite instincts, symbolised by different animals (in this case, the serpent and the bird, indeed). Already in 'The Castle in the Forest', while Jung is commenting on a vision dated 28 December 1913, the 'white bird' is said to be 'the messenger' of the 'ancient sleeper'. This can be awakened when one learns to accept their opposite nature, that is, when women discover their masculine soul, and men their feminine. In this way, people stop living in 'arbitrary and artificially created boundaries', and open to a more complete and human nature. The 'white bird', meant as 'the messenger', appears after one has broken down 'the walls that confine your view' (RB II, 2: 264). A few lines above, Jung wrote: 'when you become the one who is mocked, the white bird of the soul comes flying. It was far away; but your humiliation attracted it'. Thus the 'white bird' always represents transformation, indeed, and what follows the scene in 'The Magician', in Jung's fantasy, is that 'the serpent turned into a small white bird which soared into the clouds where she disappeared'. Then it talks to Jung's 'I' and says: 'Do you hear me? I'm far off now. Heaven is so far away. Hell is much nearer the earth. I found something for you, a discarded crown. It lay on a street in the immeasurable space of Heaven, a golden crown'. Such a crown bears an inscription which reads 'love never ends'. In this scene, the bird and the serpent come to represent 'Heaven' and 'Hell', respectively. The bird continuously turns itself into the serpent and goes to hell, and vice versa, while Jung's 'I' is hanging between sky and earth and cannot figure out what is going on around him. The inscription on the crown symbolises precisely the necessity of uniting the opposites; as the bird says: 'Everything under you is the earth, everything above you is the sky. You fly if you strive for what is above you; you are hanged if you strive for what is below you'. By explaining that, 'she' also solves the 'mystery' of the crown:

> B: "The crown and serpent are opposites, and are one. Did you not see the serpent that crowned the head of the crucified?"
>
> I: "What, I don't understand you."
>
> B: "What words did the crown bring you? 'Love never ends'—that is the mystery of the crown and the serpent."
>
> I: "But Salome? What should happen to Salome?"
>
> B: "You see, Salome is what you are. Fly, and she will grow wings". (RB II, 21, 'The Magician': 325–326)

In another fantasy from *Scrutinies* (3 May 1916), Jung's 'I' affirms that both the serpent and the bird are part of his 'soul', who 'has become multiple'. Elijah and Salome are part of *her* as well (RB *Scrutinies*, § 14: 357). Realising the identity of multiplicity and unity appears as the key to overcome what could be put as the *nonsense* perspective, namely the conflict. Only once the conflict is integrated and its contradictory nature admitted, a progress can happen; that is, a new 'God' can come to life. Later on, Jung explained his vision: 'Then my soul divided herself. As a bird she swooped up to the higher Gods and as a serpent she crawled down to the lower Gods. Soon afterward, she returned and said, troubled, "The Gods are outraged that you do not want to be obedient"'. Because he has 'broken the compulsion of the law', Jung's 'I' is considered by the 'Gods' as the devil, but such a sacrifice is necessary to overcome 'one-sidedness', therefore he is also forgiven by them (ibid.: 358). In Jung's cosmology, the bird is said to be 'heavenly soul' and the serpent is called 'earthly soul' (RB *Scrutinies*, 'Appendix A': 363).

At the end of *Liber Primus* other serpents appear, as already said. The intervention of a second serpent—the white one—in order to resolve the tension between 'forethinking' and 'pleasure' through their connection to 'longing' has been already brought out: only by admitting that the serpent has a positive meaning, by the side of its poisonous nature, can such a reconciliation take place. In fact, the serpent is also an 'instrument of sacrifice', according to *Wandlungen und Symbole der Libido*: 'It is the knife that kills, but also the phallus as symbol of the regenerative power of the grain, which, buried in the earth like a corpse, is at the same time the inseminator of the earth' (CW 5: § 676; WSL: 409). Precisely in this sense, the second modality of Jung's interpretation of the serpent symbol in *Zarathustra* is to be investigated in *Liber Novus*. The sacrifice theme appears a couple of times referring to serpents. However, such meaning is to be found in layer 2 almost exclusively; that is to say, it occurs in Jung's retrospective reflections and stylistic choices remarkably more often than in visions. As already seen, in the chapter 'Descent Into Hell in the Future', Jung's 'I' is terrified by the vision of 'small serpents on the dark rock walls, striving toward the depths, where the sun shines. A thousand serpents crowd around, veiling the sun' (RB I, 5: 237). As has been argued in the previous chapter, in this vision he comes to realise the importance of sacrifice in a perspective of development; so he reflects on his fantasy:

> Therefore I take part in that murder; the sun of the depths also shines in me after the murder has been accomplished; the thousand serpents that want to devour the sun are also in me. I myself am a murderer and murdered [Mörder und Gemordeter], sacrificer and sacrificed [Opferer und Opfer]. The upwelling blood streams out of me.
>
> You all have a share in the murder. In you the reborn one will come to be, and the sun of the depths will rise, and a thousand serpents will develop from your dead matter and fall on the sun to choke it. Your blood will stream forth. The peoples demonstrate this at the present time in unforgettable acts, that will be written with blood in unforgettable books for eternal memory. (ibid.: 239)

Nietzsche's dithyramb *Amidst Birds of Prey* reads:

Oh Zarathustra, cruelest nimrod!
Recently still a hunter of God,
The snare of all virtue,
The arrow of evil! / Now—
Hunted by yourself [von dir selber erjagt],
Your own prey [deine eigene Beute],
Bored into your self [in dich selber eingeboh]. (KSA 6: 389)

As already anticipated, in *Wandlungen und Symbole der Libido*, Jung makes use of Nietzsche's dithyramb in order to explain the meaning of the 'separation from the mother-image' (WSL: 290). A few paragraphs above, however, Jung recalls the same poem precisely in the sense of *Liber Novus*, pointing out that 'it is not torture coming from outside', but man is himself 'hunter, murderer, sacrificer and sacrificial knife' [Jäger, Mörder, Opferer und Opfermesser ist]. In Nietzsche's poem—so he carries on—'the apparent dualism in the inner conflict is resolved through the utilisation of the same symbology' (WSL: 282, my own translation). In 1952, Jung's interpretation of Nietzsche's poem does not change in regard to this point (CW 5: §§ 446–447). Furthermore, the 'Morality of sacrificial beasts' [Moral der Opferthiere] is also analysed by Nietzsche in *Daybreak* (M, 215, KSA 3: 191–192), and, in 'Of the Pale Criminal', the question is posed: 'You do not intend to kill, you judges and sacrificer [ihr Richter und Opferer], before the beast has bowed its neck?' (Za I, 6, KSA 4: 45). As already recalled, in 1945, Jung analyses that chapter indeed, while taking on the issue of 'collective guilt' in relation to the Second World War and the rise of fascism (CW 10: §§ 400–443; Bishop 1999).

Interpreting further visions, Jung understands the necessity of 'the Conception of the God'. In that circumstance he states: 'Do you think that it is dead in you? But this dead can also change into serpents. These serpents will extinguish the prince of your days' (RB I, 8, 'The Conception of the God': 243). In the *Draft* version, this passage is followed by the statement: 'But the serpent is also life. In the image furnished by the ancients, the serpent put an end to the childlike magnificence of paradise; they even said that Christ himself had been a serpent' (Shamdasani 2009, ibid.). Back to the published text, not many lines below: 'Therefore on your journey be sure to take golden cups full of the sweet drink of life, red wine, and give it to dead matter, so that it can win life back. The dead matter will change into black serpents. Do not be frightened, the serpents will immediately put out the sun of your days, and a night with wonderful will-o'-the-wisps will come over you' (ibid.: 249). Again, in the description of the sacrifice committed by Jung's 'I', the atmosphere is introduced through the image of serpents. The 'tangle of human bodies' which is immediately visible, is called 'serpent-like'. Among these, the body of a dead girl lies on the ground. The 'daimons' who 'have thrown themselves over the maiden's feet and body' have bodies that 'sleek like serpents' (RB II, 12, 'hell': 288), and so Jung reflects: 'Your bloodthirsty tiger growls softly, your poisonous serpent hisses secretly, while you, conscious only of your goodness, offer your human hand to me in greeting. I know your shadow and mine, that follows and comes with us, and only waits for the hour of twilight when he will strangle you and me with all the daimons of the night' (ibid.: 289). The vision continues, and Jung's 'I' is forced to eat the liver of the maiden, which causes him nausea and deep discomfort. Again, a similar image is evoked in order to describe the happening: 'A sickening feeling of nausea sneaks up on me, and abominable, perfidious serpents wind their way slowly and cracklingly through parched undergrowth; they hang down lazily and disgustingly lethargic from the branches, looped in dreadful knots'. He walks 'hesitantly over the boulders, avoiding every dark place for fear of treading on a serpent'. Here is the meaning of the sacrifice:

> The sacrifice has been accomplished: the divine child, the image of the God's formation, is slain, and I have eaten from the sacrificial flesh. The child, that is, the image of the God's formation, not only bore my human craving, but also enclosed all the primordial and elemental powers that the sons of the sun possess as an inalienable inheritance. The God needs all this for his genesis. (RB II, 13, 'The Sacrificial Murder': 290–291)

It has already been said that Philemon's 'wisdom' is called 'the wisdom of the serpents, cold, with a grain of poison, yet healing in small doses'. What is still to be pointed out, is the way such a wisdom operates:

> Your magic paralyzes and therefore makes strong people, who tear themselves away from themselves. But do they love you, are they thankful, lover of your own soul? Or do they curse you for your magical serpent poison? They keep their distance, shaking their heads and whispering together. (RB II, 21, 'The Magician': 315)

By paralysing, Philemon's 'poison' scares people and forces them to face themselves. Also in this case, the serpent has the function to represent a necessary sacrifice, in order to achieve transformation. The venomous nature is the linking element of this process, and it leads directly to the third point highlighted through Jung's interpretation of the serpent in *Zarathustra*. It has been already said much of this aspect; nonetheless, a few further elements can be brought out, representing significant parallels with Jung's later seminar. In this case, such meaning appears recurring with similar consistency in both layers 1 and 2. In a few sections from *Liber Novus*, another serpent is associated with Salome. She symbolises pleasure, meant as the counterpart of 'forethinking'. In the fantasy from 'The Magician', she is compared to 'the serpent that coiled around [Jung's 'I'] and pressed out [his] blood' (ibid.: 324). As discussed in Chap. 3, pleasure is the element which permits the one-sidedness of thinking to overcome itself and get rid of what has been called one-sided knowledge. Precisely in this sense, Jung's comment on 'Of the Adder's Bite' deserves a little bit of attention. The phrase 'Crush the head of the serpent and it will bite you in the heel' (SNZ I: 755) shows the same image used by Jung himself in *Symbols of Transformation*: 'If you want the snake to bruise your heel you have only to tread on its head' (CW 5: § 586). Such a metaphor, as previously argued, refers to a sentence from 'First Day'—'But the poison of the serpent, whose head you crush, enters you through the wound in your heel; and thus the serpent becomes more dangerous than it was before' (RB II, 8: 279)—which is directly linked to the meaning attributed to the serpent in the first Elijah-Salome episode (Domenici 2018). Quite ironically, in regard to 'Of the Adder's Bite', Martha Sigg suggested Jung that 'When Nietzsche wrote this part of *Zarathustra* he had just had five months of daily discussion with Lou Salomé', to which he responded: 'Ah, there he met the serpent, that is quite certain' (SNZ I: 755). In a similar sense, in his seminar on Kundalini Yoga, Jung introduces Kundalini—represented as a serpent—as the Anima: 'That is the very reason why I hold that this second center, despite the Hindu interpretation of the crescent being male, is intensely female, for the water is the womb of rebirth, the baptismal fount' (Jung 1996: 32).

Returning to the comparison with *Liber Novus*, towards the end of the book, Philemon makes clear the meaning of serpents in transformation processes, namely in their relation to the bird once more. This time, the conflict symbolised by the animals is expressed in terms of *sexuality* and *spirituality* indeed, where serpents represent the approach of 'the daimon of sexuality' to 'our soul':

> The daimon of sexuality approaches our soul as a serpent. She is half human soul and is called thought-desire.
>
> The daimon of spirituality descends into our soul as the white bird. He is half human soul and is called desire-thought.
>
> The serpent is an earthly soul, half daimonic, a spirit, and akin to the spirits of the dead. Thus too, like these she swarms around in the things of earth, making us fear them or else having them arouse our craving. The serpent has a female nature, forever seeking the company of those dead who are spellbound by the earth, and who did not find a way across to singleness. The serpent is a whore. She courts the devil and evil spirits; she is a mischievous tyrant and tormentor, forever inveigling the most evil company: The white bird is a half-celestial soul of man. He abides with the mother, descending from time to time. The bird is manlike, and is effective thought. He is chaste and solitary, a messenger of the mother. He flies high above the earth. He commands singleness. He brings knowledge from the distant ones, who have departed before and attained perfection. He bears our word up to the mother. (RB *Scrutinies*, § 11: 353)

Bird and serpent, however, complement each other and elevate human beings:

> She intercedes, she warns, but she is powerless against the Gods. She is a vessel of the sun. The serpent descends and cunningly lames the phallic daimon, or else goads him on. She bears up the too-crafty thoughts of the earthly, those thoughts that creep through every hole and cleave to all things with craving. Although the serpent does not want to, she must be of use to us. She flees our grasp, thus showing us the way, which our human wits could not find. (ibid.)

The same process is made clear at the very end of *Liber Novus*, when Philemon meets 'the shade', his 'master'. Here the reference to a serpent—or 'worm'—is expressed in Christian terms:

> But ΦΙΛΗΜΩΝ answered, "Recognize, Oh master and beloved, that your nature is also of the serpent. Were you not raised on the tree like the serpent? Have you laid aside your body, like the serpent its skin? Have you not practiced the healing arts, like the serpent? Did you not go to Hell before your ascent? And did you not see your brother there, who was shut away in the abyss?"

> Then the shade said, “You speak the truth. You are not lying. Even *so*, do you know what I bring you?”
>
> “This I know not,” ΦΙΛΗΜΩΝ answered, “I know only one thing, that whoever hosts the worm also needs his brother. What do you bring me, my beautiful guest? Lamentation and abomination were the gift of the worm. What will you give us?”
>
> The shade answered, “I bring you the beauty of suffering. That is needed by whoever hosts the worm”. (ibid., § 15: 359)

What is implied in this passage, is the identity between ‘Christ’ and the ‘Antichrist’, which—as Jung will argue later on, in *Aion: Researches Into the Phenomenology of the Self*—is expressed by the double nature of the serpent (1951, CW 9, 2: §§ 369–390).

Besides the three main characterisations of serpents in Jung’s *Zarathustra* seminar and in *Liber Novus*, there are also two further readings, definitely less recurrent, which regard their closeness to the symbols of *spider* and *scarab*, respectively. On 19 May 1937, at the moment of analysing the chapter ‘Of the Tarantulas’, Jung makes a long digression on the sexual aspect implied by the tarantula symbol. ‘Of the Tarantulas’ was preceeded by the chapter ‘Of the Rabble’, during whose analysis Jung had emphasised the predominance of a masculine element, namely of Wotan, in the recurrent image of the wind. Because Nietzsche appears nearly identified with the masculine element, a feminine presence is needed, according to Jung, in order to counterbalance its effect and prevent such an identification from succeeding. In this sense, its link with the earth and sensation in relation to Nietzsche’s intuition are particularly dealt with:

> the tarantula is found in southeastern Europe; it lives in a hole in a rock or in the ground, and it is pretty poisonous, though its sting actually kills only small animals. The legend is that anybody poisoned by a tarantula goes raving mad and is seized by an uncontrollable desire to dance, but I think that idea simply comes from the fact that the people who had been poisoned were forced to dance, which was quite reasonable, in order to induce a heavy perspiration and give the poison a chance to get out of the body. (SNZ II: 1077; see also 1075–1076)

Not too far from these lines, Jung adds: ‘A tarantula is less dangerous than a venomous snake for instance, but people make a great story about it, a sort of metaphor’ (ibid.: 1078).[7] As proposed by Miss Barbara Hannah, the tarantula can be also interpreted as ‘a symbol for the self’. In response, Jung comments:

Yes. There are dreams, for instance, where the spider appears as a jewel, perhaps a sapphire, a blue resplendent gem in the center of the web which is made of golden threads. And people make pictures like that, not knowing of course what they mean. This is the symbol of the self but in a certain condition: namely, in the condition of complete unconsciousness. [...] Now, its positive aspect is that there is a central being somewhere that has spread its golden webs throughout the world to catch the souls of man. Often, however, it is projected in its negative aspect onto the analyst who is then seen as a spider catching people, getting them under his influence and sucking them dry, but his is merely the negative aspect of a very positive thing. (ibid.: 1087)

In this sense, Jung explains Nietzsche's warning against collectivity in 'Of the Tarantulas', which is seen in terms of infection:

Those people who preach that collectivism of equal units are the ones who are afraid of the action of the spider. They feel that the spider, or the analyst, is preaching of individuation, that a hostile power is seeking them, enveloping them as a spider does. They fear that they may get stuck or caught in something, and they necessarily think that this is absolutely wrong, that they should be free. But people lose their real freedom when they really succeed in behaving in collectivism and equality. Then they are caught in their equality and there is no possibility of any differentiation any longer. It is as if all the water were in one lake where nothing moved, where there was a complete lack of potential. Now, this positive aspect of the spider of course is a symbol, but inasmuch as that symbol is a triangle it doesn't fit of course, because a triangle just means one-sidedness, while individuation means everything else but one-sidedness—it means completeness. Therefore individuation is represented by a circle and a square. (ibid.: 1087–1088)

The scarab symbol in 'Of the Vision and the Riddle' offers Jung another occasion to talk about serpents, and to relate both symbols to the rebirth theme. Jung's remarks start with the observation that 'scarabs live on rotten matter: they dig into carrion in order to bury their eggs in it, or they make balls of manure to feed on and deposit their eggs in, so they are not particularly nice animals in that respect, though they look all right'. However, he notes '[i]f they attain human size they would be quite dangerous, naturally'. He compares them to the serpents in dreams and visions, and points out the essential difference in the genetical structure of scarabs/serpents and humans, causing them to be perceived as symbols of danger:

> Now what is a scarab? It is a very typical symbol, but one can assume that this child [who dreamt of a serpent] had any notion of its meaning. [...] What is the beetle anyhow? [...] I mean the fact that it has a sympathetic nervous system and no cerebro-spinal system. To dream of a worm would have the same meaning—they stand for the sympathetic system. Now I don't know how man knows that. I assume that it is a wasp knows that the third dorsal ganglion of the caterpillar's sympathetic system is the motor ganglion and puts it sting just into that, so it lames the caterpillar without killing it; and then the eggs which the wasp deposits thrive on that knowledge as key, one can unlock the dream. (ibid.: 1300)

However, scarabs are also symbols 'of resurrection in Egypt, the transitory form of Ra when he is invoked as Cheper or Chepra, the rising sun'. Jung explains that 'Ra in the form of the Chepra is buried in the ball of dung, and then he rises at the sun. That means man in the incubation sleep, in a state of rebirth, man buried in the sympathetic system when consciousness [...] is entirely extinguished'. Not surprisingly, St John's depiction of 'Christ' appears in this discourse as well:

> In the Evangel of St. John, Christ likens himself to the serpent that was raised by Moses in the desert, against the many poisonous snakes that were killing the people. That is exactly the same motif, but instead of the beetle, it was the serpent directly. If one is at variance with one's cerebro-spinal system plus the sympathetic system, it would be expressed by the poisonous snake. Many people resist not only their sympathetic system, but the cerebro-spinal system as well, and they are of course directly threatened by the snake. The serpent becomes poisonous. [...] [Nietzsche] raised himself too high, onto the point of a needle, with his idea of the superman, so he is naturally in contradiction to his human side and that forms the black snake. (ibid.)

Although there is no reference to spiders or tarantulas in *Liber Novus*—except a quick allusion to 'spider-legged monsters' (RB I, 6, 'Splitting of the Spirit': 241)—the same meaning of renewal element attributed to the scarab appears twice. In chapter 'Descent into Hell in the Future', after having seen the head of a wounded man in a cave, Jung's 'I' comes across 'a large black scarab floating past on the dark stream' (RB I, 5: 237). Jung comments: 'the black beetle is the death that is necessary for renewal; and so thereafter, a new sun glowed, the sun of the depths, full of riddles, a sun of the night' (ibid.: 239). Also in in his scientific writings, Jung puts the scarab symbol in connection with rebirth in relation to Egyptian myth a couple of times (see CW 5: § 358 and CW 8: § 843). In 'Dies II', the same animal appears again: 'Over there a small dark beetle is crawling along, pushing a ball in front of it—a scarab'. As mentioned above, Jung's 'I' is tempted to worship the animal, due to his experience in the dryness of the desert. Differently from humans, the black scarab is *living* its 'myth'—represented by its pushing the ball; therefore, it deserves admiration (RB II, 5: 271).

4.3.2 Frogs and Swamp

Apparently, frogs and toads play only a marginal role in the evolving of *Zarathustra*. Nonetheless, Jung dedicates much of his time to the interpretation of their meaning. On 21 November 1934, he comments on Nietzsche's sentence 'Or is it this: to wade into dirty water when it is the water of truth, and not to disdain cold frogs and hot toads?', from the chapter 'On the three Metamorphoses' with these words:

> Here comes in that idiosyncrasy from which Nietzsche suffered; he always was obsessed by the idea that he ought to swallow a toad. [...] That idea often occurred to him: it is the expression of the loathsomeness of life, or of the lower man. Frogs and toads are a first attempt of nature towards making something like man—a most ridiculous, absurd attempt, of course—so they are symbols or human transformation. First there is the transformation from tadpoles, and then it is a tailless animal with arms and legs, and that, of course, impresses itself very much upon the naive mind. [...] The meaning of the frog to Nietzsche was of course the inferior man living in the swamp or mire. And it is quite clear that he feels the connection with that primitive man here, because he is going to face again the conflict with the interior man; it is still the same problem of the rope-dancer. (SNZ I: 255)

While making his comment, Jung refers to Nietzsche's dream which has already been mentioned, and which he discusses in *Symbols of Transformation*.

On 3 June 1936, Jung analyses the weight of animals in general in one's confrontation with the unconscious. He defines the relationship between men and animals as a 'chain': 'The body is the original animal condition; we are all animals in the body, and so we should have animal psychology in order to be able to live in it'. To endorse his hypothesis, he makes use of the alchemical 'symbol of Avicenna', which 'consists of an eagle flying high in the air, and from his body falls a chain which is attached to a toad creeping along on the earth'. Jung comments on the image by pointing out: 'The eagle of course represents the air, the spirit, and in alchemy it had a very particular meaning. The eagle would remind any alchemist of the phoenix, the self-renewing god, an Egyptian inheritance' (SNZ II: 967–968). On 16 November 1938, he considers the same alchemical image, and compares it to Zarathustra's animals more specifically: 'The flying eagle can be compared to Zarathustra's eagle and the toad corresponds to his serpent, the eagle representing the spirit or the mind, or a flying thought-being that consist of breath, while the toad just hops on the earth, an utterly chthonic animal' (ibid.: 1413).

Interestingly, Vischer writes in *Auch Einer*: 'Three are the swamps where one should not live: the swamp of the seas, the swamp of slackness and the swamp of the close sense of the pile that does not know of any fatherland. Do you know of any fatherland?' [Drei sind die Sümpfe, darin man nicht leben soll: der Sumpf der Seen, der Sumpf der Schlaffheit und der Sumpf des engen Pfahlsinns, der von keinem Vaterland weiss. Wisst ihr denn von einem Vaterland?] (Vischer 1878: 201). In *Liber Novus*, as partially seen, the toad occurs a few times, always with the same meaning of the seminar, and plays a crucial role in the evolving of the story. As it was with serpents, also the image of the swamp means disgust and rebirth at the same time. When it comes to depicting a dark and gloomy atmosphere, Jung makes use of that very symbol to enrich his descriptions (RB II, 2 ' The Castle in the Forest': 261; RB II, 6 'death': 273; RB *Scrutinies*, § 8: 349); on a few occasions, however, its meaning gets deeper and comes to signify a necessary step to take towards personal development. The tone of such reflections—also in this case, the swamp motif recurs more frequently in layer 2—does not differ at all from Jung's opinion in the seminar cited above. For instance, he comments on a vision he had on 29 December 1913 by stating:

> At your low point you are no longer distinct from your fellow beings. You are not ashamed and do not regret it, since insofar as you live the life of your beings and descend to their lowliness/you also climb into the holy stream of common life, where you are no longer an individual on a high mountain, but a fish among fish, a frog among frogs [ein Frosch unter Fröschen]. [...]
>
> Your heights are your own mountain, which belongs to you and you alone. [...] Becoming belongs to the heights and is full of torment. How can you become if you never are? Therefore you need your bottommost, since there you are. But therefore you also need your heights, since there you become.

[...]

Everything is riddlesome to one who is becoming, but not to one who is. He who suffers from riddles should take thought of his lowest condition; we solve those riddles from which we suffer, but not those which please us.

To be that which you are is the bath of rebirth. In the depths, being is not an unconditional persistence but an endlessly slow growth. You think you are standing still like swamp water [Sumpfwasser], but slowly you flow into the sea that covers the earth's greatest deeps, and is so vast that firm land seems only an island imbedded in the womb of the immeasurable sea. (RB II, 13, 'One of the Lowly': 266)

And, again, in the *Draft* version of 'Nox Tertia':

The lowest in you is the stone that the builders discarded. It will become the cornerstone. The lowest in you will grow like a grain of rice from dry soil, shooting up from the sand of the most barren desert, and rise and stand very tall. Salvation comes to you from the discarded. Your sun will rise from muddy swamps [aus schlammigen Sümpfen]. Like all others, you are annoyed at the lowest in you because its guise is uglier than the image of yourself that you love. The lowest in you is the most despised and least valued, full of pain and sickness. He is despised so much that one hides one's face from him, that he is held in no respect whatsoever, and it is even said that he does not exist because one is ashamed for his sake and despises oneself In truth, it carries our sickness and is ridden with our pain. We consider him the one who is plagued and punished by God on account of his despicable ugliness. But he is wounded, and exposed to madness, for the sake of our own justice; he is crucified and suppressed for the sake of our own beauty We leave him to punishment and martyrdom that we might have peace. But we will take his sickness upon ourselves, and salvation will come to us through our own wounds. (Shamdasani 2009, RB II, 16, 'Nox Tertia': 300, footnote 204)[8]

The reference to the lowest is repeated in *Scrutinies* (11 January 1916), when Jung's 'I' speaks to his soul:

Oh bitterness! You have dragged me through sheer and utter Hell, you have tormented me nearly to death-and I long for your thanks. Yes, I am moved that you thank me. The hound's nature lies in my blood. Therefore I am bitter-for my sake, since how does it move you! You are divine and devilishly great, wherever and howsoever you are. As yet I am only your eunuch doorkeeper, no less imprisoned than you. Speak, you concubine of Heaven, you divine monster! Have I not fished you from the swamp [aus dem Sumpfe]?

How do you like the black hole? Speak without blood, sing from your own force, you have gorged yourself on men. (RB *Scrutinies*, § 5: 344)

In *Zarathustra*, the protagonist meets the 'leech' for the first time while passing by a 'swamp' [Sumpf]. The character—namely a scientist involved in a meticulous analysis of leech brain—is submerged by mud and does not even look like a man (Za IV, 4, KSA 4: 309). Remarkably, in Jung's copy, this chapter presents several underlinings and readings markings. Among these, the word 'compassionately' [mittleidig] is underlined. What follows the aforementioned passage from *Liber Novus* is this:

Then my soul writhed and like a downtrodden worm turned and cried out, "Pity, have compassion." "Compassion? Have you ever had compassion for me? You brute bestial tormentor! You've never gotten past compassionate moods. You lived on human food and drank my blood. Has it made you fat? Will you learn to revere the torment of the human animal? What would you souls and Gods want without man? Why do you long for him? Speak, whore!" (RB *Scrutinies*, § 5: 344)

The 'leech' is one of the 'higher men' encountered by *Zarathustra* and invited by him to his cave for the 'Last Supper'. As all the other 'higher men', he represents to Jung Nietzsche's reluctance to deal with his own inferiority. Such understanding can be said to correspond to the role of the frog as a symbol of transformation and renewal in *Liber Novus* as well. Indeed, the 'new God' whom Jung's 'I' gives birth to is retrospectively called 'the son of the frogs'—such a phrase, as already argued, was probably borrowed by Jung from Spitteler's *Imago* (Spitteler 1906: 62; see Sect. 3.2.1). It is not easy to accept to give birth to a frog, but exactly from the overcoming of such difficulty, the transformation can take place. In chapter 'The Magician' it is written:

My soul, you adulterous whore, you became pregnant with this bastard! I am dishonored; I, laughable father of the Antichrist! How I mistrusted you! And how poor was my mistrust, that it could not gauge the magnitude of this infamous act!

What do you break apart? You broke love and life in twain. From this ghastly sundering, the frog and the son of the frog come forth. Ridiculous-disgusting sight! Irresistible advent! They will sit on the banks of the sweet water and listen to the nocturnal song of the frogs, since their God has been born as a son of frogs. (RB II, 21, 'The Magician': 327)

And again, a few lines below: 'The myth commences, the one that need only be lived, not sung, the one that sings itself I subject myself to the son, the one engendered by sorcery, the unnaturally born, the son of the frogs, who stands at the waterside and speaks with his fathers and listens to their nocturnal singing. Truly he is full of mysteries and superior in strength to all men. No man has produced him, and no woman has given birth to him' (ibid.: 328).

In *Scrutinies*, Abraxas is worshipped as 'the lord of toads and frogs, which live in the water and go up on the land, whose chorus ascends at noon and at midnight' (RB *Scrutinies*, § 8: 350). Again: 'The God of the frogs or toads, the brainless, is the uniting of the Christian God with Satan. His nature is like the flame; he is like Eros, but a God; Eros is only a daimon' (ibid., 'Appendix C': 370). Finally, there is another passage from *Scrutinies* which seems directly to refer to Jung's future interpretation of 'Of the Three Metamorphoses':

> In this moment my vision ended. And ΦΙΛΗΜΩΝ went away and I was alone. And I remained apart as I had been told. But in the fourth night I saw a strange form, a man wearing a long coat and a turban; his eyes shone cleverly and kindly like a wise doctor's. He approached me and said, "I speak to you of joy." But I answered, "You want to speak to me of joy? I bleed from the thousandfold wounds of men."
>
> He replied, "I bring healing. Women taught me this art. They know how to heal sick children. Do your wounds burn you? Healing is at hand. Give ear to good counsel and do not be incensed."
>
> I retorted, "What do you want? To tempt me? Mock me?"
>
> "What are you thinking?" he interrupted, "I bring you the bliss of paradise, the healing fire, the love of women."
>
> "*Are you thinking*," I asked, "*of the descent into the frog swamp? The dissolution in the many, the scattering, the dismembering?*"
>
> But as I spoke, the old man turned into ΦΙΛΗΜΩΝ and I saw that he was the magician who was tempting me. But ΦΙΛΗΜΩΝ continued:
>
> "You have not yet experienced the dismembering. You should be blown apart and shredded and scattered to the winds. Men are preparing for the Last Supper with you."
>
> "What then will remain of me? I cried.
>
> Nothing but your shadow. You will be a river that pours forth over the lands. It seeks every valley and streams toward the depths."

I asked, full of grief "But where will my uniqueness remain?"
"You will steal it from yourself," ΦΙΛΗΜΩΝ replied, "You will hold the invisible realm in trembling hands; it lowers its roots into the gray darknesses and mysteries of the earth and sends up branches covered in leaves into the golden air". (RB *Scrutinies*, § 13: 355, italics added)

As already discussed, references to the 'turban' and the 'Last Supper' put this passage in a more direct connection with Zarathustra. Moreover, this passage elucidates and enriches what has been said in 'The Way of What is to Come': 'The spirit of the depths, however, conquered this arrogance, and I had to swallow the small as a means of healing the immortal in me' (RB I, § 1: 230). The allusion to swallowing 'the small' undoubtedly links once more Jung's experience to his later understanding of Nietzsche's faulty individuation represented by *Zarathustra*.

4.3.3 Doves, Feminine, and Jung's 'Soul'

As discussed in the introduction, one of Jung's main criticisms to Nietzsche's experience with the 'unconscious' is the lack of acknowledgement of the Anima in *Zarathustra*. As already pointed out, sometimes this archetype is incorporated in some features belonging to *Zarathustra* (like his passion for dance); other times it is projected onto feminine personifications, such as life and wisdom. Occasionally, some of these personifications are read by Jung as a form of immature eroticism. This is precisely the case with the image of doves, whose presence in Nietzsche's text is neither particularly recurrent nor crucial, but, according to Jung, calls for a deep psychological interpretation. Such an interpretation does not differ from that of the dancing maidens in 'The Night-Song', where Jung expresses himself:

[...] A multiplicity of anima figures is only to be met with in cases where the individual is utterly unconscious of his anima. In a man who is completely identical with the anima, you might find that plurality, but the moment he becomes conscious of that figure, she assumes a personality and is definitely one. This is in contradistinction to the animus in women, who as soon as she becomes conscious of him is definitely several. [...] So from such a symbol you can conclude that Nietzsche/Zarathustra is profoundly unconscious of his anima. Yet we cannot assume, inasmuch as Zarathustra is the typical wise old man, that he would be unconscious of the nature of the anima. The myth of Simon Magus and Helena is a typical example, and the (tale of)

> Faust and Gretchen is another, but not so good because she is too unconscious and he is not wise enough. (SNZ II: 1153, 16 June 1937)

Previously, on 5 June 1935, while analysing 'The Tree Upon the Hill', Jung had said about the Anima:

> That conflict [between the Wise Old Man and the Anima] is settled, for when the anima is rescued out of the brothel of the world, she follows the wise old man, as his *sybilla*, his *somnambule*. If the anima is in the brothel the old wise man does not exist; he can only appear when the anima is redeemed from the brothel. Of course she would be the complete opposite of the wise old man when she is in the brothel, but then the opposition is so complete that the other part is invisible. (SNZ I: 530)

James, L. Jarrett, the editor of the seminar wrote in a footnote, cross-referring to Jonas (1934: 353–358): 'Simon Magus, a prominent early Gnostic, is said to have taken from a brothel in Tyre a girl in whom he recognised a reincarnation of Helen of Troy and a manifestation of the Divine Mother of all beings, including angels' (ibid., footnote 4). Allusions to Simon Magus and Helena appear again in *Memories, Dream, Reflexions* (MDR: 206).

On 25 January 1939, Jung comments on the image of the 'laughing lion with a flock of doves' in 'Of the Old and New Tables' in a similar way. First, he stresses Nietzsche's solitude once more: 'Think of the picture—a laughing lion and a circle of pigeons sitting around him. Now, I find that there is a little uncertainty about the question of being alone with oneself and going down to humanity'. Nietzsche's mistake would be to seek himself 'in such utter solitude, but only fall[s] into [his] unconscious. What is meant is, that you should be *with yourself*, not alone but with yourself, and you can be with yourself even in a crowd'. By losing oneself, one 'seeks solitude as a sure means of making him unconscious of himself'. Therefore he concludes: 'But the point is *not* to be unconscious: the point is to picture the unconscious of oneself but to be with oneself'. In this sense, 'that forced, or chosen, solitude in which Nietzsche lived was a temptation, and one of the reasons why he lost himself in the unconscious' (SNZ II:1484–1485). The image of the lion surrounded by doves is compared to 'the lion of salon, the *bel homme* in the drawing room with a flock of young girls round him. And then there is the rooster and the hens. That is a very covert metaphor for somebody whose audience contains a greater number of ladies'. Jung states: 'So the laughing lion is obviously himself with an audience, and the doves are specifically feminine birds', which he defines as 'lovebirds'; for they represent the bird of Aphrodite. They are also a symbol for 'the Holy Ghost'—that was represented as 'the mother', 'the wife of God', and 'Mary' herself in Gnostic tradition—'Sophia', or the 'Church' (which is said to be 'the embodiment of the Holy Ghost'). The lion 'is the age-old symbol of the sun, and the sun in July and August particularly, the *domicilium solis*'. The fact that this animal is said to laugh means, to Jung, that there was a moment in which it did not laugh. Therefore its laughing means that something new is about to happen, that 'fulfilment comes'. Because 'Zarathustra compares himself again and again with the setting sun and the rising sun, or the sun that comes out of the dark clouds, or out of the cave', Jung postulates the lion being Zarathustra himself, 'and he is laughing because he sees the fulfilment, senses a completion. Completion is a circle and here it is a circle of lovebirds'. He compares such an image with 'the Shakti circling round Shiva', which is 'of course a pretty grand idea and not necessarily something to laugh about. But when that becomes concrete, the animal god in Nietzsche laughs. *Then Eros comes up*, and of course everybody will say, "I always told you so, that is the end of it"'. From this point on, 'Zarathustra turns into his own opposite, practically by the law of *enantiodromia*' (ibid.: 1489–1492, first italic ours). Jung adds: 'The books begins with that great spiritual solitude, and at the end come the Dionysian dithyrambs. Now arrives the ass, beautiful and strong, but the ass is the symbol of voluptuousness, which Nietzsche, as a philologist, knew very well. And when you look through his poems you see the same element'. Jung mentions the dove as the Holy Ghost embodiment also on 15 February 1939 (ibid.: 1532). On 28 November 1934, the lion in 'Of the Three Metamorphoses' was interpreted this way: 'Here I think it is clear why Nietzsche needed the lion to symbolize an attitude which can break laws. It is the royal self-will, it is the antinomy' (SNZ I: 269). In *Concerning the Archetypes, With Special Reference to the Anima Concept* (1936/1954), in relation to Brother Klaus, Jung points out:

> In the visions that marked his initiation into the state of adoption by God, God appeared in dual form, once as a majestic father and once as a majestic mother. This representation could not be more unorthodox, since the Church had eliminated the feminine element from the Trinity a thousand years earlier as heretical. Brother Klaus was a simple unlettered peasant who doubtless had received none but the approved Church teaching, and was

> certainly not acquainted with the Gnostic interpretation of the Holy Ghost as the feminine and motherly Sophia. His so-called Trinity Vision is at the same time a perfect example of the intensity of projected contents. Brother Klaus's psychological situation was eminently suited to a projection of this kind, for his conscious idea of God was so little in accord with the unconscious content that the latter had to appear in the form of an alien and shattering experience. We must conclude from this that it was not the traditional idea of God but, on the contrary, an 'heretical' image that realized itself in visionary form; an archetypal interpretation which came to life again spontaneously, independently of tradition. It was the archetype of the divine pair, the syzygy. (CW 9, 1: § 133)

The same motif is discussed also in *The Concept of the Collective Unconscious* (1936): 'according to an early Christian-Gnostic idea, the spirit which appeared in the form of a dove was interpreted as Sophia-Sapientia—Wisdom and the Mother of Christ. Thanks to this motif of the dual birth, children today, instead of having good and evil fairies who magically "adopt" them at birth with blessings or curses, are given sponsors—a "godfather" and a "godmother"' (ibid.: § 93), and 'The dove represents the fructifying agent, the wind of the Holy Ghost' (ibid.: § 108). 'Sophia' is also closely explored in relation to the figure of 'Christ' in *Christ, A Symbol of the Self* (CW 9, 2: § 118, footnote 88), whereas the symbol of the dove in relation to the Holy Ghost in alchemy is exhaustively discussed in *Mysterium Coniunctionis* (1955/56) (CW 14: § 81).

Getting back to Jung's seminar on *Zarathustra*, according to this interpretation, Nietzsche was not able to recognise his Anima; on the one hand, he projected her onto the plurality of dancing girls or flying birds, on the other hand, he intuited her highest meaning—that is her complementary role to his personality—but because his relation to her was so undeveloped, the erotic aspect of the Anima surpassed the sacrality of her value. This situation appears to Jung as generated by Nietzsche's incapacity to face his own solitude, which would lead him to get lost within his unconscious projections. The words pronounced in relation to Nietzsche's solitude remind one of what Jung said about himself and his experience with his fantasies at the beginning of *Liber Novus*, which has been sufficiently discussed in Chap. 3. In particular, it is again the question of the desert that seems to arise: 'Is it solitude, to be with oneself? Solitude is true only when the self is a desert' (RB I, 4, 'The Desert': 236; see Sect. 3.2.1). And, also this time, Nietzsche's 'self' appears to be a desert: as already remarked, in his interpretation, Jung describes Nietzsche's meeting with the unconscious in terms of 'temptation' (SNZ II: 1485).

In 1912, Jung had a first dream of a white bird, namely 'a small seagull or a dove', that rested on his table, in the garden, and then turned into an eight-year-old girl with blonde hair who began to play with his children. After a while, the creature transformed itself into a bird again, and spoke these words to Jung: 'Only in the first hours of the night can I transform myself into a human being, while the male dove is busy with the twelve dead'. After having spoken, the dove flew away (MDR: 171–172; the dream is also reported in *Black Book* 2: 17–18). According to his *Black Books*, that dream was responsible for Jung's decision to start an affair with Toni Wolff, whom he had known for three years. More generally, in *Liber Novus* Jung identifies his soul with the 'white bird', or the 'dove', and the link between doves and feminine recurs quite often,[9] as will happen in his later works. Also in this case, therefore such a link appears in layer 2 more frequently; however, images of doves occur in visions as well. Especially towards the end of the story, one of the most significant apparitions of a 'white bird' takes place, namely in the chapter 'The Way of the Cross'. After that the black serpent had turned itself into a white one, Jung's 'I' felt confused by what was happening, and 'great weight burdened' his 'soul'. At this point, as already reported, 'the white bird that sat on [his] shoulder spoke to [him]: "Let it rain, let the wind blow, let the waters flow and the fire burn. Let each thing have its development, let becoming have its day"' (RB II, 20: 310). The images used by Jung to connect soul and feminine in *Liber Novus* are the same appearing in his published writings. At the very end of *Scrutinies*, Philemon is said to be Simon Magus. As already anticipated, on a 'hot summer day' in June 1916, while 'taking a stroll' in his garden, Jung came across Philemon again, who was 'strolling in the fragrant grass'. He wrote that when he 'sought to approach him, a blue shade came from the other side, and when ΦΙΛΗΜΩΝ saw him, he said, "I find you in the garden, beloved. The sins of the world have conferred beauty upon your countenance"'. Then he welcomed him, but the shade replied: 'Oh Simon Magus or whatever your name may be, are you in my garden or am I in yours?' And 'ΦΙΛΗΜΩΝ said, "You are, Oh master, in my garden. Helena, or whatever you choose to call her, and I are your servants. You can find accommodation with us. Simon and Helena have become ΦΙΛΗΜΩΝ and Bauci and so we are the hosts of the Gods"'. It could be stated that through the figures of Simon and Helena, as well as through the shade and the serpent, the opposites are conjuncted on a universal level, so that the final transformation can now occur. The shade's response to Philemon, which resolves the entire *Liber Novus* plot, has been previously discussed: 'I bring you the beauty of suffering. That is needed by whoever hosts the worm' (RB *Scrutinies*, § 15: 359). In the *Black Books*, the shade is said to be 'Christ' Himself. In Ovid's and La Fontaine's representations of Philemon and Baucis, the couple host the Gods. In both versions, their loyalty and hospitality are exalted and rewarded (Ovid, *Metamorphoses* VIII; de La Fontaine, 1963). On the contrary, in Goethe's story, the couple host Mephistopheles and Faust who, instead of being grateful, kill them (Goethe, *Faust* II, 5). The reference to Helena seems to allude to *Faust* again, especially to its final lines: 'All things corruptible / Are but a parable; / Earth's insufficiency / Here finds fulfilment; / Here the ineffable / Wins life through love; / Eternal Feminine / Leads us above'. Jung made use of Goethe's conception of the 'Eternal Feminine' in several texts, the most significant of which being *The Psychology of the Child Archetype* (1940) (CW 9, 1: §§ 298–299). In *Concerning Rebirth* (1939/1950), Jung writes:

> Another aspect of this fourth form [rebirth (renovatio)] is essential transformation, i.e., total rebirth of the individual. Here the renewal implies a change of his essential nature, and may be called a transmutation. As examples we may mention the transformation of a mortal into an immortal being, of a corporeal into a spiritual being, and of a human into a divine being. Well known prototypes of this change are the transfiguration and ascension of Christ, and the assumption of the Mother of God into heaven after her death, together with her body. Similar conceptions are to be found in Part II of Goethe's *Faust*; for instance, the transformation of Faust into the boy and then into Doctor Marianus. (ibid.: § 204)

In *Memories, Dreams, Reflexions*, Jung recounts:

> In the days when I first read *Faust I* could not remotely guess the extent to which Goethe's strange heroic myth was a collective experience and that it prophetically anticipated the fate of the Germans. Therefore I felt personally implicated, and when Faust, in his hubris and self-inflation, caused the murder of Philemon and Baucis, I felt guilty, quite as if I myself in the past had helped commit the murder of the two old people. This strange idea alarmed me, and I regarded it as my responsibility to atone for this crime, or to prevent its repetition. (MDR: 234)

It might be of interest to finally recall that Nietzsche reversed the meaning of Goethe's final verses in his *Lieder des Prinzen Vogelfrei*: 'The intransigency / is but your imagery! / God's interagency / Is lyric trickery … / / World rim, rolling all, / skimming aim to aim: / the must—the spited call, / Insane calls it—the game … / / The game of worlds, immane, Stains into seen and seem:—/ the ever more inane / Stains into ever—we!' (FW *Anhang*, 'An Goethe', KSA 3: 639).

Back to *Liber Novus*, the feminine plays the same role also in the resolution of the Elijah and Salome episode, where—as already pointed out—the couple of opposites are expressed in terms of 'logos' and 'eros'. Later on, Jung will comment:

> The old man represents a spiritual principle that could be designated as Logos, and the maiden represents an unspiritual principle of feeling that could be called Eros. […] The figure of an old prophet is therefore a fitting allegory for this principle, since the prophetic spirit unites in itself all these qualities. In contrast, Eros is a principle that contains a commingling of all the fundamental activities of the soul just as much as it masters them, although its purpose is completely different. It is not form-giving but form-fulfilling; it is the wine that will be poured into the vessel; it is not the bed and direction of the stream but the impetuous water flowing in it. Eros is desire, longing, force, exuberance, pleasure, suffering. […] The old prophet expresses persistence, but the young maiden denotes movement. Their impersonal essence is expressed by the fact that they are figures belonging to general human history; they do not belong to a person but have been a spiritual content of the world's peoples since time immemorial. Everyone has them, and therefore these figures recur in the work of thinkers and poets. (RB *Scrutinies*, 'Appendix B': 365)

In similar manner, in 1916, Jung writes in *Black Book* 5: 'Above you comes the dove or the celestial soul, in which love and foresight are united, just as poison and shrewdness are united in the serpent' (ibid., 'Appendix C': 370). In 'Systema Munditotius', Jung's cosmological representation, a more specific link between the dove and the Holy Ghost is given: 'The light realm of rich fullness lies to the right, where from the bright circle *frigus sive amor dei* [cold, or the love of God] the dove of the Holy Ghost takes wing, and wisdom (*Sophia*) pours from a double beaker to left and right.—This feminine sphere is that of heaven.—' (ibid., 'Appendix B': 364). In this respect, it is not to be forgotten that the Latin word 'Anima' means precisely 'soul'—in Italian it still maintains the same meaning—

though Jung's idea does not mean to stop at a pure rational understanding of the concept. Several years later—when trying to express the archetypes in more conceptual terms—Jung will make clear that his understanding of the Anima intends to denote a more complete (and complex) 'personification of the unconscious'. Similarly, in *Archetypes of the Collective Unconscious* (1934–1954), Jung writes: 'The anima is not the soul in the dogmatic sense, not an *anima rationalis*, which is a philosophical conception, but a natural archetype that satisfactorily sums up all the statements of the unconscious, of the primitive mind, of the history of language and religion' (CW 9, 1, § 54). And, in *The Syzygy: Anima and Animus*, Jung refers to Spitteler's phrase 'My Lady Soul' [Herrin meines Lebens; Strenge Frau]" (Spitteler 1906), and opposes to it with his idea of Anima:

> I have suggested instead the term "anima," as indicating something specific, for which the expression 'soul' is too general and too vague. The empirical reality summed up under the concept of the anima forms an extremely dramatic content of the unconscious. It is possible to describe this content in rational, scientific language, but in this way one entirely fails to express its living character. Therefore, in describing the living processes of the psyche, I deliberately and consciously give preference to a dramatic, mythological way of thinking and speaking, because this is not only more expressive but also more exact than an abstract scientific terminology, which is wont to toy with the notion that its theoretic formulations may one fine day be resolved into algebraic equations. (CW 9, 2: § 25)

On 28 September 1916, as reported in *Black Books* 6, Jung's 'soul' spoke to him about a 'golden bird', which 'is not the white bird [...]. It is different. The white bird is a good daimon, but the golden one is above you and under your God. It flies ahead of you. I see it in the blue ether, flying toward the star. It is something that is part of you. And it is at once its own egg, containing you'. Differently from the white one, this bird 'is no soul; it is your entire nature. People are golden birds as well; not all; some are worms and rot in the earth. But many are also golden birds'. Then she continues:

> The golden bird sits in the tree of the six lights. The tree grows out of Abraxas's head, but Abraxas grows out of the Pleroma. Everything from which the tree grows blossoms as a light, transformed, as a womb of the flowering treetop, of the golden egg-bird. The tree of light is first a plant, which is called an individual; this grows out of Abraxas's head, his thought

is one among many. The individual is a mere plant without flowers and fruits, a passageway to the tree of seven lights. The individual is a precursor of the tree of light. The lucent blossoms from him, Phanes himself. Agni, a new fire, a golden bird. This comes after the individual, namely when it has been reunited with the world, the world blossoms from it. Abraxas is the drive, individual, distinct from him, but the tree of the seven lights is the symbol of the individual united with Abraxas. This is where Phanes appears and he, the golden bird, flies ahead.

You unite yourself with Abraxas through me.

First you give me your heart, and then you live through me. I am the bridge to Abraxas. (Shamdasani 2009, RB *Scrutinies*, § 12: 354, footnote 125)

Notes

1. On an accurate analysis of all the historical interpretations of Philemon in relation to his meaning to Jung's personal psychology, see Shamdasani (2005: 62–86).
2. On Adler's reception of Nietzsche, see Brudel-Bezzel (2003, 2010).
3. Beside the *Groß-* and the *Kleinoktavausgabe*, other editions of Nietzsche's *Gesammelte Werke* were published, in both hardcover and paperback sizes. On the history of the 'Nietzsche-Archiv', see Montinari (1982: 10–21) and Hoffmann (1991). On a detailed reconstruction of the events that led to the birth of a critical edition of Nietzsche's works, see Campioni (1992: 19–67, 2001b, 2010). On fascist, idealistic, as well as nationalistic readings of Nietzsche, see Montinari (1981).
4. On Nietzsche's distinction between 'self' [Selb], 'body' [Leib], and 'soul' [Seele], see Gerhardt (2011: 1–49 and 58–86). He defines Nietzsche's understanding of the ' self ' as 'the capacity of the body to act ' (10); in fact it seems to have 'the same ontological dignity' as the 'body'. According to the scholar, these concepts appear as differentiated from each other only on a conceptual level. The 'self' would represent a sort of 'mediator between body and I', which would 'hold together physical body [Körper] and soul [Seele], body [Leib] and I [Ich]'. This would permit to perceive the body as a 'whole' [Einheit] (52).
5. The serpent is also faced *en passant* another couple of times. On 2 November 1938, while interpreting 'On The Bedwarfing Virtue', the symbol of the serpent is mentioned in relation to 'Christ' and the zodiac (SNZ II: 1384); on 30 November 1938, while discussing 'On The Three Evil Things', an analogy between some kinds of plants and serpents is proposed, referring to a similarity in their moving (ibid.: 1435; Jung speaks of 'serpentine movement').

6. The sentence 'What is beyond the human that appears in love has the nature of the serpent and the bird' can be also compared to Nietzsche's aphorism 'What is done out of love always takes place beyond good and evil' (JGB IV, 153, KSA 5: 99). Jung's personal copy of *Beyond Good and Evil* (available at Jung's personal library in Küsnacht) presents numerous underlinings, annotations, and comments.
7. Because of the link between the tarantula and intuition, Jung argues that Nietzsche 'never saw a tarantula', since in his representation it displays a triangle on its back, and that characteristic belongs to a different kind of spider, namely the *Kreuzspinne*. According to Jung, Nietzsche would not need to see a tarantula: his imagination would be guided by the intuition, so the force of the symbol would be given by Nietzsche's perception about its deep meaning. However, as pointed out by James L. Jarrett in one of the footnotes to the text, 'The European tarantula does have a small triangle on its back' (ibid., footnote 2: 1079).
8. Cfr Mt 21:42: 'Jesus said to them, "Have you never read in the Scriptures: 'The stone the builders rejected has become the cornerstone; the Lord has done this, and it is marvelous in our eyes'?"'; Mark 12:10: 'Haven't you read this passage of Scripture: "The stone the builders rejected has become the cornerstone"'; Luke 20:17: 'Jesus looked directly at them and asked, "Then what is the meaning of that which is written: 'The stone the builders rejected has become the cornerstone'?"' and Acts 4:11: 'Jesus is "the stone you builders rejected, which has become the cornerstone"'.
9. Occasionally, the biblical meaning of the dove occurs as well: 'That will be a time of salvation and the dove, and the eternal fire, and redemption will descend' (RB I, 8, 'The Conception of the God': 245); 'Be crafty like serpents and guileless like doves' (RB II, 16, 'Nox Tertia': 300). This last sentence seems to recall Matthew 10:16: 'Behold, I send you forth as sheep in the midst of wolves: be ye therefore wise as serpents, and harmless as doves'. In *Memories, Dreams, Reflexions*, Jung makes use of this verse in order to explain the lack of answers of myth for modern man, who 'has suppressed any […] attempts' to develop the meaning offered by 'the original version of myth': 'For what purpose do men need the cunning of serpents? And what is the link between this cunning and the innocence of the dove?' (MDR: 332).

References

Adler, Alfred. 1912. *Über den nervösen Charakter*. Wiesbaden: J. F. Bergmann.

———. 1933. *Der Sinn des Lebens*. Frankfurt am Main: Fischer.

———. 1933–1937. Über den Ursprung des Strebens nach Überlegenheit und des Gemeinschaftsgefühls. In *Alfred Adler, Psychotherapie und Erziehung*.

Ausgewählte Aufsätze, Band III: 1933–1937, ed. Heinz L. Ansbacher and Rowena R. Antoch. Frankfurt am Main: Fischer, 1983.
Bäumler, Alfred. 1931a. *Die Unschuld des Werdens*. Leipzig: Kröner.
———. 1931b. *Nietzsche. Der Philosph und der Politiker*. Leipzig: Reclam.
Bishop, Paul. 1993. The Jung/Förster-Nietzsche Correspondence. *German Life and Letters* 46: 319–330.
———. 1994. The Members of Jung's Seminar on Zarathustra. *Spring* 56: 92–122.
———. 1995a. *The Dionysian Self: C. G. Jung's Reception of Friedrich Nietzsche*. Berlin and New York: De Gruyter.
———. 1995b. Jung's Annotation of Nietzsche's Works: An Analysis. *Nietzsche-Studien* 24: 271–314.
———. 1999. Estrangement from the Deed and the Memory Thereof: Freud and Jung on the Pale Criminal in Nietzsche's *Zarathustra*. *Orbis Litterarum* 54: 424–438.
———, ed. 2004. *Nietzsche and Antiquity. His Reaction and Response to the Classical Tradition*. Rochester, NY: Camden House.
———. 2008. *Analtytical Psychology and German Classical Aesthetics: Goethe, Schiller, and Jung*, Vol. 1, The Development Of The Personality. 2 vols. London and New York: Routledge.
———. 2012. Jung's *Red Book* and Its Relation to Aspects of German Idealism. *The Journal of Analytical Psychology* 57: 335–353.
———. 2014. *Carl Jung*. London: Reaktion Books.
———. 2017. *On the Blissful Island with Nietzsche and Jung: In the Shadow of the Superman*. Oxon and New York: Routledge.
Bruder-Bezzel, Almuth. 2003. Nietzsche, Freud und Adler. In *Kreativität und Determination. Studien zu Nietzsche, Freud und Adler*, ed. Almuth Bruder-Bezzel and Klaus-Jürgen Bruder, 122–169. Göttingen: Vandenhoek & Ruprecht.
———. 2010. Alfred Adlers Nietzsche-Bezug und die schöpferische Kraft. In *Nietzsche und die Tiefenpsychologie*, ed. Roman Lesmeister and Elke Metzner, 91–106. Freiburg and Munich: Verlag Karl Alber.
Campioni, Giuliano. 1992. *Leggere Nietzsche. Alle origini dell'edizione critica Colli-Montinari. Con lettere e testi inediti*. Pisa: ETS.
———. 1998. *Sulla strada di Nietzsche*. Pisa: ETS.
———. 2001a. *Les lectures françaises de Nietzsche*. Paris: PUF. Republished in *Der französische Nietzsche*. Berlin: De Gruyter, 2009.
———. 2001b. Nota. In *Che cosa ha detto Nietzsche. A cura e con una nota di Giuliano Campioni*, ed. Mazzino Montinari, 196–224. Milan: Adelphi.
———. 2009. *Nietzsche. La morale dell'Eroe*. Pisa: ETS.
———. 2010. Lombrichi e tesori. La ricerca delle fonti e la 'biblioteca ideale' di Nietzsche. In *La passione della conoscenza, Volume pubblicato in onore di Sossio*

Giametta, a cura del Centro interdipartimentale di ricerca Arthur Schopenhauer e la scuola dell'università del Salento, 85–105. Lecce: Pensa Multi Media Editore.

De La Fontaine, Jean. 1693. Philémon et Baucis. In *Fables*. Paris: Barbin: Livre XII, Fable 25.

Dixon, Patricia E. 1999. *Nietzsche and Jung: Sailing a Deeper Night*. New York: Peter Lang.

Domenici, Gaia. 2014. Overleaping oder Surpassing? Die problematische Lektüre der Geschichte des Seiltänzers bei C. G. Jung. In *Nietzsches Zarathustra Auslegen. Thesen, Positionen und Entfaltungen zu "Also sprach Zarathustra" von Friedrich Wilhelm Nietzsche*, ed. Murat Ates, 207–219. Marburg: Tectum Verlag.

———. 2018. 'Crush the Head of the Serpent and It will Bite you in the Heel': A Reconstruction of Jung's Interpretation of the Poisonous Serpents in *Zarathustra* Through *Liber Novus*. *Phanês: Journal for Jung History* 1: 1–27.

Gay, Marco, and Isolde Schiffermüller, eds. 2013. *Lo Zarathustra di Nietzsche: C. G. Jung e lo scandalo dell'inconscio*. Bergamo: Moretti & Vitali.

Gerhardt, Volker. 2011. *Die Funken des freien Geistes. Neuere Aufsätze zu Nietzsches Philosophie der Zukunft*. Berlin and New York: De Gruyter.

Heidegger, Martin. 1961. *Nietzsche*. 2 vols. Pfullingen, Neske.

Hoffmann, David M. 1991. *Zur Geschichte des Nietzsche-Archivs*. Berlin and New York: De Gruyter.

Huskinson, Lucy. 2004. *Nietzsche and Jung. The Whole Self in the Union of Opposites*. Hove and New York: Brunner-Routledge.

Innamorati, Marco. 1991. La presenza dello Zarathustra di Nietzsche nelle opere di Jung. *Giornale storico di psicologia dinamica* 29: 73–93.

Jarrett, James. 1989. 'Introduction', 'Members Of The Seminar' and 'Footnotes'. In *Nietzsche's Zarathustra: Notes of the Seminar Given in 1934–9*, ed. C.G. Jung, 2nd ed. Edited by James L. Jarrett in Two Parts. London: Routledge, 1994.

Jaspers, Karl. 1935/1974. *Nietzsche. Einführung in das Verständnis seines Philosophierens*, 1981. Berlin: de Gruyter.

Johannes Valentinus Andreä. 1602/1616. *The Chymical Marriage of Christian Rosenkreutz in the Year 1459*. Strasbourg.

Jonas, Hans. 1934. *Gnosis und Spätantiker Geist*. Vol. I. Göttingen: Vandenhoeck & Ruprecht. 1934.

Jung, Carl Gustav. 1902. *On the Psychology and Pathology of So-called Occult Phenomena*. Collected Works of C. G. Jung. Vol. 1, §§ 1–150.

———. 1905. *Cryptomnesia*. Collected Works of C. G. Jung. Vol. 1, §§ 166–186.

———. 1909/1949. *The Significance of the Father in the Destiny of the Individual*. Collected Works of C. G. Jung. Vol. 4, §§ 693–744.

———. 1912a. *Wandlungen und Symbole der Libido. Beiträge zur Entwicklung des Denkens*. 2nd ed. Leipzig and Vienna: Franz Deuticke, 1925.

———. 1912b. *Psychology of the Unconscious. A Study of the Transformations and Symbolisms of the Libido. A Contribution to the History of the Evolution of Thought*. New York: Moffat, Yard and Company, 1917.
———. 1914–1920. *Some Crucial Points in Psychoanalysis. A Correspondence between Dr. Jung and Dr. Loÿ*. Collected Works of C. G. Jung. Vol. 4, §§ 576–669.
———. 1917. *On the Psychology of the Unconscious*. Collected Works of C. G. Jung. Vol. 7, §§ 1–201.
———. 1922/1931. *On the Relation of Analytical Psychology to Poetry*. Collective Works of C. G. Jung. Vol. 15, §§ 97–132.
———. 1934. *Archetypes of the Collective Unconscious*. Collected Works of C. G. Jung. Vol. 9, 1, §§ 1–86
———. 1936a. *Wotan*. Collected Works of C. G. Jung. Vol. 10, §§ 371–399.
———. 1936b–1937. *The Concept of the Collective Unconscious*. Collected Works of C. G. Jung. Vol. 9, 1, §§ 87–110.
———. 1928–1935/1938. *The Relations Between the Ego and the Unconscious*. Collected Works of C. G. Jung. Vol. 7, §§ 202–406.
———. 1945. *After the Catastrophe*. Collected Works of C. G. Jung. Vol. 10, §§ 400–443.
———. 1945–1948. *The Phenomenology of the Spirit in Fairytales*. CW 9, 1: §§ 384–455.
———. 1951. *Aion Researches into the Phenomenology of the Self*. Collected Works of C. G. Jung. Vol. 9, 2.
———. 1952a. *Symbols of Transformation*. Collected Works of C. G. Jung. Vol. 5
———. 1952b. *Synchronicity: An Acausal Connecting Principle*. Collected Works of C. G. Jung. Vol. 8, §§ 816–997.
———. 1954. *Concerning the Archetypes, with Special Reference to the Anima Concept*. Collected Works of C. G. Jung. Vol. 9, 1, §§ 111–147.
———. 1955–1956. *Mysterium Coniunctionis*. Collected Works of C. G. Jung, Vol. 14.
———. 1989. *Nietzsche's Zarathustra: Notes of the Seminar Given in 1934–9*. 2nd ed. Edited by James L. Jarrett in Two Parts. London: Routledge, 1994.
———. 1996. *The Psychology of Kundalini Yoga. Notes of the Seminar given in 1932*. Edited by Sonu Shamdasani. Princeton: Princeton University Press.
———. 2009. *The Red Book: Liber Novus*. Edited and Introduced by Sonu Shamdasani. Translated by Mark Kyburz, John Peck, and Sonu Shamdasani. New York and London: W. W. Norton & Company.
Jung, Carl Gustav, and Aniela Jaffé. 1962. *Memories, Dreams, Reflections by Carl Gustav Jung*. Recorded and Edited by Aniela Jaffé. New York: Vintage Books, 1989.
Kieser, Franz. 1606. *Cabala Chymica*. Mühlhausen.

Liebscher, Martin. 2001. 'Wotan' und 'Puer Aeternus'. Die Zeithistorische Verstrickung von C. G. Jungs Zarathustrainterpretation. *Nietzsche Studien* 30: 329–350.

———. 2002. Zarathustra – Der Archetypus des 'Alten Weisen'. *Nietzscheforschung* 9: 234–245.

———. 2003. Die 'unheimliche Ähnlichkeit'. Nietzsches Hermeneutik der Macht und analytische Interpretation bei Carl Gustav Jung. *Ecce Opus* 81: 37–50.

———. 2006. *Nietzsche und Jung*. Review of Lucy Huskinson, *The Whole Self in the Union of Opposites* (2004). *Nietzsche Studien* 35: 393–397.

———. 2012. *Libido und Wille zur Macht. C.G. Jungs Auseinandersetzung mit Nietzsche*. Basel: Schwabe.

Lindner, Michael. 2010. 'Ein tiefstes Erlebnis'. C. G. Jungs Lektüre von Nietzsches 'Also sprach Zarathustra' anhand seiner Seminare 1934–39. In *Nietzsche und die Tiefenpsychologie*, ed. Roman Lesmeister and Elke Metzner, 107–120. Freiburg and Munich: Verlag Karl Alber.

Montinari, Mazzino. 1981. *Su Nietzsche*. Rome: Editori Riuniti.

———. 1982. Die neue kritische Gesamtausgabe von Nietzsches Werken. In *Nietzsche lesen*. Berlin and New York: de Gruyter.

Nietzsche, Friedrich Wilhelm. 1878. *Human, All Too Human I*. Translated by Alexander Harvey. Chicago: Charles H. Kerr & Company, 1908.

———. 1879. *Human, All Too Human II*. Translated by Paul V. Cohn. London: George Allen and Unwin, 1911/1924.

———. 1883–1885. *Thus Spoke Zarathustra*. 2nd ed. Translated by R. J. Hollingdale. New York: Penguin Classics, 1969.

———. 1887a. *The Gay Science*. Translated by Josefine Nauckhoff. Edited by Bernard Williams. Poems Translated by Adrian Del Caro. Cambridge and New York: Cambridge University Press, 2001–2008.

———. 1887b. *Genealogy of Morals. A Polemical Tract*. Translated by Ian Johnston. Arlington, VA: Richer Resources Publications, 2009.

———. 1888–1889. *Dithyrambs of Dionysus*. www.thenietzschechannel.com.

———. 1899–1911. *Kleinoktav-Gesamtausgabe*. Leipzig: Naumann und Kröner.

———. 1930 [1883–1885]. *Thus Spake Zarathustra*. Translated by Thomas Common. New York: The Modern Library.

———. 1967–. *Kritische Gesamtausgabe der Werke Nietzsches*. Edited by Giorgio Colli and Mazzino Montinari. Berlin and New York: De Gruyter.

———. 1980–. *Kritische Studienausgabe*. Edited by Giorgio Colli and Mazzino Montinari. Berlin and New York: De Gruyter.

———. 2009–. *Digital Critical Edition*. Edited by P. D'Iorio.

Nill, Peggy. 1988. Die Versuchung der Psyche: Selbstwerdung als schöpferisches Prinzip bei Nietzsche und C. G. Jung. *Nietzsche-Studien* 17: 250–279.

Parkes, Graham. 1999. Nietzsche and Jung: Ambivalent Appreciations. In *Nietzsche and Depth Psychology*, ed. Jacob Golomb, Weaver Santaniello, and Ronal L. Lehrer, 205–227. Albany: SUNY Press.
Pezzella, Mario, ed. 1995. *Lo spirito e l'ombra. I seminari di Jung su Nietzsche.* Bergamo: Moretti & Vitali.
Schmitt, Gerhard. 1998. *Zyklus und Kompensation: Zur Denkfigur bei Nietzsche und Jung.* Frankfurt am Main: Peter Lang.
———. 2011. Vom Übermensch und Übersinn: Nietzsches Metaphorik im *Roten Buch. Recherches germaniques* 8 (special edition): 117–133.
Shamdasani, Sonu. 2005. *Jung Stripped Bare: By His Biographers, Even.* London: Karnac.
———. 2009. 'Introduction' and 'Footnotes'. In *The Red Book: Liber Novus*, ed. C.G. Jung. Edited and Introduced by Sonu Shamdasani. Translated by Mark Kyburz, John Peck, and Sonu Shamdasani. New York and London: W. W. Norton & Company.
Spitteler, Carl. 1906. *Imago.* Jena: Eugen Diederichs, 1922.
Vischer, Friedrich Theodor. 1878. *Auch Einer. Eine Reisebekanntschaft.* Leipzig: Heffe & Becker Verlag.

CHAPTER 5

Conclusion

This is how I overcame madness. If you do not know what divine madness is, suspend judgment and wait for the fruits. But know that there is a divine madness which is nothing other than the overpowering of the spirit of this time through the spirit of the depths. Speak then of sick delusion when the spirit of the depths can no longer stay down and forces a man to speak in tongues instead of in human speech, and makes him believe that he himself is the spirit of the depths. But also speak of sick delusion when the spirit of this time does not leave a man and forces him to see only the surface, to deny the spirit of the depths and to take himself for the spirit of the times. The spirit of this time is ungodly; the spirit of the depths is ungodly; balance is godly. (RB I, 5 'Descent into Hell in the Future': 238)

5.1 Introductory Remarks

From what has emerged so far, the core of what was called Jung's confrontation with Nietzsche concerns first of all the issue of the 'death of God'. In Jung's first readings, according to his later memoirs, *Zarathustra* was considered a prophetical text, where the timeless voice of something similar to his 'No. 2' imposed on the individual Nietzsche and drove him towards a powerful experience (MDR: 102). Later on, *Zarathustra* was associated with other works, whose composition was defined by Jung as 'visionary' (CW 15, §§ 139–141). Jung never ceased to attribute such prophetical capacity to *Zarathustra*; in fact, he even saw prophecies about

G. Domenici, *Jung's Nietzsche*,
https://doi.org/10.1007/978-3-030-17670-9_5

the twentieth-century wars and totalitarianisms hidden behind a few of its metaphors and images. In addition to such an impression of the text, Jung also wondered about a connection between Nietzsche's tragical fate and his experience with *Zarathustra*, that is, whether or not what Nietzsche had come across before and during the composition of his text could be linked to his final madness. As argued throughout this book, such a thought occupied Jung's mind especially at the time of his own experience with the 'timeless voice', namely while writing *Liber Novus*, especially after 1914. As argued in Chaps. 3 and 4, this text presents several references to Nietzsche which are to be read in terms of a personal confrontation. Such a confrontation lasted throughout Jung's life and emerged most loudly during his analysis of *Zarathustra* at the Psychological Club in Zurich. In that circumstance, he interpreted some sections and images from *Zarathustra* in exactly the same way he had interpreted the same images in *Liber Novus*. In both occasions, Jung's only protection against ending up like Nietzsche seemed to be giving birth to a 'new God'.

The way Jung and Nietzsche understand and react to the 'death of God' reflects an insurmountable diversity not only in their thinking but also—and more importantly—in the purpose of the two works this investigation is focussing on. In the following section, Nietzsche's and Jung's understandings of the 'death of God' more broadly, and then of Christianity more specifically, will be compared. In fact, both *Liber Novus* and *Zarathustra* come to touch and question Christianity itself. Still in accordance with this issue, in the last section of this conclusive chapter, the meaning of 'self-overcoming' will be discussed. Such concept is indeed central in both works, but the way its meaning varies from one author to the other reflects again a radical difference in their thinking, which definitely affects a hypothetical dialogue between the two—or between their spokesmen Philemon and Zarathustra—and makes it unilateral.

5.2 The 'Death of God' and the Meaning of 'Christianity'

5.2.1 Philological Experiments and Empiricist Revelations

To Nietzsche, realising that God was 'dead' came as the result of a slow investigative process. As the son of a parson, and the only male heir of an entire family of parsons—in either maternal and paternal lineage—since his youngest years, Nietzsche had been expected to study theology and become a parson himself. He moved to Bonn indeed, in 1864, in order to attend the faculty of Theology. After a few months, however, he decided to switch to Philology, and at the end of the last term, to get back to his home region and complete his education at the University of Leipzig.[1] Although Nietzsche was designated by his family to become a theologian, with his final choice, he made clear to everyone what his profession should be: he was first of all a philologist. And this has very much to do with Nietzsche's statement 'God is dead'. As stated by Jörg Salaquarda, if 'disagreement persists among Nietzsche scholars as to when, and for what reasons exactly, Nietzsche broke with Christianity', one thing which remains certain, is that 'as reason for his renunciation of Christianity, in his notes young Nietzsche offered historical criticism'. Above all, it was the 'historical relativity' of Christian doctrines to be highlighted by Nietzsche in his 'first outspoken criticism', in contrast with their 'alleged absolutism'. Besides, 'in his writings of the early 1870s Nietzsche made use of two additional arguments. Together with Overbeck he mocked the poverty of contemporary Christian trends. He also tried to unmask the inconsistency or "mendacity," not only of individual Christians, but of Christian doctrine as such. In the 1880s Nietzsche's criticism became more aggressive and psychological in orientation' (Salaquarda 1996: 92–93).[2]

As made clear by Andreas Urs Sommer, it is important to maintain a distinction between Nietzsche and the 'Madman' [der Tolle Mensch] from the aphorism 125 of *The Gay Science*, who announces that 'God is dead'. Neglecting the fictional function of 'madman' could lead to consequences which do not really differ from those deriving from the identification between Nietzsche and Zarathustra. In fact, the same statement 'God is dead' is attributed to the 'devil' in *Zarathustra* chapter 'Of the Compassionate' (Sommer 2006: 77). Considering that in Nietzsche's notes the 'madman' was originally named 'Zarathustra', not only does Sommer's hypothesis make sense, but it also aids to reflect on Nietzsche's position about Christianity. Indeed, although Sommer emphasises Nietzsche's latest criticism of Christianity as meant in the broader sense of his 'experimental' and 'sceptic' philosophy, he also points out that such criticism has to be read in terms of historical analysis. In this sense, he states that Nietzsche's atheism does not have to be confused with a substitutive dogma for the old Christian values; on the contrary, it represents the starting point of a creative process of 'experimental self-liberation' [experimentelle Selbstbefreiung] (ibid.: 87–90). Following this line, it can be argued that the sentence 'God is dead' achieves its highest value when thought of as the result of a careful philological analysis of the history of culture, namely as a necessary process in the bigger project of Nietzsche's extreme experimentation. As reported in the preface of *Twilight of the Idols*, the 'hammer' used by Nietzsche—key symbol of his *Umwertung* ('transvaluation')—is not meant as a violence tool, but as the same instrument used by physicians in order to auscultate body cavities. As Nietzsche points out, such 'hammer' should be somehow interpreted as a 'tuning fork'. His intent, namely ***sounding out idols***, is to show emptiness in all of our old values, even in those *most fervently believed*. In this circumstance, Nietzsche calls himself a 'psychologist'; for his task, his *great declaration of war*, intends to deconstruct human beliefs psychologically, that is to say, by disclosing the original link between human mental attitudes and the developing of 'eternal idols' (GD *Vorrede*, KSA 6: 57–58). Again, in Nietzsche's retrospective comment on *Human, All Too Human*, written in *Ecce Homo*—where the philosopher puts himself as a 'psychologist' several times—a similar perspective is to be found:

> The term "free spirit" does not want to be understood in any other way: a spirit that *has become free*, that has taken hold of itself again. The tone, the sound, has completely changed: you will find the book clever, bold, under certain circumstances harsh and sarcastic. A certain spirituality of *noble* taste seems to be constantly fighting a more passionate current in order to stay on top. [...] If you look more closely you will find a merciless spirit who knows all the hiding-places where the ideal is at home,—the mountain where its dungeon lies and, as it were, its ultimate security. With a steady torch in hand, this *underworld* of the ideal is illuminated with a searing clarity. It is war, but a war without powder or fumes, without belligerent posturing, without pathos and contorted limbs—all this would still be "idealism". One mistake after another is calmly put on ice, the ideal is not refuted, it is *frozen to death*. (EH III, 14, KSA 6: 323)

In the specific discourse on *Twilight of the Idols*, it has to be mentioned that the way such a method operates consists of slowly analysing all 'idols', one by one, and showing the relativity of their fundamentals. What comes after this process is a more active individual awareness in dealing with values, which should lead to the aforementioned 'experimental self-liberation': maintaining the old idols; giving them a new meaning; or creating new ones are precisely expressions of this kind of freedom. Even though Nietzsche's revaluation concept was defined in terms of a real project in 1886–1888, several notes concerning the issue of values and re-evaluating are present among Nietzsche's writings already at the beginning of the eighties, that is, at the time of *Daybreak* and *The Gay Science*. In particular, as pointed out by Thomas Brobjer, in *The Gay Science*, 269, it is stated: 'In *what do you believe?*—In this, that the weights of all things must be determined anew' (Brobjer 2010: 14–17, see FW, 269, KSA 3: 519). And 'all things' must include also 'God', meant both as a broad symbol for any kind of safe and steady guidance, and as the Christian God indeed. In the preface to *The Anti-Christ*, Nietzsche puts himself in the position of being 'born posthumously': 'my day won't come until the day after tomorrow'. His anti-Christian experiment can be indeed understood only if possessing 'courage for the *forbidden*' and being 'honest':

> The conditions required to understand me, and which in turn *require* me to be understood,—I know them only too well. When it comes to spiritual matters, you need to be honest to the point of hardness just to be able to tolerate my seriousness, my passion. You need to be used to living on mountains—to seeing the miserable, ephemeral little gossip of politics and national self-interest *beneath* you. You need to have become indifferent, you need never to ask whether truth does any good, whether it will be our undoing ... The sort of predilection strength has for questions that require more courage than anyone possesses today; a courage for the *forbidden*; a predestination for the labyrinth. An experience from out of seven solitudes. New ears for new music. New eyes for the most distant things. A new conscience for truth that have been kept silent until now. *And* the will to the economy of the great style: holding together its strength, its *enthusiasm* ... Respect for yourself; love for yourself; an unconditional freedom over yourself. (AC *Vorwort*, KSA 6: 167)

Not too differently from Nietzsche, Jung's religious crisis—which took place in his teens—came as the result of an intense quest. According to *Memories, Dreams, Reflexions*, Jung experienced God's almightiness for the first time at the age of 11, in Basel, when 'one fine summer day', on his way back from school, an undesired thought concerning God and the new Cathedral took possession of his mind. Following his description, he tried not to 'go on thinking' for nearly three days, during which he could not sleep and a certain discomfort was visible to anyone around him. The reason why he did not intend to let his thought come up was because that was a 'sin against the Holy Spirit', which would condemn him to Hell forever. At the end of the last day, however, he realised that even sinning could respond to God's will: Adam and Eve were 'created directly by God, who intentionally made them as they were', that means that 'God in His omniscience had arranged everything so that the first parents would have to sin. *Therefore it was God's intention that they should sin*'. That possibility 'liberated' Jung, who 'now knew that God Himself had placed [him] in this situation'. God would want him to 'show courage' and follow the divine will, against his faith and morals. Thus he decided to let his thought go and felt relieved: 'I saw before me the cathedral, the blue sky. God sits on His golden throne, high above the world and from under the throne an enormous turd falls upon the sparkling new roof, shatters it, and breaks the walls of the cathedral asunder'. This event made him question his father's faith:

> That was what my father had not understood, I thought; *he had failed to experience the will of God*, had opposed it for the best reasons and out of the deepest faith. And that was why he had never experienced the miracle of grace which heals all and makes all comprehensible. He had taken the Bible's commandments as his guide; he believed in God as the Bible prescribed and as his forefathers had taught him. But *he did not know the immediate living God who stands, omnipotent and free, above His Bible and His Church*, who calls upon man to partake of His freedom, and can force him to renounce his own views and convictions in order to fulfill without reserve the command of God. In His trial of human courage God refuses to abide by traditions, no matter how sacred. In His omnipotence He will see to it that nothing really evil comes of such tests of courage. If one fulfills the will of God one can be sure of going the right way. (MDR: 40, italics added)

Interestingly, he also reports: 'Oddly enough, I did not think for a moment that the devil might be playing a trick on me. The devil played little part in my mental world at that time, and in any case I regarded him as powerless compared with God. But from the moment I emerged from the mist and became conscious of myself, the unity, the greatness, and the superhuman majesty of God began to haunt my imagination' (ibid.: 39).

One thing, therefore, was the Bible and its doctrine; another thing was 'the immediate living God' experienced by Jung. But precisely such a discovery upset Jung's beliefs:

> It was obedience which brought me grace, and after that experience I knew what God's grace was. One must be utterly abandoned to God; nothing matters but fulfilling His will. Otherwise all is folly and meaninglessness. From that moment on, when I experienced grace, my true responsibility

> began. Why did God befoul His cathedral? That, for me, was a terrible thought. But then came the dim understanding that God could be something terrible. I had experienced a dark and terrible secret. It overshadowed my whole life, and I became deeply pensive. (MDR: 40)

The new aspect of God that Jung was experiencing also increased his 'sense of inferiority' and made him compare himself with a 'devil'. He then began to read the Bible seriously, especially the New Testament: 'I wanted to find out whether other people had undergone similar experiences, I never succeeded in discovering so much as a trace of them in others. As a result, I had the feeling that I was either outlawed or elect, accursed or blessed'. In this new situation, Jung had a new 'secret'. His first 'secret' was the revelation in the famous dream of the phallus, which occurred to him when he was only three years old and 'haunted' him 'for many years'. In that dream, 'a huge thing, reaching almost to the ceiling', 'made of skin and naked flesh, and on top there was something like a rounded head with no face and no hair. On the very top of the head was a single eye, gazing motionlessly upward' was sitting on a throne in the middle of a subterranean 'rectangular chamber' under the meadow of the vicarage where he was staying with his family at that time (ibid.: 11–12). Jung's second secret was his wooden manikin, carved and coloured by himself at the end of a ruler, dressed up and jealously kept in a pencil case (ibid.: 21). In Jung's years as a teenager, the experience of a twofold God, lord of both good and evil, played an important role. Also in his case, most of his family members were parsons, and, as already said, his father was a parson himself. In all of them, as noted, Jung could see only one of the two sides of faith, namely the speculative, theological part; but the 'secret of grace' was missing (ibid.: 41–42).

Such an approach to Christianity in particular and religion in general remained consistent in Jung's life. In *Psychology and Religion* (1937/1940), he writes: 'Religion, as the Latin word denotes, is a careful and scrupulous observation of what Rudolf Otto aptly termed the *numinosum*, that is, a dynamic agency or effect not caused by an arbitrary act of will. On the contrary, it seizes and controls the human subject, who is always rather its victim than its creator'. Indeed, he also specifies: 'At all events, religious teaching as well as the *consensus gentium* always and everywhere explain this experience as being due to a cause external to the individual. The *numinosum* is either a quality belonging to a visible object or the influence of an invisible presence that causes a peculiar alteration of consciousness'.

Although this is said to be 'the general rule', a few exceptions may occur, 'when it comes to the question of religious practice or ritual', in which individuals can effect their conscious state themselves, by 'producing at will the effect of the *numinosum*'. Such practices or rituals are, for instance: 'invocation, incantation, sacrifice, meditation and other yoga practices, self-inflicted tortures', and so on. However, 'a religious belief in an external and objective divine cause is always prior to any such performance'. More specifically, the definition given by Jung to the word 'religion' regards 'a peculiar attitude of mind which could be formulated in accordance with the original use of the word *religio*, which means a careful consideration and observation of certain dynamic factors that are conceived as "powers"'. Even though 'creeds' are 'originally based on the one hand upon the experience of the *numinosum* and on the other hand upon *πίστις*', by 'religion' Jung does not intend to mean only 'creeds'. In fact, '"religion" designates the attitude peculiar to a consciousness which has been changed by experience of the *numinosum*' (CW 11: §§ 6–9; see Otto 1917: 5–7).

The psyche appears as an independent phenomenon from the individual personality; however, it also comprehends the individual personality itself, along with all the unconscious manifestations. In this sense, Jung regards religions as attempts to represent the complexity of the psyche. In particular, he dwells upon Catholicism and dogmas, and compares their representative capacity with scientific theories by affirming: 'Dogma expresses the psyche more completely than a scientific theory, for the latter gives expression to and formulates the conscious mind alone. Furthermore, a theory can do nothing except formulate a living thing in abstract terms. Dogma, on the contrary, aptly expresses the living process of the unconscious in the form of the drama and repentance, sacrifice and redemption' (CW 11: § 82). Apart from religion, a similar attempt would have been made by philosophy as well. For example, Jung associates the philosophers' quest for a 'round substance' with a similar motif recurring in dream symbolism, where circle and quaternity images play the main part; as if all these were *projections* of something else (ibid.: § 95). However, Jung makes clear that 'God is an "unscientific" hypothesis', or a '"mystical" idea', and that his 'observations' 'prove only the existence of an archetypal God-image, which [...] is the most we can assert about God psychologically'. Shortly after he adds though: 'But as it is a very important and influential archetype, its relatively frequent occurrence seems to be a noteworthy fact for any *theologia naturalis*. And since experience of this archetype has the quality of numinosity, often in very high degree, it comes into the category of religious experiences' (ibid.: §§ 101–102).

Previous theoreticians of the unconscious such as Carus, von Hartmann, or Schopenhauer are seen by Jung as spokesmen for the acknowledgement of the unconscious as something bigger than 'a mere absence of consciousness'. Their attempt to describe the unconscious in terms of 'world-creating principle' would reflect that 'they were only summing up all those teachings of the past which, grounded in inner experience, saw the mysterious agent personified as the gods'. Following this argument, two kinds of errors are 'unavoidable' when dealing with 'God': the materialistic and the psychologising one. 'Since the throne of God could not be discovered among the galactic systems, the inference was that God never existed'; because 'God is anything, he must be an illusion derived from certain motives—from the will to power, for instance, or from repressed sexuality'. Such mistakes recall the attitude of Christian missionaries towards the 'idols of heathen gods'. The difference is that whereas 'the early missionaries were conscious of serving a new God by combatting the old ones, modern iconoclasts are unconscious of the one in whose name they are destroying old values'. Nietzsche himself is taken as an example in this sense:

> Nietzsche thought himself quite conscious and responsible when he smashed the old tablets, yet he felt a peculiar need to back himself up with a revivified Zarathustra, sort of alter ego, with whom he often identifies himself in his great tragedy *Thus Spake Zarathustra*. Nietzsche was no atheist, but his God was dead. The result of this demise was a split in himself, and he felt compelled to call the other self "Zarathustra" or, at times, "Dionysus". In his fatal illness he signed his letters "Zagreus", the dismembered god of the Thracians. The tragedy of *Zarathustra* is that, because his God died, Nietzsche himself became a god; and this happened because he was no atheist. He was of too positive a nature to tolerate the urban neurosis of atheism. It seems dangerous for such a man to assert that "God is dead": he instantly becomes the victim of inflation. Far from being a negation, God is actually the strongest and most effective "position" the psyche can reach, in exactly the same sense in which Paul speaks of people "whose God is their belly". (Phil. 3:19). (ibid.: §§ 141–142)

'God', therefore, represents all those phenomena which appear stronger than human consciousness and possess it—as Jung puts it, 'Anything despotic and inescapable is [...] "God"' (ibid.); this is why he cannot die, but just be projected onto a new symbol'. As he states a few paragraphs below, indeed, '[t]he individual ego is much too small, its brain is much too feeble, to incorporate all the projections withdrawn from the world'. Moreover, 'when Nietzsche said "God is dead", he uttered a truth which is valid for the greater part of Europe. People were influenced by it not because he said so, but because it stated a widespread psychological fact'. Consequences of such a statement are, according to Jung, 'the fog of -isms' and 'the catastrophe' thereafter (ibid.: § 145).

The idea of God as both 'good and evil' is also at the core of Jung's polemic against the definition of evil as *privatio boni*; it is therefore central in his peculiar relationship with Victor White. In *A Psychological Approach to the Trinity* (1942/1948), Jung expresses his argument this way:

> This classic formula [*privatio boni*] robs evil of absolute existence and makes it a shadow that has only a relative existence dependent on light. Good, on the other hand, is credited with a positive substantiality. But, as a psychological experience shows, "good" and "evil" are opposite poles of a moral judgment which, as such, originates in man. A judgment can be made about a thing only if its opposite is equally real and possible. The opposite of a seeming evil can only be a seeming good and an evil that lacks substance can only be contrasted with a good that is equally non-substantial. Although the opposite of "existence" is "non-existence", the opposite of a non-existing good can never be a non-existing evil, for the latter is a contradiction in terms and opposes to an existing good something incommensurable with it; the opposite of a non-existing (negative) evil can only be a non-existing (negative) good. (ibid.: § 247)

On the grounds that '[i]f [...] evil is said to be a mere privation of good, the opposition of good and evil is denied outright', Jung wonders: 'How can one speak of "good" at all if there is no "evil"?'. So, he concludes. 'if you allow substantialilty to good, you must also allow it to evil. If evil has no substance, good must remain shadowy, for there is no substantial opponent for it to defend itself against, but only a shadow, a mere privation of good. Such a view can hardly be squared with observed reality' (ibid.). Moreover, the not substantial essence of evil cannot certainly get along well with the issue of the 'devil' in Christianity, if regarded as of independent nature from God's will (ibid.: §§ 248–249). Jung also reports a Gnostic belief, according to which 'the devil' would be 'God's first son', and 'Christ [...] the second'. Then he adds: 'a further logical inference would be the abolition of the trinity formula and its replacement by a quaternity' (ibid.: § 249). In *Foreword to White's 'God and the Unconscious'*

(1952), Jung makes clear that in 'the doctrine of the *privatio boni* [...] the theologian has a certain right to fear an intrusion on the part of the empiricist'. In fact: 'evil is in itself nothing, a mere shadow, a trifling and fleeting diminution of good, like a cloud passing over the sun'. However, 'it is self-evident to the empiricist that the metaphysical aspect of such a doctrine must be left out of account, for he knows that he is dealing only with moral judgments and not with substances'. Here is his main argument:

> We name a thing, from a certain point of view, good or bad, high or low, right or left, light or dark, and so forth. Here the antithesis is just as factual and real as the thesis. It would never occur to anyone [...] to define cold as a diminution of heat, depth as a diminution of height, right as a diminution of left. With this kind of logic one could just as well call good a diminution of evil. [...] If your evil is in fact only an unreal shadow of your good, then your so-called good is nothing but an unreal shadow of your real evil. If he does not reflect in this way he is deceiving himself, and self-deceptions of this kind have dissociating effects which breed neurosis, among the feeling of inferiority, with all their well-known attendant phenomena.
>
> For these reasons I have felt compelled to contest the validity of the *privatio boni* so far as the empirical realm is concerned. For the same reasons I also criticize the dictum derived from the *privatio boni*, namely: "Omne bonum a Deo, omne malum ab homine"; for then on the one hand man is deprived of the possibility of doing anything good, and on the other he is given the seductive power of doing evil. The only dignity which is left him is that of the fallen angel. (ibid.: §§ 456–458)

In this circumstance, already at the beginning of his lecture *Psychology and Religion* Jung calls himself an empiricist and points out that he does not intend to get involved in metaphysical issues. Nonetheless, he does not reject that an archetypal background might exist, which pushes human mind to create 'mythologems, folklore motifs, and the individual formations of symbols', namely images or ideas contradicting empirical experience (ibid.: § 459). Lastly, the issue is faced again in *Answer to Job* (1952). In the *Prefatory Note*, Jung writes that 'psychological experience shows that whatever we call "good" is balanced by an equally substantial "bad" or "evil". If "evil" is not existent, then whatever there is must needs be "good"' (ibid.: *Answer to Job*, *Prefatory Note*). Furthermore, such a theory implies that 'it is impossible for the consciousness of a good God to produce evil deeds' (ibid.: § 600, footnote 13). Indeed, Jung defines the *privatio boni* as a 'nonsensical doctrine'. More specifically, the concepts of

'Summum Bonum' and *privatio boni* are said to be incompatible with the Old Testament figure of Yahweh (ibid.: § 685).

It can be stated that whereas Nietzsche felt the need for *experimenting*, Jung searched for stability, in order to justify the power he truly *experienced*. Nietzsche's 'God' was an empty idol to revaluate, beyond—and before—all the ethical implications of that name; Jung's 'God' was a real and tangible experience to defend, that summed up his *empirical* experience of 'evil' and the subordination of his will to an external entity. Like Jung, Nietzsche too stresses the necessity of 'evil gods', by the side of 'the good ones: after all, people do not exactly owe their own existence to tolerance and love of humanity ... Why bother with a god who does not know about anger, revenge, envy, scorn, cunning, violence?' (AC, § 16, KSA 6: 182). But whereas, to Nietzsche, ethics has no substantial essence in itself; to Jung, it is at the base of human perception and action, although he admits 'that clear-cut *moral* distinctions are the most recent acquisition of civilized man. That is why such distinctions are often so hazy and uncertain, unlike other antithetical constructions which undoubtedly have an archetypal nature and are the prerequisites for any act of cognition' (*Foreword to White's 'God and the Unconscious'*, CW 11: § 459).

5.2.2 Nietzsche and the Issue of Imitation: Socrates, Wagner, Christ

Even if not expressly investigated, the problem of imitation has been implicitly central in Nietzsche's speculation since *Birth of Tragedy*. Addressing his criticism against Plato, Nietzsche brings out that the supremacy of logics over ethical issues attributed to Socrates was in fact still part of Socrates's instinctual acting. Plato did not seem to realise the difference, therefore he would take such an attitude for a normative rule and would build his own philosophy around it. In this sense, Nietzsche's aim is *Socratism*, rather than Socrates, whose instinctual acting was contemplated through him 'as [...] through a shadow'. He writes, indeed:

> Now, we see here a grotesque defect in mythical consciousness, so that Socrates can be considered specifically a non-mystic man in whom the logical character has become too massive through excessive use, just like instinctive wisdom in the mystic. On the other hand, it was impossible for that logical drive, as it appeared in Socrates, to turn against itself. In its unfettered rush it demonstrates a natural power of the sort we meet, to our shud-

> dering surprise, only in the very greatest instinctive powers. Anyone who has sensed in the Platonic texts the merest scent of the god-like naïveté and confidence in the direction of Socrates's teaching has also felt how that immense drive wheel of Socratic logic is, at it were, in motion behind Socrates and how we have to see this behind Socrates, as if we were looking through a shadow. (GT 13, KSA 1: 91)

Nietzsche's relationship with Socrates is deep and complex; it started off during Nietzsche's years as a young philologist, and evolved throughout the development of his thinking. As pointed out by Giuliano Campioni, at the beginning, Socrates did not hold a particular appeal on Nietzsche, who felt more attracted to Democritus; however, Nietzsche's 'confrontation' with Socrates has been carried on with such 'passion, vehemence, excess', that it can be compared only with Nietzsche's relation to Wagner. In fact, especially in Nietzsche's latest texts, both Socrates and Wagner represent decadence and sickness (Campioni 2009: 75–79). In the discourse on Nietzsche and Socrates, however, a standard feature is to be found in the issue of Socratism. In *The Gay Science*, 340, 'The Dying Socrates' [Der sterbende Sokrates], through his revelation about owing 'Asclepius a rooster', Socrates would let his 'pessimism' come out, that is, he would reveal his fear of dying, as well as his hatred for life, which brings sufferance and pain (FW 340, KSA 3: 569–570). In a previous aphorism, 'To Harm Stupidity', Nietzsche wrote:

> Ancient philosophy, by contrast, taught a quite different main source of misery [Unheil]: from Socrates onwards these thinkers never tired of preaching, "Your thoughtlessness and stupidity, your way of living according to the rule, your subordination to the opinion of your neighbor is the reason why you so seldom achieve happiness—we thinkers are, as thinkers, the happiest". (FW 328, KSA 3: 555)

In the section from *Twilight of the Idols* entitled 'The Problem of Socrates', such aspect is related to Socrates's 'ugliness' and 'sickness' of life. His 'hypertrophy of logic', together with his 'emblematic rachitic spite', become 'symptoms' of decadence; whilst his 'daimon' is regarded as 'auditory hallucinations'. Also in this case, Socrates appears as struggling against his 'anarchy of instincts' (GD II, KSA 6: 67–74): he perceives and reflects all of the aspects of a transition, namely, the beginning of an era of decadence. Again, Socrates is not to blame for being the first decadent; Socratism, as the typical attitude of decadence, instead, is the kernel of Nietzsche's argument. The moment that Socrates's rational instinct was hypostatised corresponds to the very beginning of the decadence, whose approaching was already experienced by Socrates as a symptom.

In similar manner, a steady point of Nietzsche's ambivalent relationship with Wagner is 'Wagnerism'. Nietzsche never stopped to acknowledge Wagner as a talented musician; nor did he cease to regard him and his wife Cosima as models, and to confront with them. Nietzsche's unpublished *Five Prefaces* [*Fünf Vorreden zu fünf ungeschriebenen Büchern*] were indeed dedicated by him to Cosima Wagner in Autumn 1872 (KSA 1: 754). In the very last letters written by Nietzsche in Turin just a few days before his one-way journey in the world of madness (January 1889), he addressed Cosima by comparing her to Ariadne and himself to Dionysus (eKGWB, letters n. 1241, 1242 a). According to Cosima's diaries, both herself and her husband felt hurt by Nietzsche's estrangement (Campioni 1998: 199). Nietzsche met Wagner for the first time in 1868. The musician and his wife immediately exerted a significant influence over him, who became an assiduous guest of their house in Tribschen (Lucerne). The starting point of Nietzsche's estrangement from Wagner is normally said to coincide with the first Bayreuth Festival in 1876 and with Nietzsche's fourth *Untimely Meditation* (1876). Reading the text, however, it is clear that the aim of Nietzsche's passionate considerations are Wagnerians and not Wagner himself. 'In Bayreuth'—so Nietzsche—'even the spectator is a spectacle worth seeing, there is no doubt' [ist auch der Zuschauer anschauenswerth, es ist kein Zweifel] (UBWB, KSA 1: 432). What Nietzsche's perception is characterised by, is Wagner's relationship with his audience. As Campioni highlights in one of his studies on Nietzsche and Wagner, Bayreuth *idealism* and 'Germanism' appeared to Nietzsche as a 'tremendous accumulation of deformation and falsification' (Campioni 2001: 110, 2009: 136). Indeed, as reported by Nietzsche himself in *Ecce Homo*: 'Wagner had been translated into German. The Wagnerians had gained control over Wagner!—*German* art! The *German* master! *German* beer' (EH III, 15, KSA 6: 323). Nietzsche's reaction corresponds to the same attitude he had taken in his first *Meditation* on David Strauss (1873), where he had expressed himself against the Germans and the 'barbarising element' [barbarisiendes Element] of their 'men of culture' [Kultur-Menschen] (UBDS, KSA 1: 206). Similar themes are brought out also in Nietzsche's lectures *On the Future of our Academies* [Über die Zukunft unserer Bildungsanstalten] (1872) (KSA 1:

641–753) and *Philosophy in the Tragic Age of the Greeks* [Die Philosophie im tragischen Zeitalter der Griechen] (1873) (KSA 1: 799–872). The tension between political strength and cultural impoverishment is also treated in relation to the educational role of a teacher in Nietzsche's third *Untimely Meditation*, *Schopenhauer as an Educator* (1874). The aim of his criticism, therefore, are the political interconnections hiding behind the relationship between music and spectators. As argued by Campioni, Wagner's 'theatricality' would play a part in his relationship with the German people in the sense that, his main accent being on the 'actor', meant as a creator and counterpart of the 'mime' (the usual protagonist of French drama), he would give his audience the illusion of creating something, rather than merely imitating (as the 'mime' does). In this way, he would assure German supremacy over other countries. Wagner's whole life would be, therefore, transformed into a theatre (Campioni 2001: 111). Interestingly, in Wagner's last works, his vicinity to Schopenhauer and Christianity appears in contradiction of his first revolutionary writings, in which the strongest echoes came from Feuerbach's philosophy (in particular *Art and Revolution* [Kunst und Revolution], 1849, and *Opera and Drama* [*Opera und Drama*], 1852). Such a change seems indeed to reflect Wagner's stress on theatre as an element of power and domination. Nietzsche's later criticisms of Wagner will also concern this aspect. In the *The Case of Wagner*, the issue will be defined in terms of decadence, and Wagner's music will be regarded as an example of German 'cloudy education' [Wolkenbildung] (WA 10, KSA 6: 37). Lastly, in the preface to *Nietzsche Contra Wagner*, Nietzsche will distance himself from the 'Germans' by counterpoising the *psychological* purpose of his essay to their reading ability: 'I have my readers everywhere, in Vienna, in St Petersburg, in Copenhagen and Stockholm, in Paris, in New York—I do *not* have any in Europe's flatlands, Germany … And I might drop a word into the ears of my dear Italians, who I love as much as I love myself … *Quosque tandem, Crispi* … Triple alliance: an intelligent people can only enter into a *mésalliance* with the "*Reich*"' (NcW *Vorrede*, KSA 6: 415). Already in Summer 1875, while working on *Richard Wagner In Bayreuth*, Nietzsche wrote: 'Here the artist Wagner is now a symptom of contradiction. It is the spirit of negation speaking from within himself; but also the feeling of the deepest compassionate, the helpful, that takes on the fight with necessity: the Promethean of artists' [Hier ist nun der Künstler Wagner ein Symptom des Entgegengesetzten. Es spricht der Geist der Verneinung des Bisherigen aus ihm; ebenfalls aber das Gefühl des tiefsten

Mitleidens, des Hülfreichen, das den Kampf mit der Nothwendigkeit aufnimmt: das Prometheische des Künstlers] (NF 11[3] KSA 8: 189).[3]

A similar discourse has to be made in regard to the figure of 'Christ'. In *The Anti-Christ*, Nietzsche distinguishes between Jesus as a historical character and 'Christ' as the son of God. He states that 'Christianity can only be understood on the soil where it grew,—it is *not* a counter-movement to the Jewish instinct, it is its natural consequence, a further conclusion drawn by its terrifying logic'. Here, 'the psychological type of the Galilean is still recognizable, but it had to assume a completely degenerated form (simultaneously mutilated and full of alien features) before it came to be used as a *redeemer* of humanity'. In fact, he explains that the Jews 'defined themselves in *opposition* to all the conditions under which peoples so far had been able to live [...]—they took religion, cults, morality, history, and psychology, and twisted them around, one after the other, to the point where they were in irreversible *contradiction to their natural values*'. He describes them as 'the people with the toughest life force', and adds:

> when transplanted into impossible conditions they took sides with all the instincts of decadence and they did this freely and out of the most profoundly shrewd sense of self-preservation—*not* because they were dominated by these instincts, but rather because they sensed that these instincts had a power that could be used to prevail *against* "the world". The Jews are the opposite of decadents: they had to act like decadents to the point of illusion, they knew, with a *non plus ultra* of theatrical genius, how to put themselves at the forefront of all movements of decadence [...] so they could make these movements into something stronger than any *yes-saying* defenders of life. [For the] priestly type, decadence is only a means: this type of person has a life-interest in making humanity sick and twisting the concepts 'good' and "evil", "true" and "false" to the point where they endanger life and slander the world. (AC 24, KSA 6: 191–193)

Through the history of Israel, some 'priestly agitators' gained power and interpreted 'all happiness as a reward, all unhappiness as a punishment for disobeying God, for "sin"' (ibid.: 25, KSA 6: 194). In this sense, Christianity as a religion was founded by Paul, who—as Nietzsche explains later in the text, '*invented for himself a history of the first Christianity.* Even more, he falsified the history of Israel once again, to make it look like the prehistory of his *own* actions: all the prophets have talked about *his* "redeemer" ... Later, the church even falsified the history of humanity into the prehistory of Christianity'. Paul appears as in search of the 'type of the redeemer'; 'he needed the death on the cross *and* something else besides'. Indeed, Nietzsche wonders: '*What* was the only thing that Mohammed would later borrow from Christianity? Paul's invention, his method of priestly tyranny, of forming the herds, the belief in immortality—*which is to say the doctrine of the "judgement"*' (ibid.: 42, KSA 6: 215–217). Other than a 'redeemer', and differently from Paul's psychology, the 'type' represented by Jesus is the 'idiot': 'We are familiar with a condition where the *sense of touch* is pathologically over-sensitive and recoils from all contact, from grasping any solid objects. Just follow this sort of physiological *habitus* to its ultimate consequences—as an instinct of hatred for *every* reality, as a flight into the "unimaginable", into the "inconceivable", as an aversion to every formula, to every concept of space and time, to everything solid' (ibid.: 29, KSA 6: 200).[4]

What distinguishes Christianity from other systems of values is the fact that 'Christians are not characterized by their "faith": Christians act, they are characterized by a *different* way of acting. By the fact that they do not offer any resistance, in their words or in their heart, to people who are evil to them' (ibid.: 33, KSA 6: 205). But this appears to be only an external attitude, which has nothing to do with its origins: 'Nothing is less Christian than the *ecclesiastic crudity* of God as a *person*, of a "kingdom of God" that is *yet to come*, a "kingdom of heaven" in the *beyond*, a "son of God" as the *second person* in the Trinity' (ibid.: 34, KSA 6: 206). Christianity came after Jesus and his life. Even more, it started immediately after his death and evolved through centuries as a 'misunderstanding' of its 'symbolism':

> the history of Christianity—starting [...] with the death on the cross—is the story of the progressively cruder misunderstanding of an original symbolism. Every time Christianity expanded to greater and cruder masses of people whose presuppositions were increasingly remote from the presupposition under which it arose, it became increasingly necessary to vulgarize Christianity and make it barbaric,—Christianity soaked up doctrines and rites from all the subterranean cults of the imperium Romanum and bits of nonsense from all kinds of sick reason. [...] Sick barbarism itself finally achieved power in the church,—the church, this form of deadly hostility to everything honest, to every height of the soul, to every discipline of spirit, to everything kind and candid in humanity. (ibid.: 37, KSA 6: 209)

Christian attitude has nothing to do with its original meaning: 'Every practice at every moment, every instinct, every value judgement that people act *on* is anti-Christian these days: what *miscarriages of duplicity* modern people are, that in spite of all this they are *not ashamed* to call themselves Christians!' (ibid.: 38, KSA 6: 211). Even more radically, Nietzsche states:

> Even the word "Christianity" is a misunderstanding—, there was really one Christian, and he died on the cross. The "evangel" died on the cross. What was called "evangel" after that was the opposite of what he had lived: a "bad tidings", a dysangel. It is false to the point of absurdity to think that Christians are characterized by their "beliefs", like a belief in salvation through Christ: only the practice of Christianity is really Christian, living like the man who died on the cross ... A life like this is still possible today, for certain people it is even necessary: true, original Christianity will always be possible ... Not a believing but a doing, above all a not-doing-much, a different being ... States of consciousness, any sort of belief, as such as taking something to be true, are (as every psychologist knows) trivial matters of fifth-rate importance compared to the value of the instincts: to put it more rigorously, the whole idea of spiritual causation is false. To reduce Christianity, to reduce being Christian to a set of claims taken to be true, to a simple phenomenalism of consciousness, is to negate Christianity. In fact, there have never been any Christians. "Christians", the people who have been called Christian for two thousand years, are just a psychological self-misunderstanding. Examined more closely and in spite of all 'belief', they have been governed only by instincts,—and what instincts they are! (ibid.: 39, KSA 6: 211–212)

And, again:

> Jesus could not have wanted anything more from his death itself than publicly to give his doctrine its strongest test, to prove it ... but his disciples were far from being able to forgive this death,—which would have been evangelical in the highest sense; or even more, from offering themselves up for a similar death in the sweet and gentle calm of the heart ... Revenge resurfaced, the most unevangelical feeling of all. It was impossible for his death to be the end of the matter: "retaliation" was needed, "judgement" [...]. Once again, the popular expectation of a messiah came to the fore; it was considered a historical moment: the 'kingdom of God' will come to judge its enemies ... But this is a misunderstanding of everything: the "kingdom of God" as a closing ceremony, as a promise! The evangel was precisely the existence, the fulfilment, the actuality of this "kingdom". (ibid.: 40, KSA 6: 213–214)

According to Nietzsche's reconstruction, Christianity arose and developed by promoting 'pity', that is, '*practice* of nihilism', '*negation of life*', and winning 'people over to *nothingness*'. Also in this case, Nietzsche speaks of a 'depressive and contagious instinct' which 'runs counter to the instincts that preserve and enhance the value of life: by *multiplying* misery just as much as by *conserving* everything miserable, pity is one of the main tools used to increase decadence' (ibid.: 7, KSA 6: 173).[5] In fact, Christianity 'falsifies, devalues and negates reality [Wirklichkeit]' (ibid.: 15, KSA 6: 181).

In a sense, it is possible to read the issue of Paul's relation to Christianity in no other way than Plato's relation to Socratism and Wagnerians' relation to Wagner. What is common to all of these cases is the *imitating* attitude of followers, all symbols of *decadent* peoples: the Greeks, the Germans, and the Jewish lower classes, moved by their resentment towards the Pharisees (ibid.: 46, KSA 6: 214). As visible in chapters from *Zarathustra* such as 'Of the Bestowing Virtue' and 'The Intoxicated Song', however, such 'believers'' attitudes are to be rejected, for they do not belong to the 'man of knowledge'. Instead, they reflect that believers 'have not found themselves yet' (Za I, 22, KSA: 4, 101). What was called 'shadows of God' in *The Gay Science* (FW 108–109, KSA 3: 467–469) comes back in the discourse on the decadence in terms of weakness. Decadence, indeed, means nothing more than a form of sickness; as pointed out for the first time by Bourget in his *Essays de psychologie contemporaine* (1883) and taken again by Nietzsche, it signifies the supremacy of the single part over the totality, or, as Bourget puts it: 'A style of decadence is that where the wholeness of a book breaks down to leave room for the independence of the sentence, and so the sentence, to leave room for the independence of the word' (Bourget 1883: 14). Similarly to Bourget, Nietzsche puts himself as a 'psychologist'; but his idea of being a psychologist coincides with being also a 'philologist ' and a 'physiologist': he intends to disclose relations and interconnections at the root of contemporary society, while proposing a cure for its sickness at the same time. Such a cure appears to deal with the issue of imitation; more precisely, with a return to 'nature'. He writes, in his 'law against Christianity' at the end of *The Anti-Christ*, that 'every type of anti-nature is a vice. The priest is the most vicious type of person: he *teaches* anti-nature' (AC *Gesetz wider das Christenthum*, KSA 6: 254). But what does a return to nature mean, if not getting rid of emulation? Any model imposing from outside does nothing but put itself as anti-vitalistic, suffocating individual inclinations and self-experimentation; with Nietzsche's words, waging 'a war to the death against this higher type of person', making 'the strong human being' a 'depraved' (AC 5, KSA 6: 171). In fact, Nietzsche's 'great style' proposed in the preface represents the opposite idea of a decadent style: while the latter loses the idea of *totality*, the former finds its meaning in 'holding together its strength, its *enthusiasm*' (AC *Vorwort*, KSA 6: 167).

Ironically, Nietzsche's opinion on the *Imitatio Christi* seems to anticipate Jung's dialogue with the librarian in the asylum scene from *Liber Novus* which precedes the encounter with the alleged Nietzsche:

> The *Imitatio Christi* is one of those books that I cannot pick up without a physiological feeling of repulsion: it exudes a scent of the eternal-feminine, which is all right if you happen to be French—or Wagnerian ... this saint talks about love in a way that makes even Parisan woen wonder.—They say that this book was the source of inspiration for that cleverest of Jesuits, A. Comte, who wanted to lead his Frenchmen to Rome on the *round-about* path of science. I believe it: 'the religion of the heart'. (GD IX, 4, KSA 6: 113)

Despite several interesting markings and underlinings in Jung's copy of *Twilight of the Idols*, however, this particular passage does not show any sign of interest from Jung. The *Imitatio Christi* is ultimately mentioned by Nietzsche in a note dating Winter 1887–88, where he faithfully transcribes an unpublished note from Baudelaire's on 'the pleasure of love':

> Once, in my presence, it was asked in what lay the greatest pleasure of love. Some one answered naturally: in receiving, and another: in giving one's self. The former said: pleasure of pride; and the latter: delight of humility! All these blackguards spoke like the Imitation of Christ.—Finally, an impudent Utopian came forward to affirm that the greatest pleasure of love is to create citizens for the fatherland. As for me, I said: The one and the supreme bliss of love rests in the certainty of doing evil. Both man and woman know, from birth, that in evil lies all bliss. (NF [11]174, KSA 13: 77–78; Baudelaire 1919: 213)[6]

5.2.3 Jung and Christ's Archetypal Nature

In *Psychology and Religion* (1937/1940), Jung states that 'The life of Christ is understood by the Church on the one hand as an historical, and on the other hand as an eternally existing, mystery'. Indeed, he lived a double life: as a concrete, unique individual and as an archetype presenting 'numerous connections [...] with worldwide myth-motifs'. Such a duplicity is what 'constitutes the meaning of the gospels', and represents difficulty for researchers looking for historical data. Because 'the life of Christ is archetypal to a high degree, it represents to just that degree the life of the archetype. But since the archetype is the unconscious precondition of every human life, its life, when revealed, also reveals the hidden, unconscious ground-life of every individual. That is to say, what happens in the life of Christ happens always and everywhere'. He then makes clear that he does not address himself to 'the happy possessors of faith, but to those many people for whom the light has gone out, the mystery has faded, and God is dead'; for these people, 'there is no going back, and one does not know either whether going back is always the better way'. The disappearance of God, other than such a psychological condition, is also an archetypical pattern, eternally recurrent in several religions and beliefs; the same Christian mystery is a representation of it: 'Christ always dies and always he is born; for the psychic life of the archetype is timeless in comparison with our individual time-boundedness'. As narrated in the Bible, after the crucifixion, Jesus's body could not be found, and, according to some gospels, he descended into hell and spent there three days. By drawing a more detailed psychological parallel, Jung sees in Jesus's body 'the outward, visible form, the erstwhile but ephemeral setting for the highest value'; while the descent 'describes the sinking of the vanished value into the unconscious, where, by conquering the power of darkness, it establishes a new order, and then rises up to heaven again, that is, attains supreme clarity of consciousness. The fact that only a few people see the Risen One means that no small difficulties stand in the way of finding and recognizing the transformed value' (CW 11: §§ 146–149).

In *Aion. Researches into the Phenomenology of the Self* [*Aion: Untersuchungen zur Symbolgeschichte*] (1951), Jung depicts 'Christ' as 'the still living myth of our culture', and adds: 'He is our culture hero, who, regardless of his historical existence, embodies the myth of the divine Primordial Man, the mystic Adam'. Not only this, 'Christ' even 'exemplifies the archetype of the self. He represents a totality of a divine or heavenly kind, a glorified man, a son of God sine macula peccati, unspotted by sin'. In this sense, Christ is said by Jung to represent the embodiment of God 'before the fall', which—psychologically—symbolises the moment in which such 'God-image' is 'damaged and corrupted' within the human body. Thanks to Christ's soul descending 'to hell', the restoration 'through God's grace' can take place: Christ's descent represents the 'integration' indeed; 'its work of redemption embracing even the dead'. Still in a depth psychological framework, this corresponds to 'the integration of the collective unconscious which forms an essential part of the individuation process' (CW 9, 2: §§ 69–72). Lastly, as an archetype, Christ also represents 'wholeness'. But, due to the church's unilateral view again, and to the doctrine of the *privatio boni*, such wholeness cannot be admitted:

> There can be no doubt that the original Christian conception of the imago Dei embodied in Christ meant an all-embracing totality that even includes the animal side of man. Nevertheless the Christ-symbol lacks wholeness in the modern psychological sense, since it does not include the dark side of things but specifically excludes it in the form of a Luciferian opponent. Although the exclusion of the power of evil was something the Christian consciousness was well aware of, all it lost in effect was an insubstantial shadow, for, through the doctrine of the *privatio boni* first propounded by Origen, evil was characterized as a mere diminution of good and thus deprived of substance. According to the teachings of the Church, evil is simply "the accidental lack of perfection." This assumption resulted in the proposition "omne bonum a Deo, omne malum ab homine." Another logical consequence was the subsequent elimination of the devil in certain Protestant sects. (ibid.: §§ 73–74)

As a consequence, the complementary side of 'Christ' is projected onto his opposite character, the 'Antichrist':

> Thanks to the doctrine of the privatio boni, wholeness seemed guaranteed in the figure of Christ. One must, however, take evil rather more substantially when one meets it on the plane of empirical psychology. There it is simply the opposite of good. In the ancient world the Gnostics, whose arguments were very much influenced by psychic experience, tackled the problem of evil on a broader basis than the Church Fathers. For instance, one of the things they taught was that Christ "cast off his shadow from himself." […] The Antichrist develops in legend as a perverse imitator of Christ's life. He is a true *ἀντιμιμὸν πνεῦμα*, an imitating spirit of evil who follows in Christ's footsteps like a shadow following the body. (ibid.: § 75)

In this sense, Jung calls the 'Antichrist' the 'shadow of the Self':

> The psychological concept of the self, in part derived from our knowledge of the whole man, but for the rest depicting itself spontaneously in the products of the unconscious as an archetypal quaternity bound together by inner antinomies, cannot omit the shadow that belongs to the light figure, for without it this figure lacks body and humanity. In the empirical self, light and shadow form a paradoxical unity. In the Christian concept, on the other hand, the archetype is hopelessly split into two irreconcilable halves, leading ultimately to a metaphysical dualism the final separation of the kingdom of heaven from the fiery world of the damned. (ibid.: § 76)

The 'Antichrist' is said to equally represent the Self, but it incarnates its 'dark aspect'. It is as important as the two thieves crucified together with Jesus: 'the progressive development and differentiation of consciousness leads to an ever more menacing awareness of the conflict and involves nothing less than a crucifixion of the ego, its agonizing suspension between irreconcilable opposites' (ibid.: § 79). This way, he also points out that the most significant attempt to integrate evil in Christian symbolism has been made by the Gnostics. Jung then goes back over the history of Christianity and finds evidence for his ideas in Gnostic theories, as well as in alchemy. In particular, he associates the symbol of the 'fish' of the earliest Christians with the alchemical *lapis philosophorum*: both these images reflect psychological attempt to express the 'wholeness' of the 'Self'. In order to be grasped as such, such 'wholeness' has to be *revealed*, and not simply represented; for a representation would show only one of its sides, but not its 'numinosity'. The 'Self' appears as expressed universally, and its 'wholeness' is normally indicated through the unification of opposites, which is usually perceived as a paradox, 'since a union of opposites can be thought of only as their annihilation'. Indeed, '[p]aradox is a characteristic of all transcendental situations because it alone gives adequate expression to their indescribable nature'. Ultimately, the importance of 'redemption' in Christianity becomes meaningful because of its attributing 'moral accentuation' to the 'Self', thus recognising only the divine element of the 'Self'. If a Christian 'voluntarily takes the burden of completeness on himself, he need not find it "happening" to him against his will in a negative form'; but if he follows his religious teaching, then the opposites within himself become unreconcilable. Similarly to Eastern religions, such a conflict did not exist in the Old Testament (ibid.: §§ 122–126).

5.3 Self-Overcoming

In a *Zarathustra* seminar session dated 29 January 1936, while introducing his comment on 'Of the Bestowing Virtue', Jung explains Nietzsche's symbol of the 'golden ball' in terms of 'a reaction against the Christian spirit, since Christ really did not die for the earth but for the spirit'. So, he continues: 'The golden ball has that meaning; it symbolizes Nietzsche's most important idea, the relation to the earth' (SNZ, II: 788). A bit later, he adds: 'So this chapter and the idea of the bestowing virtue in itself, has not only a Christian aspect, but a Christian *value*, there is no doubt about it. You see, when Zarathustra, or Nietzsche, returns to life, he surely will be forced to participate in the life of mankind as it is in that moment, and then he will see the positive values of it' (ibid.: 791). As can be read through these lines, Jung understands a return to collectivity as the essential element not only to interrupt Nietzsche's inflation, but also to *overcome* the unilateral perspective of Christianity; that is to say, to integrate the opposites and reach a new and more complete psychological state. The issue of self-overcoming is the main element in both *Zarathustra* and *Liber Novus*. These texts can be regarded as peculiar lenses, through which the two radically different perspectives on the 'death of God' and Christianity analysed above can be investigated. In both texts, indeed, self-overcoming is strongly linked with the 'death of God'.

As argued above, Nietzsche's criticism of Christianity aims at emulation and imitation, at the Christian attitude of pure exteriority; it can be inserted in the same line of his criticism to Socratism and Wagnerism as *decadent* attitudes. A life like that of Christ—as already remarked—'is still possible today, for certain people it is even necessary: true, original Christianity will always be possible' (AC 39, KSA 6: 211). For 'types' like Jesus, such a life can happen regardless of time or space. Only in Jesus's life, however, speaking of 'Christianity' makes sense; for what is meant today by that word is nothing but the attitude of imitating followers. As previously said, this all has to be contextualised in the wider framework of Nietzsche's experimental philosophy, his continuous challenge of: 'How much truth can a spirit tolerate, how much truth is it willing to *risk*?' [Wie viel Wahrheit erträgt, wie viel Wahrheit wagt ein Geist?], which 'increasingly became' Nietzsche's 'real measure of value' [Werthmesser] (EH *Vorrede*, 3, KSA 6: 259). In such consistent experimenting, all the old 'values' have to die, also 'God' and his 'shadows'. One of the symbols for the repugnancy towards revaluation is represented in *Zarathustra* by 'the spirit of gravity' [der Geist der Schwere]. This is Zarathustra's archenemy, that is, the resistance against changing, and this is precisely the kind of attitude needing to be overcome. Zarathustra warns his pupils against himself; indeed, he embodies the spirit of Nietzsche's radical experimental philosophy, and such a philosophy cannot teach any truth.

Differently, in his published writings, Jung sees in 'Christ' also the representation of a timeless symbol, an archetype, that needs to be integrated by consciousness and reunited to his 'shadow'—the 'Antichrist'—to finally reunify earth and heaven, nature and spirit, and achieve the wholeness of the Self. 'Christ' being a symbol, his meaning and representation are expected to change and live accordingly with the evolving of human beings' representative patterns (see Jung's definition of 'symbol', published as an appendix of *Psychological Types*, 1921, CW 6: §§ 814–829). Jung criticises the exteriority of the *Imitatio Christi* too, but, because of the symbolic meaning of 'Christ', he does not admit the possibility that such a life could occur again on earth. The self-overcoming described in *Liber Novus* is always oriented towards the realisation of a 'new God'. Among the many meanings of the phrase 'new God', giving a sense to the aridity of concepts deserve to be remarked; in other words, it is crucial to integrate irrationality in the contemporary rational mind. Jung's God—or at least his presence—has been *experienced* by Jung himself, for this reason he cannot die without being brought to life again. After all, Jung calls himself an 'empiricist', and the Latin inscription above his entrance door in Küsnacht reads 'vocatus atque non vocatus Deus aderit' (whether or not you call Him, God will be here), indeed. If Nietzsche's purpose is to overcome the *Geist der Schwere*, Jung's inspirational inner voice, responsible for the fantasies narrated in *Liber Novus*, is the *Geist der Tiefe*, the 'spirit of the depth'. This symbolises the communication with the deepest—timeless—spirit, necessary to overcome the static perspective of the 'I'. As pointed out in the introduction, the whole *Liber Novus* seems to teach how to overcome the dichotomy between 'sense' and 'nonsense' towards the 'supreme meaning'; Jung's *faith* in a 'supreme meaning' is represented by Philemon, whose teachings guide Jung's 'I', and appear as the only possible way to overcome the one-sidedness of rationality.

Both Nietzsche and Jung, lastly, can be said 'untimely'. Nietzsche called himself that way several times, and often considered his ideal readers as yet to come, thus orienting his hope towards the future. Jung, in a similar sense but in a radically different perspective, waits for his fate to be accomplished. Nietzsche's being 'untimely' concerns the understanding of his thinking, he is untimely to his contemporaries; Jung is 'untimely' in the sense that he tries to overcome the barrier between his time and the time of the 'spirit of the depth'. Indeed, as argued since the beginning, the leading thread of 'visionary' works is the *prophetical* nature of their composition. Precisely in this sense the diversity in their conceptions of 'self-overcoming' has to be understood. In fact, whereas Zarathustra intends to overcome the 'Three Evil Things', namely 'Sensual pleasure, Lust for power, Selfishness' (Za III, 10, 'Of the Three Evil Things', KSA 4: 235–240),[7] Jung looks forward to the 'Three Prophecies' announced by his 'soul': 'The misery of war, the darkness of magic, and the gift of religion' (RB II, 18, 'The Three Prophecies': 306). In other words, Nietzsche's 'self-overcoming' is oriented towards a higher self-responsibility which denies obscure explanations, faith attitudes, or beliefs, and it has to be understood only in relation to his *experimental* philosophy; Jung aims at opening up and embracing the totality of the unknown, trying to preserve its irreducibility to logical categories, by stressing a certain human need for *meaning*. Finally, all this can also shed more light on Jung's interpretation of Nietzsche: as retrospectively remarked by Jung in relation to 'The Magician', 'One can teach the way that leads to chaos, but one cannot teach magic' (RB II, 21: 314). Magic is therefore something which follows chaos and brings wholeness. But it cannot be taught. Nietzsche, instead, would stop there, when he claimed that 'one must have chaos in one, to give birth to a dancing star' (Za I, *Prologue* 5, KSA 4: 18). Therefore, from Jung's standpoint, Zarathustra's attempt to *teach* how to 'give birth' to such a 'dancing star' might be read as his mistake, namely as the reason for his failure as a teacher. Consequently, Nietzsche's inability to admit the importance of magic could be considered responsible for his falling into madness. The main implicit criticism of Nietzsche in *Liber Novus* concerns precisely the fact that, in spite of Zarathustra's consistent rejection of emulation, Nietzsche is not able to propose any alternative model of teaching. Philemon, by contrast, leads Jung's 'I' to realise the divine exclusively by showing the necessity of magic. Both Zarathustra's 'doctrine' and Philemon's teaching can be indeed read in terms of *empty* teachings in which teachers do not provide their disciples with contents, but rather allow them to find solutions themselves. But whereas Zarathustra struggles to *teach* the *Übermensch* and the eternal return—although meant as mere hypotheses—Philemon puts himself as a magician, and rejects Jung's 'I' as a disciple. In *Zarathustra*, disciples have to learn how to reject their teachers; the succeeding teacher in *Liber Novus* rejects his own disciple. Again, what in *Zarathustra* assumes an epistemological tone—that is, the absence of truth—in *Liber Novus* becomes a religious issue. If *Zarathustra* is meant as 'a book for all and none', *Liber Novus* can be essentially considered as a book valid for Jung only. *Liber Novus* represents indeed Jung's unique experience with his own realisation of the divine. Should anyone else try to walk the same path, it would be nothing but imitation, and there would be no difference with Christianity and its relation to the figure of 'Christ'.

Notes

1. Pretty much simultaneously, Nietzsche's teacher and guide, the philologist Friedrich Ritschl, made the same decision of teaching in Leipzig, after an argument with his colleague Otto Jahn.
2. As the scholar points out, it is quite controversial to date Nietzsche's estrangement from Christianity: 'In the corpus of his early notes, we find testimonies of a living faith as late as 1861. But these notes conflict with other texts in which Nietzsche submitted Christian teachings to a sober analysis or penned rather blasphemous remarks. At any rate, from 1862 or so, Nietzsche was clearly already estranged from Christianity, and in 1865, when he confined his studies exclusively to classics, he overtly broke with it irrevocably' (ibid.: 92).
3. On a detailed representation of how Nietzsche's idea of decadence can be combined with his criticism to Wagner, see Thomä 2008: 107–127.
4. The target of Nietzsche's polemic is Ernest Renan, who depicted Jesus as a 'hero' and a 'genius' (Renan 1863). Nietzsche is most likely to have borrowed the phrase 'idiot' from Dostoevsky's *The Idiot* (*Идиот*, 1869).
5. Nietzsche's criticism also aims at Schopenhauer, who was equally *hostile to life* (ibid., KSA 6: 174).
6. The last paragraph of Baudelaire's note is quoted by Nietzsche in French: 'Moi, je dis: la volupté unique et suprême de l'amour gît dans la certitude de faire le mal. Et l'homme et la femme savent, de naissance, que dans le mal se trouve toute volupté'.
7. Interestingly, in his *Zarathustra* seminar, Jung interprets these elements as prophecies on Freud, Adler, and himself, respectively (see SNZ II: 1450–1451).

References

Baudelaire, Charles. 1919. Intimate Papers from the Unpublished Works of Baudelaire. In *Baudelaire. His Prose and Poetry*, ed. T.R. Smith. Translated by Joseph T. Shipley. New York: The Modern Library.

Bourget, Paul. 1883. *Essays de psychologie contemporaine*. Paris: Plon-Nourrit.

Brobjer, Thomas H. 2010. The Origin and Early Context of the Revaluation Theme in Nietzsche's Thinking. *The Journal of Nietzsche's Studies* 19 (Spring): 12–29.

Campioni, Giuliano. 1998. *Sulla strada di Nietzsche*. Pisa: ETS.

———. 2001. *Les lectures françaises de Nietzsche*. Paris: PUF, 2001. Reprint in Giuliano Campioni. 2009. *Der französische Nietzsche*. Berlin: De Gruyter.

———. 2009. Socrate *monstrum*: egoismo e decadenza. In *Nietzsche. La morale dell'eroe*, 71–120. Pisa: ETS.

Dostoevsky, Fyodor. 1869. *The Idiot: A Novel in Four Parts*. New York: The Macmillan Company, 1913.

Jung, Carl Gustav. 1921. *Psychological Types*. Collected Works of C. G. Jung. Vol. 6.

———. 1937–1940. *Psychology and Religion*. Collected Works of C. G. Jung. Vol. 11, §§ 1–168.

———. 1942/1948. *A Psychological Approach to the Trinity*. Collected Works of C. G. Jung. Vol. 11, §§ 169–295.

———. 1951. *Aion: Researches into the Phenomenology of the Self*. Collected Works of C. G. Jung. Vol. 9, 2.

———. 1952a. *Foreword to White's 'God and the Unconscious'*. Collected Works of C. G. Jung. Vol. 11, §§ 449–460.

———. 1952b. *Answer to Job*. Collected Works of C. G. Jung. Vol. 11, §§ 553–758.

———. 1989. *Nietzsche's Zarathustra: Notes of the Seminar Given in 1934–9*. 2nd ed. Edited by James L. Jarrett in Two Parts. London: Routledge, 1994.

———. 2009. *The Red Book: Liber Novus*. Edited and Introduced by Sonu Shamdasani, Translated by Mark Kyburz, John Peck, and Sonu Shamdasani. New York and London: W. W. Norton & Company.

Jung, Carl Gustav, and Aniela Jaffé. 1962. *Memories, Dreams, Reflections by Carl Gustav Jung*. Recorded and Edited by Aniela Jaffé. New York: Vintage Books, 1989.

Nietzsche, Friedrich Wilhelm. 1882/1887. *The Gay Science*. Translated by Josefine Nauckhoff. Edited by Bernard Williams. Poems Translated by Adrian Del Caro. Cambridge and New York: Cambridge University Press, 2001–2008.

———. 1883–1885. *Thus Spoke Zarathustra*. 2nd ed. Translated by R. J. Hollingdale. New York: Penguin Classics, 1969.

———. 1888–1989. *The Anti-Christ, Ecce Homo, Twilight of the Idols, and Other Writings*, 2007. Translated by Judith Normann. Cambridge: Cambridge University Press.

———. 1967–. *Kritische Gesamtausgabe der Werke Nietzsches*. Edited by Giorgio Colli and Mazzino Montinari. Berlin/New York: De Gruyter.

———. 1980–. *Kritische Studienausgabe*. Edited by Giorgio Colli and Mazzino Montinari. Berlin/New York: De Gruyter.

———. 2009–. *Digital Critical Edition*. Edited by P. D'Iorio.

Otto, Rudolf. 1917. *Das Heilige—Über das Irrationale in der Idee des Göttlichen und sein Verhältnis zum Rationalen*. Breslau, 1920.

Renan, Ernest. 1863. *Vie de Jésus*. Paris: Nelson/Colman Lévy.

Salaquarda, Jörg. 1996. Nietzsche and the Judaeo-Christian Tradition. In *The Cambridge Companion to Nietzsche*, ed. Bernard Magnus and Kathleen Higgins, 90–118. Cambridge and New York: Cambridge University Press.

Sommer, Andrea Urs. 2006. 'Gott is tod' oder 'Dionysos gegen den Gekreutzigten'? In *Atheismus: Ideologie, Philosophie oder Mentalität?* ed. Richard Faber and Susanne Lanwerd, 75–90. Würzburg: Königshausen & Neumann.

Thomä, Dieter. 2008. Umwertungen der Dekadenz. Korrespondenzen zwischen Richard Wagner, Friedrich Nietzsche und Sergej Eisenstein. In *Nietzsche und Wagner. Geschichte und Aktualität eines Kulturkonflikts*, ed. Armin Wildermuth, 103–140. Zurich: Orell Füssli.

Index[1]

[1] Note: Page numbers followed by 'n' refer to notes.

G. Domenici, *Jung's Nietzsche*,
https://doi.org/10.1007/978-3-030-17670-9

The manufacturer's authorised representative in the EU is Springer Nature Customer Service Centre GmbH, Europaplatz 3, 69115 Heidelberg, Germany. If you have any concerns regarding our products, please contact ProductSafety@springernature.com

Printed and bound by CPI Group (UK) Ltd, Croydon, CR0 4YY
05/10/2026
02228125-0007